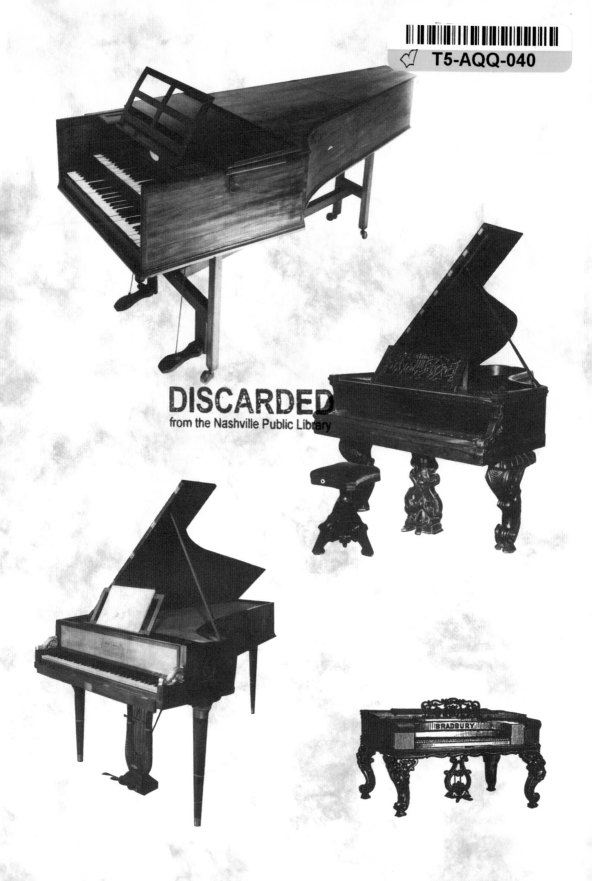

MUSICAL HIGHLIGHTS
FROM THE
WHITE HOUSE

Elise K. Kirk

KRIEGER PUBLISHING COMPANY
Malabar, Florida
1992

Original Edition 1992
Based on Music at the White House:
A History of the American Spirit

Printed and Published by
KRIEGER PUBLISHING COMPANY
KRIEGER DRIVE
MALABAR, FLORIDA 32950

Library of Congress Cataloging-in-Publication Data

Kirk, Elise K. (Elise Kuhl), 1932–
    Musical highlights from the White House / by Elise Kirk.
        p.   cm.
    Rev. ed. of: Music at the White House. c1986.
    Includes bibliographical references (p.) and index.
    ISBN 0-89464-664-8 — ISBN 0-89464-699-0 (pbk.)
        1. White House (Washington, D.C.) 2. Music—Washington (D.C.)—
History and criticism. 3. Concerts—Washington (D.C.)—4. Music—
United States—History and Criticism. 5. Washington (D.C.)—Buildings,
structures, etc. 6. Public buildings—Washington (D.C.)
I. Kirk, Elise K. (Elise Kuhl), 1932–   Music at the White House.
II. Title.
ML200.8.W3K57   1992
780.78'753--dc20   91-43346
                                                                              CIP
                                                                              MN

    10   9   8   7   6   5   4   3   2

To my mother—my own first lady
whose loving heart and joyous spirit
touched many pages of this book

CONTENTS

PREFACE TO THE NEW EDITION

No book is ever finished. This is particularly true of a historical work whose events unfold chronologically. In this new edition of my original book, *Music at the White House: A History of the American Spirit* (University of Illinois Press, 1986), I have added the administration of George Bush, which I feel brings the musical life of the mansion full circle, conjuring up images of the more informal, intimate early days of White House musical history. To allow ease in perusing the three major functions of White House music—family music-making, guest entertainment and ceremonial practices—I have added three appendixes. Appendix A, for example, provides an overview of first family scores and their repositories, which will encourage performance of these richly varied collections of early presidential music. Finally, I have focused primarily on the historic highlights: those programs, performers and attitudes that were especially significant in shaping the White House musical scene from its earliest days. In this edition I have endeavored to retain many aspects of the original edition, especially the moods, stories and surrounding cultural background that place these highlights in their human environment.

I offer my special thanks to the American Society of Composers, Authors and Publishers for honoring *Music at the White House* with the 1987 ASCAP/Deems Taylor Award for outstanding books in the field of music. I am also grateful to the White House Historical Association for sponsoring a series of concerts and lectures relating to my book during the White House bicentennial in 1992, and to Krieger Publishing Company for recognizing my work through its new edition: *Musical Highlights from the White House*.

PREFACE

"Pardon me, ma'am, but you'll have to work somewhere else now," said the White House guard politely one morning. "The president likes to come in here at noon and browse through the books." I left—fast—gathering up my notes, pencils, glasses, and briefcase that had been sniffed both inside and out by two large dogs dutifully searching for bombs. The White House is not equipped to handle researchers. The office of the curator is very small, so that day the gracious staff had situated me in the elegant Federal-style library on the ground floor, where I had been taking notes for several hours with the Gilbert Stuart portrait of George Washington looking over my shoulder and the soft gray and rose tones of the Tabriz carpet under my feet.

I had grown to love this great, white citadel of democracy. Situated among the green parks of Washington, D.C., like a charming "English clubhouse," as Charles Dickens described it when he visited President John Tyler in 1841, the mansion is both imposing and intimate, awesome and warm—the home of every American. I felt that it had been my home, too. For as I left the White House that day I could hear Mrs. John Quincy Adams at her Babcock pianoforte, the young Teresa Carreño playing for Abraham Lincoln, Madam Schumann-Heink serenading Theodore Roosevelt, the legendary Hofmann, Paderewski, Rachmaninoff at the East Room Steinway, and Eubie Blake on the White House lawn. I nodded my thanks to the guard. I would be back—very soon.

How did I come to write a book on the musical history of the White House? The idea occurred to me while I was researching material for my doctoral thesis on the French composer, Charles Koechlin. This erudite master had come to the United States with a mission of French scholars and was entertained at the White House by President Woodrow Wilson in 1918, only two days after the Armistice. Surely there would be ample, accessible information about this event, I thought. But I was wrong. The sources for White House history are widely diffused, and sifting through them to find a specific piece of information is a major undertaking. Official records of the social activities of the White House and its inhabitants were not kept until the turn of the century. But even after this time, published studies of the mansion's social life are rare—and a history of its cultural activities nonexistent. Not until 1961 was the White House curatorial office established by Mrs. John F. Kennedy to amass and preserve the historic furnishings of the mansion. But the *musical* history of our nation's oldest "performing arts center" still needed to be studied and appreciated.

Despite the obstacles, researching a topic that examined American musical practices from a fresh interdisciplinary springboard was tempting. I knew that the White House—both home and governmental institution—could tell us much about our nation if we asked the right questions. But in order to do this, the historian must be willing to roam widely within and beyond his or her own discipline and to chart new landscapes. I would have to become, in the words of Richard Crawford, a mapmaker rather than a prospector, broadening my focus from Music with a capital M to *music-making*—or from the product to the process. Thus, in examining the role of the White House in accepting, reflecting, or promoting certain kinds of music, a new image of America would emerge.

And so the adventure began. I found it essential to explore the resources and insights of several different disciplines to place the details of my study in an appropriate setting. Many of my basic sources were nonmusical: manuscripts and published accounts relating to the White House, presidential papers, newspaper reports, private diaries and letters, oral histories, government documents, and financial accounts. To interpret the facts gleaned from these sources and to relate specific White House events to the musical life of the nation at large, I examined the approaches of various social and cultural historians. Political history was also a vital area to consider; the exigencies of foreign policy, the trauma of war, and the personal lives and tenets of individual presidential families all influenced the musical activities of the White House. Finally, my own experience as a musicologist provided tools for interpreting the various programs, scores, and musical data and determining their significance to the primary theme of my book—that the musical life of the White House is a story of America, of the gradual emergence of the American national character through the growing acceptance of its indigenous creative treasures and lessening dependence upon European culture.

My research, in turn, led to avenues, moments, and memories that have become just as much a part of this book as the documents themselves. Meeting President and Mrs. Reagan and the Bushes. Conversing with Rosalynn Carter, Betty Ford, and Lady Bird Johnson. Chatting with the chief usher, Rex Scouten, in his second-floor office at the White House. Trying out the East Room Steinway as I left the PBS "In Performance at the White House" rehearsal. Interviewing numerous prominent musicians, first family members, and White House staff. But strongest of all is the memory of the great house itself, whose doors opened for me a vital new area of history. As E. V. Smalley, a New York correspondent, wrote in 1884: "There is probably no building in the world where more history has centered than in this shining White Mansion. Heroic men have died here. . . . There have been marriages and merry makings, too, jovial feasts and ceremonial banquets; grave councils of state that shaped the destiny of the nation. . . . The history of the White House is a history of the United States from 1800 to this day."

But no one book can tell the whole story. While *Musical Highlights from the White House* and its parent book, *Music at the White House: A History of the American Spirit* (University of Illinois Press, 1986), have unearthed various artifacts, many treasures remain. The scholarly investigation of American music and its role in society is still in its infancy, and the White House offers but one approach to the exploration of this vast panorama. If my book leaves the doors open and invites further research and interpretation, it will have accomplished my aims. It is hoped that readers with both broad and specialized interests will find information in this study that will provide them with new directions and fresh perspectives about America, its people, and the manner in which they perceived their art.

INTRODUCTION

The White House, first inhabited by John and Abigail Adams in 1800, is the nation's oldest important showcase for the performing arts. It is a stage like no other. As both home and office of the president of the United States, it is private, domestic, and intimate but at the same time public, visible, and powerfully linked with the people. While entertainment at the White House is usually presented to only 200 or 300 by invitation, it is open to millions through television. Few edifices in the world can boast the variety and excellence of its music, yet few concert halls or opera houses have been so conditioned by changing political attitudes. No other single arts institution has been as progressive and at the same time as conservative as the great white mansion. No other aspect of White House life can define the presidential image quite like the music performed at the chief of state's residence. Yet this image is a two-way channel. Powerful, elusive, joyous, persuasive, poignant, elegant, and brash, White House musical fêtes are a true mirror of America, a glimpse of court life in a democracy—a barometer of the nation's irrational, romantic, secular spirit.

There is a part of each of us in the music that is performed at the White House: the ceremonial pageantry and tradition that harks back to the age of romantic chivalry; the amateur's joy in making music in the privacy of his or her home; the inspiring thrill of hearing the world's finest performing artists in concert. Where else but at the White House can one find this *Gebrauchsmusik*, this trio of socially "useful" music, embodied in a single institution? And if we take a moment to glance back into history, we will note that our American tradition of changing administrations has affected the style of this music in a unique way. The personal and political tastes of the various first families have influenced the choice of music at the mansion, but even more so have the surrounding mood, cultural milieu, and world events of the era. The intensity of the Depression, for example, brought the White House programs at the close of the Hoover era closer to those of FDR, forming a type of cultural bridge between these two politically disparate administrations. The famous Kennedy arts philosophy was forecast by the Eisenhowers, whose White House concerts during their last years reflected the cultural explosion of the late 1950s. Today, however, technology, probably more than any one element, has ensured that the White House is America's stage. New attitudes in journalism and telecommunications have brought the Executive Mansion as a vital medium of artistic expression closer to the public than ever before.

Music for ceremonies and state entertainment played an important part in the history of the "President's House" from its earliest days. The eight-member U.S. Marine Band was the first musical ensemble to perform at the mansion, functioning as a form of European *Harmonie*, or small social ensemble, for the Adamses' first reception on New Year's Day, 1801. For almost 100 years the Marine Band of from thirty to seventy players performed for thousands in public concerts on the White House lawn. Under Francis Scala, John Philip Sousa, William Santelmann, and other noted leaders, it brought to America the latest Italian operas and newest works of Wagner, Brahms, and other European composers at a time when the city of Washington knew no other regular performing ensemble. The Marine Band, moreover, is our nation's oldest continuous musical organization. Now greatly expanded, it comprises a wide variety of ensemble units to meet the needs of virtually every social, artistic, and ceremonial occasion at the White House.

Despite its location in the culturally primitive capital of Washington, the White House in the early decades of the nineteenth century became an important center for elegant entertainment and informal musical programs. Like the Parisian *salon*, these artistic evenings reflected the fine European tastes of the first six presidents and first ladies. With industrialization and the great railroad expansion, touring artists began to perform at the White House during the 1840s. Among the first were the singing families and balladeers with their social and political messages in song: the Hutchinsons, William Dempster, and the Baker Family. Opera singers, such as the young diva Meda Blanchard from Washington, Etelka Gerster from Hungary, and the black soprano Marie Selika from Cincinnati, followed under Abraham Lincoln and Rutherford Hayes. Most of these programs were informal musicales, as the Hayeses called them, held in the Red or Green Room with light refreshments following. The White House staged its first formal East Room concert, preceded by supper, during Chester Arthur's administration and saw what appears to be its first printed program under Benjamin Harrison.

In 1903 Steinway & Sons presented the East Room with its first grand piano, and world-renowned pianists came to perform at the mansion—Ferruccio Busoni, Ignacy Paderewski, Josef Hofmann, Olga Samaroff, Fannie Bloomfield Zeisler, Sergei Rachmaninoff, and a host of others. This piano was replaced in 1938 by another Steinway concert grand, which remains in the White House today. Guest artists performed for the numerous diplomatic dinners and musicales during the early part of the century, but harpist Mildred Dilling, who entertained the king and queen of Siam under Herbert Hoover, was the first to be invited to play for a chief of state. Opera was first staged, albeit modestly, during Franklin Roosevelt's administration, and serious chamber music was performed at the mansion as early as William McKinley's time. But while opera, ballet, chamber music, and jazz all appeared at the mansion before 1940, it was the administration of John F. Kennedy in the early 1960s that gave these styles a clearly defined focus, establishing the White House as a prominent center for America's artistic achievements.

The choice of musical programs at the White House has tended to be more conservative than innovative, more reflective than prophetic. But there have been some notable exceptions. Beginning with Theodore Roosevelt and relying on the assistance of Steinway & Sons in arranging the programs, chamber music, the modern French and Russian schools, and especially American music were featured at a time when these styles were barely recognized in this country. "In this labor of love," wrote the *National Magazine* in 1916, "the Steinways have preserved a patriotic motif. They have maintained the policy that has long distinguished the White House, of encouraging American music and American artists." What other institution can boast this claim over so long and continuous a period in history?

Recognizing brilliant young talent has also been part of White House artistic philosophy from its earliest days. Teresa Carreño, Etelka Gerster, Erica Morini, Vladimir Horowitz, Pablo Casals, Dorothy Maynor, Ruggiero Ricci, and Eugene List are only a few of the noted artists who performed for a president before they were thirty. But obtaining world-renowned talent is not always easy, especially today when artists are in great demand and jet all over the world under tightly controlled contracts. Despite the coveted honor of playing for the president, artists such as Joan Sutherland and Luciano Pavarotti have had to turn down command performances because of their schedules and commitments. Isaac Stern, who has played many times at the White House, recalls the time he barely made it there for a reception. "I had the orchestra in Buffalo change the order of the program so I played in the first half and had a police escort to the airfield where a private jet flew me to Andrews Air Force Base. The White House had a car waiting, and it drove me to the reception." On another occasion, Stern had to apologize to the president, vice-president, and secretary of state: a jet was waiting to take him to his next engagement. If he did not leave, the Washington airport would close down. "Even the White House couldn't get them to hold the airport open for me so that I could stay a few minutes longer and chat with the president," he chuckled.

Television today has opened to the world the first family as arts supporter in a way unparalleled in past decades. We view the president and first lady in the White House enjoying their excellent "Young Performers" series and at various Kennedy Center functions, Ford's Theater, and other cultural affairs. But is presidential interest in the performing arts a mere image-making ploy? Presidents and their families throughout history have genuinely enjoyed music in various degrees as a relaxing diversion, and they have recognized the value of culture to the nation and the human spirit. Thomas Jefferson and Harry Truman were clearly not the only presidents for whom music was a "companion to divert and delight," as our third president professed. Time and again music's persuasive powers have moved the heart and mind of a tormented, weary chief of state. Impulsively. Joyously. Quietly. We need look no further than to George Washington, John Quincy Adams, John Tyler, Abraham Lincoln, Rutherford Hayes, Chester Arthur, Woodrow Wilson, Franklin Roosevelt, Dwight Eisenhower, Richard Nixon, Jimmy Carter, Ronald Reagan, and many others.

Like a vast pendulum swinging back and forth, history ensures that every tone from the past raises an echo today. Thus we can discern certain patterns within the political and cultural climate of the United States and in her leaders. A look backward to five consecutive administrations during the nineteenth century, for example, reveals a striking parallel with five consecutive periods in the twentieth. The Civil War and World War II brought to

Lincoln and FDR the musical voices of the troubled masses; the postwar periods of both Grant and Eisenhower enjoyed the military "court" musicians of the mansion; Hayes and Kennedy refreshed the nation with renewed visibility of the performing arts; Arthur and Lyndon Johnson nurtured those legacies; Cleveland and Nixon added a touch of levity through the popular music they brought to the mansion. And so the pendulum continues to swing—dynamically, creatively. Perhaps one day we will see an important U.S. premier televised from the White House or a major American composition commissioned by the President. Indeed, there will be many new directions to explore as the performing arts in America continue to gain vitality and significance.

Despite the expanded focus on the presidency by today's media, the perception of this great office has not changed much over the years. Presidential power, performance, and integrity have always been essential to a public that has tended to deify or revere its chief executives from the days of Washington. Harold Laski once said that the president, unique among world leaders, is both "more or less a king and more or less a prime minister." Thus the ceremonial tradition, the pageantry associated with this highest of American offices, still plays as significant a role today as it did during the earliest decades of the presidency—in many ways, even more vital. Through White House musical traditions, our spirits seem to cling to a bygone era, to an age of romantic chivalry in a time of burgeoning technology and commercialism. "In a sense," wrote Anatole Broyard, a critic with the *New York Times*, "America was discovered because European romanticism had nowhere else to go. It had exhausted its poetic impulse in chivalry, kings, castles and cathedrals."

Perhaps then, those words offer an explanation for that unique American phenomenon—White House music. America's early leaders had no indigenous American courtly culture to draw upon, but they had some knowledge of Haydn's work at Esterhazy, aristocratic *Hausmusik* in Vienna, "The King's Private Band" of Charles II, or a Rameau comédie-ballet at the royal palace at Versailles. Curiously, by the early twentieth century our state musical traditions became more visible and established, as many of those in Europe declined. Certain practices that we borrowed from abroad, such as the "command performance," and the gala after-dinner state entertainment by famous artists, barely exist anymore in the major European countries. Have they been transferred to the New World where they are enjoyed as lingering vestiges of romanticism? Might they be useful tools to gain support for the arts in a nation that lacks the extensive government subsidies found in Europe? Is the music of the White House merely an image, after all? Perhaps. But it is a lyric image, a joyous vision, and the most graceful language of glory the president will ever know. Music will always be a vital part of the American adventure of discovery, and the White House will remain a prime mover in the voyage.

PART ONE

1789–1901

CHAPTER 1

MUSICAL LIFE IN THE PRESIDENT'S HOUSE

Nothing is more agreeable, and ornamental, than good music.

George Washington
June 4, 1777

GEORGE WASHINGTON

The windows were thrown open wide at Number 3 Cherry Street during those warm summer days in 1789. Anyone walking nearby could hear ten-year-old Nelly Custis practicing on her new pianoforte, a gift from her stepgrandfather, George Washington, shortly after he became president. Pleyel sonatas in the incipient stages of virtuosity? A childish rendering of the "top ten" of the day's ballad-opera tunes? Scotch, Irish, or English melodies? Perhaps. For Nelly was made to practice four and five hours a day by her doting grandmother, Martha Dandridge Custis Washington.[1] Indeed, the White House from its earliest days resounded with musical tones and airs reflecting early America's perennial fascination with the keyboard—a family hearth, a replica of gentility, a burgeoning industry, a titillating idol of the American inventive spirit. And in the president's mansion, the piano reigned in yet another fashion—as an elegant image of court life in a democracy.

Washington occupied three executive mansions during his two terms in office, yet not one of them was in the city that bears his name. The graceful house on Cherry Street in New York City built by Walter Franklin, one of the city's wealthiest merchants, afforded a view of New York Bay, Long Island, and the East River. Washington took possession of the first "Presidential Palace" only a few days before his inauguration on April 4, 1789. His wife, the former widow Martha Custis whom Washington married in 1759, and her two grandchildren, Eleanor (Nelly) Parke Custis and George Washington (Tub or Little Wash) Parke Custis, joined him the following month.[2] As winter approached the family realized that their home was too small, so they moved to a large mansion on Broadway near Trinity Church. In 1790 Philadelphia became the temporary capital, and there the Washingtons occupied the home of Robert Morris, financier of the Revolutionary War, until the president retired from office in 1797. Washington lived on his beloved plantation at Mt. Vernon, Virginia, for slightly more than two years before his death in 1799 at the age of sixty-seven.

Music at the president's home in those early days was an intimate

The first President's Palace at Number 3 Cherry Street, New York, as it appeared in the 1850s, shortly before it was demolished. Ironically, Nelly Custis practiced the piano several hours a day in the building that later housed one of the nation's most flourishing piano manufacturers and music publishers, Firth, Pond and Company (formerly Firth, Hall and Pond). *Leslie's Weekly, 1856.*

amusement. If a "concert artist" performed for the Washington family, it would have been one of Nelly's teachers, such as Alexander Reinagle, a long-time acquaintance of Washington. Perhaps this gifted immigrant composer ran through some of the tunes from his latest comic opera for the president or tried out one of the fine new piano sonatas he composed in the 1790s. Reinagle was often at the president's home instructing Nelly. Another early "White House artist" was Nelly herself, who was expected to perform for the ambassadors, foreign dignitaries, and members of Congress who came to visit. Once she played for over an hour in an attempt to "attune the souls" of "two homely Spaniards," one of whom she described as "a crazy count."[3]

Washington enjoyed music and the theater and was especially fond of dancing. George Washington Parke Custis's *Recollections* noted that the general was conspicuous for his graceful execution of the minuet, a dance associated with European aristocracy and considered old-fashioned by the turn of the century. At a time when some churches called dancing "a pollution of the body," Washington's diaries are filled with accounts of the various balls he attended. During his brilliant inaugural ball on May 7, 1789, he danced with nearly every lady—except Mrs. Washington who could not

Harper's Bazar.
A Repository of Fashion, Pleasure, and Instruction.

Vol. XXII.—No. 19.
Copyright, 1889, by Harper & Brothers
All Rights Reserved.

NEW YORK, SATURDAY, MAY 11, 1889.

TEN CENTS A COPY.
WITH SUPPLEMENTS.

President George Washington dancing the minuet at his inaugural ball, as shown on the cover of *Harper's Bazaar*, May 11, 1889. The issue commemorated the centenary of his inauguration.

make the long journey from Mt. Vernon to New York in time to attend. The president also attended plays (usually interspersed with music), English ballad operas, or concerts, sometimes five or six times a season, and a special box was reserved for him at several of the theaters.

One of the first musical events the president attended after taking office was a bawdy little ballad opera called *The Clandestine Marriage*, presented in New York City by the Old American Company on June 13, 1789. The president also lightened his cumbrous duties periodically with renditions of *Beau Strategem*, *The Lock and Key* (called "a comic opera in 2 acts"), *The Way to Get Married*, and *Animal Magnetism* all of which he saw in Philadelphia. The last two works were staged on February 27, 1797, by the Reinagle-Wignell Company at the spacious, elegant New Theater on Chestnut Street. But the general's favorite was William Shield's little comic opera, *Poor Soldier*, first performed in London in 1783.

More than any other president, Washington has been sentimentalized, emulated, monumentalized, and deified. And among the panegyrics are the tales of his musical prowess, his abilities to play the flute and violin. He played neither, although he may have picked up a fipple flute on occasion and blown a note or two to entertain his "grandchildren." When Francis Hopkinson, one of the signers of the Declaration of Independence and an accomplished musician, dedicated to Washington his "Seven Songs for the Harpsichord" (published by J. Dobson in Philadelphia in 1788), the general admitted, "I can neither sing one of the songs, nor raise a single note on any instrument to convince the unbelieving."[4] Washington made sure his stepchildren played musical instruments, however; John played the violin and Martha (Patsy) the spinet. An invoice of goods from London in 1767 lists "6 Bridges for a fiddle" and "Best Roman fiddle strings" for "Master Custis 14 yrs old" among such mundane items as "1 Silver Laced Hatt" and "1 small Breeches Buckle."[5] An earlier invoice indicated that Washington had ordered for Patsy, then six years old, a "very good Spinit, to be made by Mr. Plinius [*sic*], Harpsicord Maker in South Audley Street Grosvener Square," with a "good assortment of spare strings."[6] Ordered two years after Washington's marriage to Martha, the harpsichord, made by John Plenius, remained in the family and was played often by Patsy until her untimely death before she turned seventeen. In 1789 the instrument was traded for a piano for Patsy's niece, ten-year-old Nelly.

Naturally gifted, witty, and beautiful, Nelly Custis was the daughter of John Parke Custis, Martha Washington's son by a previous marriage. Several weeks after the family occupied the presidential home, Mrs. Washington wrote to her niece: "Nelly shall begin Musick next week . . . she is a little wild creature and spends her time at the window looking at carriages etc. passing by."[7] The Washingtons paid more for Nelly's music lessons than for any other part of her education. They made certain she had all the music she needed and purchased numerous items for her up to the final days of the presidency.

As soon as she received her piano from the president, Nelly started lessons with Reinagle. Washington originally planned to have the old Plenius spinet thoroughly restored for her, and he had it shipped to New York from Mt. Vernon by schooner. He was reluctant to give it up. It had provided many happy hours of music for dancing, a favorite pastime at Mt. Vernon. However, on June 30, 1789, Washington paid Thomas Dodds "16 Guineas, 4 Guineas

Five-octave, two-manual harpsichord was purchased by George Washington from Longman and Broderip, London, in 1793. Both this instrument and a Dodds pianoforte were played by Nelly Custis while she lived in the Presidential Home in Philadelphia.

being allowed for an old Spinnett,"[8] and the first "White House" piano made its way to Cherry Street. Thus one of the earliest items purchased for the "White House" by a president was a musical instrument, one of the first pianos built in America.

Nelly's pianoforte, as the early pianos were called, was brought to Philadelphia when the family moved there in 1790. Records show that it was tuned periodically along with the fine new harpsichord Washington bought her in December 1793. The five-octave, two-manual harpsichord was ordered from Longman and Broderip, No. 26 Cheapside and No. 13 Haymarket, London. Nelly also owned an English guitar, which bears her initials "E P C" on the ivory rosette that decorates the instrument. Since the guitar, too, came from the firm Longman and Broderip, it may have been ordered about the same time as the harpsichord. It was believed to have been a birthday gift to Nelly from the president.

What did Nelly Custis play on her elegant instruments in the presidential mansions? At the end of the eighteenth century and well throughout the nineteenth, playing the piano was primarily a lady's art, with the gentlemen amateurs aspiring to the somewhat more "intricate" techniques of the violin or German flute. To be educated, a young American woman usually studied history, arithmetic, geography, and languages, as well as music, sewing, and "Dancing with Fancy Work only if required." In addition to offering a fine overview of period styles and practices, Nelly's large personal collection of music provides insight into her musical education and preferences. (See Appendix A.) But while her teacher, Alexander Reinagle, readily challenged her with works of J. C. Bach, Pleyel and Haydn, Nelly's favorite may have been the real hit of the day—Kotzwara's bombastic warhorse, "Battle of Prague" (1789). With its bugle calls, cannon shots, and other battle appurtenances written into the music, the work's enormous success on both sides of the Atlantic was dubbed "a petty plague that seemed unabatable through the decades."[9] On those warm summer evenings at the "President's Palace" when Nelly tried out this piece, she may have closed the windows. Perhaps it was best.

JOHN ADAMS

"How lonely are my days? How solitary are my nights?" wrote Abigail Adams to her husband John one bleak winter evening in 1778. "How insupportable the idea, that three thousand miles and the vast ocean now divide us!" But an old Scotch song seemed to ring in her ears like a dusty echo of bygone loves. "How oft has my heart danced to the sound of that music?" she wrote. "The native simplicity of it had all the power of a well-wrought tragedy. When I could conquer my sensibility I begged the song, and Master Charles [aged eight] has learned it, and consoles his mamma by singing it to her. I will enclose it to you. It has beauties in it to me, which an indifferent person would not feel perhaps."[10]

Indeed, music became a potion "to divert a melancholy hour" on more than one occasion for Abigail. Long separations often kept her apart from John Adams. Especially during his diplomatic missions abroad as commissioner to France and later minister to the Netherlands and England, Abigail Adams bore the loneliness, responsibilities, and struggles of her husband's ministerial career. Quietly she paid the price for his accomplishments, reflecting the dilemma, still unstudied and unsung, of women in America's early diplomatic life.

Vain, cantankerous, and extremely brilliant, John Adams served for two terms as vice-president under George Washington. On March 4, 1797, he was inaugurated as the second president of the United States. Due to ill health, Abigail remained for long periods at the Quincy farm while Adams served in the capital at Philadelphia. The site for the "Federal City," as George Washington called it, had been determined by Congress in 1790 and formally named the City of Washington the following year. On October 13, 1792, the cornerstone for the "President's Mansion" was laid after a prize of $500 for designing the house was awarded to Irish-born architect James Hoban. With the capital established at Washington in 1800, President Adams moved into the President's Mansion on November 1 of that year. Abigail arrived two weeks later, only to face what she called a "great castle" in a "wilderness city" of mud, cowpaths, and wooden huts. None of the rooms was finished. Damp plaster chilled the walls, and obtaining firewood regularly was impossible. The main stairway to the second floor would not be erected for months. Still "this house," wrote Abigail to her daughter, "is built for ages to come."[11] How right she was! But could she have realized—as she hung her laundry in "the great unfinished audience-room"—that the future East Room would one day become the stage for the finest performing artists in the world?

The Adamses had lived in the White House only about four months when the presidency went to Adams's bitter opponent, Thomas Jefferson, on March 4, 1801. During this short period in the home, the couple hardly had time to unpack, let alone transport a fragile piano or other musical instruments to the drafty, unfinished mansion. There are no records indicating that either John or Abigail owned musical instruments or purchased them for the White House with government funds. Charles Adams sang "with his light and pleasant voice," and John Quincy played the flute, but both boys were grown when their parents lived in the White House.[12]

President and Mrs. Adams, however, were responsible for bringing the first musical ensemble to the new White House, an indication of the importance they placed on music as a vital part of the spirit and social flair of the White House. The young U.S. Marine Band, which later became known as "The President's Own," played for the Adamses' first reception held on New Year's Day, 1801. This event established the tradition of the Marine Band's performances at the White House that exists to the present day. We cannot be certain of the exact instrumentation of the band at this time. On August 31, 1800, Commandant William Burrows wrote Lieutenant Hall: "Procure and send . . . 2 French Horns, 2 C Clarinets, 1 Bassoon, 1 Bass Drum, 2 feet and ½ long and 2 feet in diameter. . . . You will pay $180. . . . I think the price of the Instruments very high." The instruments arrived on November 6, and Burrows urged that "there must be no time lost in instructing them."[13] While the bass drum would not have been used for indoor social events, two oboes and an additional bassoon may have been added later to the ensemble. Thus, like the *Harmonie* of European courts and British military units in America during the Revolution, the Marine Band functioned in a social as well as ceremonial capacity from its earliest days.

Dressed in their scarlet coats faced and edged in blue, the musicians must have added a festive image to the scene. An early report specifies their uniforms at that time also consisted of "blue pantaloons with scarlet seams and gaiters to the knees" and "three-cornered hats edged with yellow." What they played, however, must be pieced together from accounts of Marine Band repertory during this early period: "The President's March" ["Hail Columbia"] and some fife and drum tunes from the Revolutionary War, such as "Dog and Gun," "Rural Felicity," and "Yankee Doodle." And there were others: "Friend and Pitcher," "Marseillaise Hymn," "Battle of the Kegs," "Around the Huge Oak," and "He's Aye a Kissing Me."[14] Or could Abigail Adams perhaps have made a special request (as succeeding first families often did) for her favorite Scotch song, "There's nae Luck about the House"?

Unlike John Quincy and Louisa Catherine Adams, the John Adamses had only modest musical talents and interests. Though inherently bright, Abigail lacked the education of her successors. "I was never sent to any school," she said. "In those days it was fashionable to ridicule female learning."[15] Both she and John typified a rather austere Puritanism, reflected in Adams's comment to Mercy Warren in 1795 that he had no pleasure or amusement which possessed any charms for him: "balls, assemblies, concerts, cards, horses, dogs never engaged any part of my [his] attention . . . business alone."[16] Yet his European experiences showed that dogs and concerts were at least put into separate categories within his frame of mind. The varied cultural opportunities abroad must have had a lasting effect on the Adamses' memories and tastes.

While they were in France, John and Abigail Adams attended concerts, operas, ballets and choral programs. John Adams found the opera "a sprightly amusement, having never seen anything of the kind before," but he also noted in his diary that "the Words are unintelligible, and if they were not, they are said to be very insignificant."[17] Although Abigail seemed more receptive to French grand opera than her husband, her New England concern for morals led her to describe the ballet almost entirely from the viewpoint of its propriety: "Girls, clothed in the thinnest silk and gauze, with their petticoats short, springing two feet from the floor, poising themselves in the air, with their feet flying, and as perfectly showing their garters and drawers as though no petticoat had been worn, was a sight altogether new to me." But while she was "ashamed to be seen to look at them," Abigail also admitted that she was growing used to "the habits, customs, and fashions, which at first disgusted me."[18]

After she returned to the United States, Abigail Adams reported hearing a program of a very different nature. One month after John Adams was inaugurated as president, she attended an historical musical event on April 25, 1798, at the New Theatre on Chestnut Street in Philadelphia: the first performance of "Hail Columbia," America's celebrated national song. Internal tension between Federalists and anti-Federalists was mounting daily at this time, and many felt that war with France was inevitable. The singer and actor Gilbert Fox, worried about filling the theater for his benefit performance, had asked Joseph Hopkinson to write a patriotic song adapted to the tune of Philip Phile's popular "President's March." The day after the performance the first lady described her vivid reactions to Mary Cranch:

> My Dear Sister:
>   I inclose to you a National song composed by this same Mr. [Joseph] Hopkinson. . . . I had a Great curiosity to see for myself the Effect . . . they called again for the song, and made him [Fox] repeat it to the fourth time. And the last time, the whole ("Gallery" cancelled) Audience broke forth in the Chorus whilst the thunder from their Hands was incessant, and at the close they rose, gave 3 Huzzas, that you might have heard a mile—My Head aches in consequence of it.[19]

As President Washington was often immortalized in music, the virtues of John Adams became the subject of a song called "Adams and Liberty." "Her pride is her Adams—his Laws are her choice" sounded America's voice in 1798. It was a bold attempt to pit Federalist conservatism against liberal Jeffersonian democracy—bolder still when one considers these words by Thomas Paine were set to the tune of an old British drinking song, "To Anacreon in Heaven," which later achieved immortality as "The Star-Spangled Banner."[20]

Thomas Jefferson, a fine amateur violinist and devotee of the arts, considered music to be his "favorite passion." This well-known painting by Rembrandt Peale (1800) hangs in the Blue Room of the White House.

THOMAS JEFFERSON

When Thomas Jefferson moved into the White House shortly after becoming president on March 4, 1801, the mansion was still far from being completed. Benjamin Latrobe, commissioner of public buildings and grounds, reported that the roof and gutters leaked so severely that the furniture had to be protected from damage. By 1804 there were still no cellars, and a few years later visitors were still appalled at the "ancient rude state" of the residence. "In a dark night," described one foreigner in 1807, "instead of finding your way to the house, you may, perchance, fall into a pit, or stumble over a heap of rubbish."[21]

Jefferson found life in the new capital rather desolate and lonely. For a cultured man, a fine amateur performer, and lover of good music, the city of Washington left much to be desired. He found a population of about four thousand citizens whose main entertainment consisted of dancing assemblies, magic shows, comic plays, the "Alla-Podrida" (or mish-mash), and a learned pig that could spell, read, and tell the days of the week. Washington's first theater had just opened in the summer of 1800. Called the United States, it was merely a small room seating 130 in Blodgett's Hotel, designed by James Hoban and located near the President's House. Records do not indicate what theatrical events the president attended while in office, although he did buy tickets to a rope-walking show on December 22, 1806, during which Signor Manfredi precariously danced a Spanish fandango over two dozen eggs.[22]

Thomas Jefferson, in fact, regarded music as "the favorite passion of my soul." At the age of seventy-four he considered the art to be "invaluable where a person has an ear. It furnishes a delightful recreation for the hours of respite from the cares of the day."[23] Jefferson's inventive mind, pursuit of excellence, abilities as a performer, and concern for the education of his daughters and granddaughters are well documented in Helen Cripe's *Thomas Jefferson and Music*. His extensive collection of family music is housed in the University of Virginia Library and reflects the tastes of a diligent collector who accumulated every variety and arrangement of music that he, his family, and friends could perform. More than any other president, Jefferson has been recognized by historians as a devotee of the joys of music—his "delightful recreation."

How and when Jefferson learned to play the violin are not known. He was a competent violinist by the age of fourteen, however, and played regularly with the noted gentlemen amateurs of Virginia. He and Patrick Henry often played their fiddles together. During his student and early professional years in Williamsburg in the 1760s, Jefferson performed with harpsichordist Robert Carter, the wealthy planter of Nomini Hall, and violinist/cellist John Tyler, whose bow arm Jefferson had admired. Tyler's son, also named John, became our nation's tenth president in 1841.

What compositions did the young lawyer play with his musical confrères? Jefferson's own catalogue, compiled in 1783, provides a clue. Listed under the category "Instrumental Music"—along with a few country dances and Scotch and Irish airs—are over 100 collections of compositions, such as the concertos of Corelli and Vivaldi, sixty overtures from the operas and oratorios of Handel, and various sonatas of Martini, Boccherini and Carlo Antonio Campioni (1720—88).[24] Jefferson seemed to be especially fond of Campioni's trio sonatas, opp. 1–6. On a hand-written note in the family music collection he advises: "On this paper is noted the beginning of the several compositions of Campioni which are in possession of T. Jefferson. He would be glad to have everything else he has composed of Solos, Duets, or Trios. Printed copies would be preferred; but if not to be had, he would have them in manuscript."[25]

Jefferson's wife, Martha Wayles Skelton, died at the age of thirty-four after having borne six children. Only two lived to adulthood—Martha (Mrs. Thomas Mann Randolph, Jr., nicknamed "Patsy" like Washington's stepdaughter), and Mary (Mrs. John Wayles Eppes). Both young women lived in the White House for several months during 1802–3 with their husbands, who were members of Congress. Like their mother, both girls were talented, and the widower Jefferson gave them every opportunity to develop their musical gifts. "Music, drawing, books, invention and exercise will be so many resources to you against *ennui*," he once wrote to fifteen-year-old Patsy.[26] He purchased for each of the young women a fine Kirkman harpsichord, and Patsy had lessons in Philadelphia with the noted English teacher, John Bentley.

When Jefferson was minister to France from 1785 to 1789, Paris was the European center of trade, commerce, and the arts. The girls studied harpsichord, guitar, and dancing with the finest Parisian masters. Jefferson took advantage of every concert, opera, private musicale, and dramatic spectacle that he possibly could. The girls, too, became acquainted with a rich new world of artistic expression. Whether an *opéra comique* by Grétry, a new Italian opera by Niccolò Piccinni, a performance by the famed violinist Giovanni Viotti, or a vocal concert at the Tuileries—Jefferson relished all. The Concert Spirituel, which left John Adams dissatisfied, so fascinated Jefferson that he was drawn back time and time again.

But the pomp and elegance of European court life, which attracted both George Washington and Adams, was abhorred by President Jefferson. Adams, who continued the more formal traditions of Washington, sniffed: "Jefferson and Rush were for liberty and straight hair. I thought curled hair was as Republican as straight."[27] When Anthony Merry, His Britannic Majesty's minister to the United States, went in full dress to present his credentials, he was shocked by Jefferson's attire in "an old brown coat, red waistcoat, old corduroy small clothes, much soiled woolen hose and slippers without heels." Jefferson abolished the weekly levees of his predecessors and held more frequent, informal dinners preferring "democratic" circular tables. He was a gracious host—but to the diplomatic circle, his was a "raw and rude court."

Jefferson officially dropped the title "Presidential Palace" when he took office, and informed the citizens that his home was known as the President's House. He held only two official levees at the mansion each year—one on New Year's Day and the other on the Fourth of July. The latter is of special interest to White House musical history. It represents the earliest description of actual performers and musical selections at the mansion. Jefferson's first reception on July 4, 1801, attracted considerable attention—especially noted was the fact that the president shook hands with everyone instead of bowing.

But it was the music, above all, that "awakened patriotic feelings as well as gaiety," recounted Margaret Bayard Smith, wife of the *National Intelligencer*'s publisher.[28] In a letter to her sister, she observed: "Martial music soon announced the approach of the marine corps of Captain Burrows who in due military form saluted the President, accompanied by the President's march [probably 'Hail Columbia'] played by an excellent band attached to the corps. After undergoing various military evolutions, the company returned to the dining room, and the band from an adjacent room played a succession of fine patriotic airs."[29]

And accompanied by the Marine Band, a strong baritone voice rang clear and true—"the ladies said it was divine." The singer was Captain Thomas Tingey, handsome commandant of the newly established Washington Navy Yard. The *Intelligencer* added: "the band of music played with great precision

Captain Thomas Tingey, U.S. Navy, first commandant of the Navy Yard, Washington, D.C., and the earliest known musical soloist to perform for a White House program. Print from a painting by Charles Saint Memin.

and with inspiring animation. . . . Captain Tingey then sang with happy animation a patriotic song, composed for the occasion by Mr. [Thomas] Law, which was received with loud plaudits."

> Hail Columbia! happy land,
> Hail ye patriots, heaven born land
> Who Independence first proclaimed . . .
> Immortal be that glorious day
> When first we cast our chains away.[30]

This account shows how the term "composed for the occasion" or "newly composed" can be easily misinterpreted unless care is taken by historians to compare texts with preexisting songs. In the early days of our nation especially, parody was very common, particularly in songs that had a great national appeal. Jefferson's Fourth of July gala did not present the first performance of "Hail Columbia" (still called "The President's March" for some time to come); rather, it featured a new set of lyrics that celebrated the first Independence Day gala at the White House. Jefferson must have enjoyed vocal soloists, because five years later at the July 4, 1806, White House reception, a "Mr. Cutting" sang a song set to the tune of "Anacreon in Heaven." Eight years later this popular tune was immortalized as "The Star-Spangled Banner," when it received new lyrics by Francis Scott Key.

There is a legend that Jefferson asked Colonel William Burrows to enlist some musicians in Italy as Marines and bring them back to expand the Marine Band. The tale could indeed be true. Jefferson once had expressed the desire to import from Italy for his Virginia plantation persons who could provide domestic and musical needs simultaneously, in other words, a "court band," American style:

> In a country where like yours music is cultivated and practised by every class I suppose there might be found persons of those trades who could perform on the French horn, clarinet or hautboy and bassoon, so that one might have a band of two French horns, two clarinets and hautboys and a bassoon, without enlarging their domestic expenses. . . .

Without meaning to give you trouble, perhaps it might be practicable for you in ordinary intercourse with your people to find out such men disposed to come to America.[31]

This plan seems to have been realized after Jefferson became president and about the same time that his conceptions for the decoration of the U.S. Capitol Building developed. Jefferson arranged through his friend Filippo Mazzei to bring sculptors from Carrara, Italy, to Washington. The first of these fine artisans arrived in October 1805, and over the ensuing decades the Capitol was emblazoned with the painting, frescos, sculpture, and carving of more than forty Italian specialists.[32]

The story of the Sicilian musicians who arrived in Washington one month before the sculptors from Carrara is less dramatic but no less colorful. The little "band" not only left its mark on the history of the Marine Band, but ultimately on the cultural life of the city of Washington itself. On September 19, 1805, upon orders from William Burrows, commandant of the Marine Corps, sixteen musicians arrived in Washington, several with their wives and children. Tired, disheveled and frightened, they were unable to communicate in a foreign tongue, in a strange new home that their leader, Gaetano Carusi, described as "a desert . . . a place containing some 2 or 3 taverns and a few scattered cottages and log huts, called the City of Washington, the Metropolis of the United States of America."[33] All were led off to their quarters in the Marine Barracks, where, according to Carusi, "men, women, boys and children, 30 or more in all, were obliged to bundle together in a single chamber and sleep upon the bare floor."[34] Four days later, the *National Intelligencer* noted, the Sicilians made their debut as "the elegant Italian Band" that performed at the banquet celebrating the victory of Captain Bainbridge over the Tripolitans.

How elegant the Sicilians felt, however, is open to conjecture. They must have been separated from the main unit because accounts of the time regularly indicate that there was both an "Italian Marine Band" and a "Marine Band." Although the versatile Gaetano Carusi was a teacher, composer, and performer who played five instruments, the musical backgrounds of the others is uncertain. Most came from Catania, the birthplace of Vincenzo Bellini and a city that abounded with music both day and night. While the Sicilians probably learned the simple, jaunty American tunes with ease, did they long for their gentle vesper hymns, modal carnival songs and the plaintive angelus striking at dawn from the cathedral tower—or for the magnificent tones of the Baroque organ at the Benedictine Monastery?

Records indicate that the Italian Marine Band played at the White House for special events, notably for the reception for Tunisian ambassador, Sidi Mellimelli, with his long black beard, four-foot pipe, and gold-embroidered cloak. But the career of the band was brief and inglorious. All the members were dismissed from the corps after only one-half of their three years were served, although several made their way back into the band. One in particular, Venerando Pulizzi, remained with the band for twenty-one years serving as its leader during the presidencies of James Monroe and John Quincy Adams.

Gaetano Carusi, however, spent most of his lifetime engaged in legal battles with the U.S. government. He claimed he had been "lured by false and deceitful promises" and that even his music had been confiscated by the "ruthless" commandant. At the age of seventy-two he petitioned Congress for the sum of $1,000 as compensation for his many grievances, but was turned down.[35] The ironic grand finale to the Carusi drama is that the maestro's three sons, Lewis, Samuel, and Nathaniel, became highly successful impresarios, composers, and teachers in Washington. In 1822 Lewis restored a building that for several decades was the scene of many inaugural galas, balls, and concerts attended by the presidents and their families—a kind of primitive John F. Kennedy Center for the Performing Arts.[36]

Jefferson's enjoyment of music has been studied and documented, and yet his personal musical activities during his eight years in the White House remain a tantalizing enigma. Did he perform music alone or with friends? Did he invite guests to play after his numerous friendly dinner parties?[37] Was there a pianoforte or harpsichord in the White House during his administration? Did the president's musical daughters play when they visited the mansion? True, the presidency weighed heavily upon Jefferson: "He held to a Spartan regimen in his duties, spending from ten to thirteen hours a day at his desk, and allowing himself a bare four hours a day for riding, dining and 'a little unbending.' "[38] He was fifty-seven years old when he took office and sixty-five when he left. But accounts indicate that he still enjoyed music when he retired to Monticello and played his violin on occasion when not bothered by a bad wrist.[39]

Jefferson managed to escape to Monticello frequently during his presidential years. Even though his daughter Martha kept her Kirkman harpsichord there, and Jefferson probably enjoyed relaxing musical moments at his estate, it is inconceivable he was without a keyboard instrument for the entire time he was president. He was fascinated with the new pianoforte, although he played neither piano nor harpsichord. In 1771 he wrote to London for a pianoforte for his future wife, Martha Wayles Skelton. While details about the instrument are obscure, Jefferson was among the few Americans to own a piano at a time when the harpsichord was still preferred in more affluent American parlors.

An inveterate tinkerer and inventor, Jefferson also bought an experimental keyboard instrument from John Isaac Hawkins of Philadelphia for $264 in 1800. The feisty little "portable grand" was promptly returned to Hawkins because it did not stay in tune "a single hour." But when Jefferson was furnishing the White House in 1802 through Thomas Claxton's assistance, he refused Claxton's suggestion that a "skilled person" select a pianoforte, an instrument that would be "pleasing to everyone." Jefferson felt that "no doubt a Pianoforte would be a perfectly proper piece of furniture. But in the present state of our funds, they will be exhausted by articles more indispensable."[40]

Despite the fact that Jefferson was known to have been a good amateur violinist and is believed to have owned at least five violins (one of these may have been a kit, or dance master's fiddle), only scant reference to these instruments exists in Jefferson's correspondence and account books. Perhaps he played a Cremona—or some other fine rare instrument—for diversion during his days in the White House. While "Jefferson violins" seem to keep emerging over the years, their stories remain only partly credible.[41]

While Jefferson was president, he had several sheaves of music bound into volumes—a sign he valued their preservation. In the family collection at Charlottesville are several volumes with green covers containing some early quartets and trios of Pleyel, Clementi, Mozart, and others. Perhaps the president propped up their parts on the fine stand he designed especially for chamber music and in his casual democratic way invited in a Marine Band player or two. Gaetano Carusi himself may have filled in as flutist or violinist, topping off a relaxing evening with a Sicilian hymn or folk song for the president.[42] Without a doubt the strains of music drifted from the White House on many an evening—when it was dark and the pasture grounds surrounding the mansion were deserted, and Jefferson thought no one was listening. For he was often very tired, and music was his "companion" to divert, delight, and "sweeten many hours."[43]

MADISON AND MONROE

The White House of Thomas Jefferson had a master but no mistress. The administration of James Madison, from 1809–17, began a new, dynamic period in the history of the mansion. Having assisted Jefferson with his entertaining when her husband was secretary of state, First Lady Dolley Madison continued Jefferson's informal, egalitarian style, but she did so with flair, imagination, and a touch of pomp. With the help of polished Frenchman John Pierre Sioussat, her "master of ceremonies," Dolley managed to maintain an oasis of civilization in a muddy, lonely city that was only beginning to acknowledge its social needs. She transformed Jefferson's cabinet room into a state dining room, expanded the frequency and size of his dinner parties, and established a weekly series of Wednesday night "drawing rooms," in what is now the Red Room, making sure everyone was invited to attend. These were evenings of "blazing splendor," according to Washington Irving, who was often a guest during this period. Dressed in her fine French ensembles with their elaborate headdresses, "Queen Dolley," as she was affectionately called, reigned with elegance and ease.[44]

Music under the Madisons became a vital element of their hospitality. The Marine Band played frequently at various events, as it did on the New Year's Day in 1811 described by Catherine Mitchell: "When we reach'd the grand entrance the sound of sweet music struck our ears. . . . Upon entering the spacious hall we beheld on one side a number of Musicians seated round a table playing, on different instruments, enlivening airs, for the entertainment of the company as they were ushered into the inner apartments. . . . The Musicians continued playing at intervals, until we had all taken our departure."[45]

There are no indications that either the president or first lady played the piano, but their guests performed often at small receptions and dinners— mostly ladies, in the true American domestic tradition. Mrs. William Seaton relates: "Mrs. Madison insisted on my playing on her elegant grand piano a waltz for Miss S[mith] and Miss M[agruder] to dance, the figure of which she instructed them in."[46] A former Quaker, the first lady had obviously subjugated her strict heritage to the worldly glamour of the waltz, which many called "hugging set to music." But while waltzes were being published in America as early as 1795, they did not become a part of Washington society

Oil portrait of Dolley Madison as first lady by Bass Otis, 1816. Mrs. Madison, one of our nation's most gracious hostesses, purchased the first piano and collection of music for the White House.

until the Carusi Dancing Assemblies brought them to life in the 1820s. Still, Dolley Madison's light steps were delightfully immortalized in the earliest piece of music dedicated to a first lady—"Mrs. Madison's Waltz," published by Willig in Philadelphia between 1810 and 1812.

From the Madison administration we have the first evidence that a piano was purchased specifically for the White House. On March 17, 1809, Benjamin Latrobe, who was furnishing the mansion for Dolley, wrote to the first lady that he had found in Philadelphia the answer to her request. After inquiring about two pianos, he settled upon a third "imported especially for a private family." It cost $530, but Latrobe managed to buy it for $450. "It is of such superior tone in strength and sweetness," he said, "that I would by all means recommend its being taken at that price. I have left with my brother Mr. Hazelhurst the necessary instructions."[47] Clementis, Broadwoods, and Astors were being imported at this time, but we may never know the details of the piano's maker. The instrument was destroyed along with the furnishings of four presidents when the British set fire to the mansion on August 24, 1814.[48]

Another purchase that Dolley Madison made for the White House is unique to the mansion's history. Through her agent at the time, Latrobe, she bought a fascinating collection of musical scores—illustrating further the importance she placed on the role of music in her household.[49] Printed in Philadelphia in 1810, Madame Le Pelletier's elegantly engraved *Journal of Musick* is an important reflection of French influence in an American culture still dominated by English practices. (See Appendix A.)

The Madisons, like Washington and Jefferson before them, enjoyed French furnishings and culture. Elegant imported articles were emblematic of the finest American tastes, and it is somewhat ironic that the pre-fire White House under Dolley Madison boasted hardly any French furniture.[50] Madison was a Republican with pro-French political sympathies, but his taste for French culture was probably stimulated by his good friend, James Monroe. A family of dignity and wealth, the Monroes cherished courtly luxuries. Not long after Monroe took office on March 4, 1817, he purchased a large quantity of furniture from France, and the first family moved into the White House in time to hold a gala reception there on New Year's Day, 1818.

Like the Madisons, the Monroes purchased a fine pianoforte for the White House. The graceful furnishing cost 2,200 francs, the most expensive item listed for the Sitting Room (probably today's Red Room), and was shipped on September 15, 1817, with other furniture for the mansion on the *Resolution* bound for Alexandria. It was described as "a piano made by Erard Brothers, decorated with bronze, having three legs ('colones') and four pedals and a 'tambourin.'"[51] At this time the prestigious firm of Erard frères (whose first piano was built by Sébastien Erard in 1777) had achieved an international reputation, and its instruments were played by Ludwig van Beethoven and other great artists.

A special feature of the piano was its multiple pedal mechanism, which allowed for theatrical colors and sound effects to serve the era's new descriptive piano pieces. Pedals could render a plucked sound (pizzicato or lute), reedy sound (bassoon), or perhaps more mellow ones (moderator) by means of cloth placed between the strings and the hammers. The "tambourin" of the Monroes' Erard was produced either by a fifth pedal or a sideways-moving "genouillère," which worked a drum (or triangle—or both) built into the bass of the piano. Thus, one can hear the White House halls reverberating with Swiss echo airs, Turkish marches, and battle pieces with their Janissary effects made popular by the European military bands of the time.

Elizabeth and James Monroe appear to be the first presidential couple to have attended the theater in Washington. On March 26, 1819, they saw the *School of Reform* at the Washington Theater (later Carusi's Saloon) during which a "Mr. Russell" danced a "hornpipe in real iron Fetters."[52] What their reaction to this gala spectacle was we may never know. But the first family who succeeded them was a truly musical one, and evidence of the Adamses' interests in the art of music exists in several sources.

JOHN QUINCY ADAMS

Both John Quincy Adams and Louisa Catherine Adams had a broader European heritage than any of their presidential predecessors. John Quincy, son of our second president, spent many vital years of his life in diplomatic service abroad before becoming president in 1825. He lived in Russia, Holland, France, and England, and his revealing diaries detail the numerous operas, concerts, and theatrical events both he and Louisa attended before and after their marriage in 1797.

Music to Adams had a special power and message that remained with him into his most mature years. When he left the presidency in 1829 upon failure of his reelection, he commented bitterly:

> In the French opera of Richard Coeur-de-Lion, the minstrel, Blondel, sings under the walls of his prison a song beginning:

> O, Richard! O, mon roi!
> L'univers t'abandonne.
> [O, Richard!, O, my king!
> The universe has abandoned you.]

When I first head this song forty-five years ago, at one of the first representations of that delightful play, it made an indelible impression upon my memory, without imagining that I should ever feel its force so much closer home. In the year 1829 scarce a day passed that did not bring it to my thoughts.[53]

John Quincy Adams had definite views about the status of American culture. He felt that "American genius was very much addicted to painting . . . but that we had neither cultivated nor were attached much to music." Why this was true he was not certain. Perhaps it was due to "some particular construction of our fibres." While the French enjoyed rousing patriotic music, the Americans who fought seven years and more for their liberty did not write a single tune that "electrified every soul." As for his own attitudes, "I am extremely fond of music," he said, "and by dint of great pains have learnt to blow very badly the flute—but could never learn to perform upon the violin, because I never could acquire the art of putting the instrument in tune."[54]

If John Quincy questioned the reasons for Americans lagging behind Europeans in their musical pursuits, his own stern republicanism—reflected vividly and poignantly in his attitudes toward his wife—provided an answer. Born in London of a wealthy Anglo-American family, Louisa Catherine Johnson was our only first lady born outside of the United States. She grew up in a musical family, played the harp and pianoforte as a young girl, and had a naturally lovely singing voice. It was her talent, in fact, that initially attracted twenty-eight-year-old John Quincy Adams while he was in England. His diaries contain many accounts of her entertaining him with her two sisters in their gracious home.[55] During their courtship John Quincy and Louisa sang and played together often; one of their favorite pieces was the aria "Angels Ever Bright and Fair" from Handel's oratorio *Theodora*.

Yet to John and Abigail Adams, Louisa Catherine was never wholly American. She was tainted by the "empty baubles of life connected with courts," the breeding ground of luxury, frivolity and vice. Even music-loving John Quincy once snapped that Louisa's playing the harp was "a trivial accomplishment," providing neither intelligence nor virtue. Music could give little "domestic happiness," he said, and he would willingly give up any of his pleasures in music if she would improve herself.[56] Improve herself, indeed! In the same breath, John Quincy promulgated that intellectualism and politics had no place in the life of a woman. Louisa's biographer, Joan Challinor, summarized her dilemma as follows: "As an ambitious woman, born when ambition was prohibited for women, she could never fully admit to, or act on, her own feelings. Caught in a web spun by the culture and her husband's extreme republicanism, Louisa suffered from ambivalences and paralyzing guilt. At no time was she able to face herself and her desires squarely and honestly."[57]

Louisa's life as the wife of a diplomat was fraught with struggle, loneliness and grief, and her bouts of deep depression only intensified when her son committed suicide in 1828. Still, the first lady made every effort to be a gracious hostess, and according to Washington society, she succeeded. In December of that same year, she and the president brought dancing to the White House, where it was described as a "novel feature of the evening's entertainment."[58]

The Marine Band not only accompanied the dancing as a small social orchestra, but it also performed for one of the decade's most significant historic events—the ground-breaking ceremony for the excavation of the Chesapeake and Ohio Canal, attended by President John Quincy Adams. "Noiseless," reported the *National Intelligencer* of July 7, 1828, "the people moved forward on the bank of the canal, keeping even pace with the long line of boats whilst airs, now animated, now plaintive, from the Marine Band, placed in the forward boat lightened the toil of the walk." Among the selections were "Rural Felicity," "Roslin Castle," "The Star-Spangled Banner," Reinagle's "America, Commerce and Freedom" from his ballet pantomime *The Sailor's Landlady* (1794), Thomas Moore's "The Meeting of the Waters," and a favorite with the first lady, Whitaker's "Oh Say not Woman's Heart is Bought."

But the most significant piece historically was "Hail to the Chief." Derived from an old Gaelic air, the tune had been adapted to a scene from Sir Walter Scott's *The Lady of the Lake* by English composer James Sanderson. In Sanderson's version of the play, Highland Chieftain Sir Roderick Dhu (actually an outlaw) is heralded by the lilting boat song "Hail to the Chief." Scott's play had many musical settings, including one by Henry Rowley Bishop. But the Sanderson version, first performed in New York in 1812, caught on instantly and was successful for many years thereafter. The July 4th celebration of 1828 appears to be the song's first association with a president. And this may have been merely by accident. The canal boats—rather than the "Chief"—might have dictated the selection for the day:

> Hail to the chief, who in triumph advances,
> Honor'd and blessed be the evergreen pine!
> . . . .
> Row, vassals, row, for the pride of the Highlands!
> Stretch to your oars for the evergreen pine![59]

While the Marine Band celebrated a national event with spirit and joy, Louisa Adams found in music her own quiet messages. She sat at the pianoforte just as she had when she was young, a tired little lady—somewhat resembling Empress Josephine—with her curls bobbing and a faint, elusive smile on her lips. She was afraid to play too often, but the moments she had alone were special. The upstairs drawing room of the president's mansion was very quiet. Gently she fingered one of her favorite pieces, her sweet voice almost a whisper:

> Oh say not Woman's Love is bought
> With vain and empty treasure!
> Oh say not Woman's heart is caught
> By every idle pleasure.[60]

This lovely ballad by John Whitaker appears not only in the famous portrait of Louisa Adams by Charles Bird King, but also among the first lady's personal collection of music (see Appendix A). Like many other pieces

March and Chorus from *The Lady of the Lake* by James Sanderson, published by G. E. Blake ca. 1812. The song was the source for "Hail to the Chief," which was first associated with a president in 1828.

Five- and one-half octave mahogany and rosewood pianoforte made by Alpheus Babcock, Boston, 1825–29. Mrs. Adams's pianoforte, harp, and two volumes of music are on exhibit in the First Ladies Hall, National Museum of American History.

in the collection, such as the melancholy songs of Thomas Moore, Whitaker's ballad conjurs up a poignant image of this unique first lady—an image only music can express.

Bound into two volumes with "L. C. Adams" tooled in gold on the covers, the music is housed at the Smithsonian Institution's Museum of American History along with Mrs. Adams's harp, music stand, and pianoforte. The collection comprises the first musical objects owned by a presidential family member during her years at the White House that are still preserved. Louisa's pianoforte, made by Alpheus Babcock of Boston, dates about 1825–29 and is believed to have been in the White House during the administration of John Quincy Adams. It is uncertain whether the piano was Mrs. Adams's own or purchased for the White House. Louisa enjoyed her American-made piano at a time when the Monroes' French tastes were criticized, and Congress had directed that the president's house should contain American-made furniture "as far as practicable."[61] The 5½ octave mahogany and rosewood instrument lacks the one-piece cast iron frame for which Babcock and his partner John Mackay achieved national recognition on December 17, 1825. But Babcock's pianos of this time won several prizes for their "excellent finish, tone and touch."[62]

When John Quincy Adams left the White House, defeated and bitter, an era had ended. The old customs soon would be modified and incorporated into a new stream of entertainment styles; the intimate family drawing rooms would open their doors to famous guest performers as technology, industry, and transportation carried their musical messages—sometimes graceful, sometimes brash—to the Executive Mansion. Presidents would be sung into office. Gentle serenades would become screaming protest. A civil war would bring to the White House music with a depth and intensity the nation had never known. For the history of the White House is the history of America. And underpinning this heritage are the ubiquitous sounds of music—tones which captured the event and the human spirit simultaneously.

CHAPTER 2

POLITICS, PROTEST, AND THE CHANGING AMERICAN CULTURE

Liberty is our motto,
And we'll sing as freemen ought to
Till it rings through glen and grotto
From the Old Granite State
That the tribe of Jesse,
That the tribe of Jesse,
That the tribe of Jesse,
Are the friends of equal rights.

Hutchinson Family
"The Old Granite State"

ANDREW JACKSON

In his sociable, democratic dealings with the American people, Andrew Jackson was closer to the spirit of Thomas Jefferson than to that of his stately predecessor, John Quincy Adams. Jackson was the product of pioneer philosophy, a self-educated man who had risen to affluence as a prosperous Tennessee planter. His father was a farmer in a backwoods area of the Carolinas, and Andrew Jackson's popularity with the voters was founded on his rough, fearless career as soldier and statesman. Like the presidents before him, Jackson was welcomed into office with the usual run of dedicatory marches, gala parades, and balls. For "Old Hickory," however, there was something extra. His inauguration on March 4, 1829, featured a performance of *Belle's Strategem*, an "elegant comedy" (and one of George Washington's favorites).[1]

The White House of Andrew Jackson was simpler in its customs, ambiance, and attitudes than it had been under Adams or Monroe. It was the people's house and its public receptions with doors open to one and all were clearly the people's pleasure. The designation "White House" was used now with more regularity, gradually replacing the term President's Palace or President's House until eventually it became the legal name under Theodore Roosevelt. The East Room was tastefully furnished; however, "it was mortifying to see men with boots heavy with mud, standing on the damask-satin-covered chairs and sofas," wrote one eyewitness about the inaugural reception. "Negroes, boys, women, and children took possession of the house and

Popular ballerina Celeste Keppler dances for President Andrew Jackson and his cabinet in a caricature by H. R. Robinson, 1836. "I've not lost all my penchant for pretty women," says Jackson in the drawing. Seated at far right is Vice-President Martin Van Buren.

scrambled, romped and fought in the rooms," commented another.[2] During the Jackson terms food, music, and congeniality were abundant. At his first Fourth of July reception the general treated his guests to a 1,400 pound "Mammoth Cheese" while the Marine Band played the president's favorite tune, "Auld Lang Syne."[3]

Jackson's wife, Rachel Donelson, died on the Christmas Eve before the general's first inauguration, and his niece, Emily Donelson, and later his daughter-in-law, Sarah Yorke Jackson, served as hostesses. Music was enjoyed informally during these years. Sarah Jackson played the guitar, and her fine imported six-stringed instrument, made by Cabasse Visinaire l'aîné, is the property of The Hermitage, Jackson's home in Tennessee. On November 21, 1831, a "rosewood pianoforte of six octaves" was purchased for the White House from Thompson and Homans "for $300 less $100 for second hand piano exchanged."[4] The new piano was probably exchanged for the "French grand piano," the old Erard that was still in the mansion on March 12, 1830.[5]

Music and pretty ladies seemed to have gone hand in hand with President Jackson. Some of them played the piano—others danced. Whether or not it was Jackson's fondness for feminine glamour that attracted him to the graceful ballerina "Mlle. Celeste," we may never know. But during the 1836 campaign, well-known political caricaturist Henry R. Robinson used an imaginary scene at the White House for some whimsical anti-Jacksonian propaganda. He showed the charming French dancer performing for the president and members of the cabinet. Barely sixteen when she arrived in

New York from Paris in 1827, Celeste Keppler was one of the first to dance *en pointe* in the United States. With her spectacular pirouettes and other tours de force, she exhibited her well-rounded legs to the delight of her audience.[6] The lithograph, called *The Celeste-al-Cabinet*, was an obvious spoof on the notorious scandal between Secretary John Eaton and Peggy Timberlake—a political war of nerves that split Jackson's cabinet in 1831.

VAN BUREN AND WILLIAM HARRISON

Ironically, the year after the *Celeste* caricature appeared, another famous ballerina actually did visit the White House. Fanny Elssler and her voluptuous, hip-swaying cachucha complete with Spanish castanets took Washington by storm. So popular was the provocative Fanny that during one of her tours it was decided that Congress would meet only on the days she was *not* dancing. Martin Van Buren, a widower who was inaugurated as president in March 1837, attended one of her performances and promptly invited the pretty dancer to the Executive Mansion the next morning. "I think his demeanor is very easy, very frank and very royal," she noted respectfully.[7]

Not all agreed. And the president's "royal" attitude became the subject of satire and song as the campaign of 1840 took firm hold on the nation. Congressman Charles Ogle of Pennsylvania branded Van Buren as an effete voluptuary whose "Asiatic Mansion" contained imported carpets, exotic artificial flowers, and even a "bathtub!" In the "yellow drawing room" (Red Room) stood an "elegant gilt-mounted pianoforte" with "damask satin-covered music stools." At the eastern end of the hall during receptions, noted Ogle, the Marine Band was stationed and "with all their fine instruments in full tune 'at the same identical moment' [they] strike up one of our most admired national airs."[8] Benjamin Perley Poore, however, thought differently about these "admired airs": "The Marine Band . . . is always ordered from the Navy Yard and stationed in the spacious front hall, from whence they swell the rich saloons of the palace with 'Hail to the Chief!' 'Wha'll be King but Charley?' and other humdrum airs, which ravish with delight the ears of warriors who have never smelt powder."[9]

Poore's reference to "Hail to the Chief" indicates that the presidential march was played in the White House during Van Buren's administration. The piece had been in the Marine Band repertory, as noted earlier, as far back as John Quincy Adams, but there is no way of knowing how closely it was identified with the chief of state. During these years it may have been just another underpinning of the festive social scene—just another "humdrum" air.[10]

The Whigs' effort to elect William Henry Harrison and John Tyler in the "log cabin and hard cider" campaign of 1840 evoked a frenzied and persuasive outburst of singing. But practically overnight the joyous songs became mournful dirges. On March 4, 1841, Harrison was inaugurated; exactly one month later, he was dead. Commemorative music was composed and published hurriedly, notably Dielman's "President Harrison's Funeral Dirge, as performed on the occasion of his burial at Washington City, April, 1841." The piano arrangement of Dielman's march traveled into thousands of American homes, complete with fanfares ("The last trumpet peal"), diminished seventh chords ("The Widow's Shriek"), and other programmatic devices. The public heard the somber tale again and again through music in a way that surpassed any newspaper. But the historical value of the piece lies in the lithograph on the cover depicting bands marching in procession from the White House; it is the earliest known iconographical source linking music with the president's home.

JOHN TYLER

The decade of the 1840s—the terms of John Tyler, James Knox Polk, and Zachary Taylor—was forecast eloquently in John Greenleaf Whittier's *Ballads and Anti-Slavery Poems* written in 1838. His popular "Stanzas" and "The Moral Warfare" were grim, moving messages of a self-conscious era. The opera house, gala new site of both culture and social persiflage during Jackson's terms, became the stage for one of the century's most spectacular riots on May 10, 1849. At least twenty were killed in the Astor Opera House in New York during the infamous Macready-Forrest feud caused by anti-English sentiments. Through their heated promulgations, the actors managed to ignite the emotions of the audience in a way like no other. Even singers such as Henry Russell and the Hutchinson Family were making strong social statements in song during this period, as were the newly founded Christy Minstrels of 1842 and the Virginia Minstrels of the following year, who toured in various parts of the country. It is little surprise, then, that among the earliest guest artists to perform at the White House were those whose musical pleasures had political overtones.

John Tyler, the Democrat-turned-Whig who followed Harrison in the White House, came from a distinguished line of Virginia planters as had his predecessor. He had fifteen children, eight by his first wife, Letitia Christian, who died in 1842, and seven by his second wife, Julia Gardiner, whom he married in 1844, a few months before he left office. Tyler inherited his father's love of music and often turned to music "to escape from all the environments of political and social cares and duties," his daughter Letitia ("Letty") recalled: "In spite of the comparatively quiet life at the White House, my father's time was rarely ever his own. 'Now sing, Letty,' he would say when we found ourselves far from the maddening crowd enjoying the quiet of some country road. And then I would sing his favorite songs, the old Scotch ballads we loved so well. . . . Nobody sings 'Barbara Allen' and 'Ye Banks and Braes' these days."[11]

The Tyler White House was socially active. Julia Gardiner, a queenly woman whose regal attitudes earned her the title "Mrs. Presidentess," reputedly gave instructions to the Marine Band to play "Hail to the Chief" whenever the president made an official appearance. By the time of Polk's inauguration, the piece was associated with the president in a ceremonious tribute maintained to the present. President and Mrs. Tyler enjoyed the weekly outdoor Marine Band concerts initiated earlier during their administration by Francis Scala. A stocky young man of nineteen who spoke no English, Scala had joined the Marine Band in 1842 shortly after arriving in America from his native Naples and became its leader under President Pierce. When he left the band in 1871, he had served nine presidents and had decidedly improved the organization's balance, technique and repertory. The outdoor concerts, open to the public, were held from spring to fall on the South Lawn of the White House on Saturday evenings—a custom that continued until the administration of Herbert Hoover.[12]

The Marine Band of this period comprised up to twenty players from at least six countries: America, England, Germany, Spain, Italy, and Austria. A survey of its repertory indicates a balance of musical styles represented by polkas, waltzes, quickstep arrangements of popular songs, and especially operatic selections. Italian opera—new to American shores in the 1820s and 1830s—became immediately popular and was transformed into piano parlor pieces, dances, and other arrangements. Indeed, Scala, born into the traditions of Italian opera, often arranged for band an operatic aria or chorus shortly after its European or American premier. The parts for "Scena e aria" from Donizetti's *Lucia di Lammermoor*, for example, are dated 1842, and the opera was given its American premier in New Orleans only the year before— with its New York premier the year *after*. Band parts for operas by Auber, Bellini, Boieldieu, Donizetti, Flotow, Gounod, Meyerbeer, Offenbach, Rossini, Verdi, and von Weber are represented in the Scala archives. Thus, under the baton of Francis Scala, White House guests were treated to all the titillating operatic airs that were invading America at this time.

Shortly after he became president, Tyler purchased two pianos for the White House from Emilius N. Scherr, a Philadelphia piano and guitar maker who had migrated from Denmark. The instruments cost $600 and $450 and were bought "by two second hand pianos taken in exchange" on July 21, 1841. One of the pianos was described as a "large new concert piano with double grand action,"[13] and most likely it was this instrument that the Bohemian-born composer, Anthony Philip Heinrich, played when he performed for President Tyler. Called "America's Beethoven," Heinrich had come to Washington to present his newest composition to the president. In his *Shadows on the Wall*, John Hill Hewitt describes accompanying Heinrich to Washington: "Poor Heinrich! I shall never forget him. He imagined he was going to set the world on fire . . . two or three hours of patient hearing did I give to the most complicated harmony I had ever heard . . . wild and unearthly passages." Hewitt goes on:

> At a proper hour we visited the President's mansion. . . . We were shown into the parlor. . . . The composer labored hard to give full effect to his weird production; his bald pate bobbed from side to side, and shone like a bubble on the surface of a calm lake. At times his shoulders would be raised to the line of his ears, and his knees went up to the keyboard, while the perspiration rolled in large drops down his wrinkled cheeks. . . .
>
> The inspired composer had got about half-way through his wonderful production, when Mr. Tyler arose from his chair, and placing his hand gently on Heinrich's shoulder, said:
>
> "That may all be very fine, sir, but can't you play us a good old Virginia reel?"
>
> Had a thunderbolt fallen at the feet of the musician, he could not have been more astounded. He arose from the piano, rolled up his manuscript, and taking his hat and cane, bolted toward the door, exclaiming:

Anthony Philip Heinrich, a Bohemian composer who emigrated to America in 1810, performed for President John Tyler in the 1840s. Anonymous drawing made from a contemporary silhouette.

"No, sir; I never plays dance music!"
I joined him in the vestibule. . . . As we proceeded along Pennsylvania Avenue, Heinrich grasped my arm convulsively, and exclaimed:
"Mein Gott in himmel! de peebles vot made Yohn Tyler Bresident ought to be hung! He knows no more about music than an oyshter!"[14]

The elegant Scherr piano was treated more subtly, though no less expressively, when two noted singing families came to the White House with messages ringing loud, clear, poignantly—with voices of reform, humanitarianism, rugged nationalism, and idealistic sentiment. "We have come from the mountains . . . of the " 'Old Granite State,' " sang the Hutchinsons. "We're a band of brothers . . . And we live among the hills. With a band of music . . . We are passing round the world."

For over a period of twenty years, the "Tribe of Jesse," as the four (sometimes five) singers were called at first, became a stirring symbol of the Yankee spirit in music. The ensemble came from rural New Hampshire and were the most popular of the singing families of the 1830s, 1840s, and 1850s, such as the Rainers (the "Tyrolese Minstrels"), the Bakers, the Cheneys, the Peakes, and the Gibsons. Through their rich harmonizations and clear diction, the Hutchinsons expressed their genuine concern for human misery and social reform in subjects involving woman's suffrage, alcohol, war, prisons, and especially slavery.

Tyler was the first of seven presidents who would hear the Hutchinsons sing in the decades ensuing. But the ensemble's first concert in the White House, on January 30, 1844, was rather subdued in tone, more patriotic than polemic. The reception packed numerous guests into the East Room, and Asa noted that there were "many pretty good looking maidens there but I pitied them laced up as they were so that they could scarcely breathe and with their dresses and shoes hardly fit for summer wear. I can't describe—music by a

Hutchinson Family Singers, known as "The Tribe of Jesse," in a sketch by Margaret Gillies, 1846. In various combinations, the group sang for seven presidents.

poor band, some dancing. . . . I hate false fashions. 'A life in the wildwood free.' "[15] The program included "The Land of Washington," "Happy and Free," "A Little Farm Well Tilled," and "The Origin of Yankee Doodle." At the close of the program was the perennial "The Old Granite State," which the group often sang in antiphonal style—solo with chorus in echo fashion—characteristic of gospel hymnody. There was scarcely a program given by the Hutchinsons that did not open or close with this piece; it became their theme song.

POLK AND TAYLOR

President and Mrs. James Knox Polk allowed no dancing, cards, or "frivolities of any kind" during their term in the White House from 1845 to 1849. Sarah Childress Polk was a talented woman whose father had given her a fine Astor pianoforte when she was a young girl.[16] As a student at the Moravian Female Academy in Salem, North Carolina, she composed music and was especially well educated in the arts. Music to Mrs. Polk had a significant place in American life, but its graceful tones were meant only to be listened to, and it was not until the administration of Benjamin Harrison that dancing became an active part of White House social life again.

One of the first musicians to entertain the Polks was William Dempster, whose popular ballads harked back to the sentimental Scotch and Irish traditions still popular in America at this time. Dempster's "Lament of the Irish Immigrant" (Boston, 1840) was composed at a time when the Irish began to arrive in America in large numbers. A melancholy little mood piece, it tells of loved ones lost and a cherished homeland.

Music to the president, however, was a mystical language that could fortify the spirits of those who knew no other means of communication. On April 30, 1846, he wrote in his diary that between twenty and thirty blind and deaf-mute children called on him and demonstrated their skills in literature, mathematics, and music. America at this time was only beginning to form an awareness of her less fortunate brothers and sisters; the Perkins Institute for the Blind, for example, was a searchlight for those deprived of sight. The president does not say from what institution the pupils came, only that "altogether it was an interesting exhibition, and impressed me sensibly with the benevolence and great value of the discovery by which these unfortunate persons could be taught to communicate their thoughts. . . . One of the females performed on the piano; one of the males (a boy) on the violin, and several of them sung very well."[17]

On March 4, 1849, Zachary Taylor was inaugurated as the nation's twelfth president. He served until his sudden death on July 9, 1850. Like Harrison, Taylor was a soldier and had won the respect of a grateful nation for his bravery during the war with Mexico. "Old Rough and Ready" became America's idol, and his feats were eulogized in a panoply of songs and parlor piano pieces churned out by American publishing houses in vast quantities. "General Taylor was an old-fashioned soldier who put on no airs whatever," said bandmaster Scala. "In fact, he was rather gruff than otherwise. . . . He was fond of older martial music."[18]

Not long before the century reached its halfway mark, President Taylor and his family heard a singing group at the White House that resembled the Hutchinsons in style and origins. On April 24, 1849, the Baker Family presented a program that included some of their most popular songs.[19] Like the Hutchinsons, the Bakers came from New Hampshire, but their four-part harmonizations and moralizing verses, composed or arranged by John C. Baker, bore more sentiment than social commentary. "Rarely has it been my happiness to be more agreeably entertained than at the concert given by these charming vocalists on Wednesday night last,"wrote the *Intelligencer* about the Bakers' recent program in Washington.

> The "family" consists of two sisters and four brothers, of youthful appearance, each possessing a natural, strong, and finely-cultivated voice, blended with unassuming manners; . . . and it is the "moral influence" inculcated in these concerts, that, to me, gives them their chief charm and renders them so inviting; . . . no one can hear them, as well as many of those sung by the "Hutchinson family," without having his feelings awakened, and who will not leave the concert in heart a better person.

A "better person"? The value of the "moral influence"? America's feelings were being awakened, to be sure. But something else was emerging—something like "a war between intellect and affection; a crack in Nature which split every church in Christendom." As Ralph Waldo Emerson wrote, "The key to the period appeared to be that the mind had become aware of itself. . . . The young men were born with knives in their brain."[20]

MILLARD FILLMORE

While national sensibilities sharpened, a new spirit of self-confidence arose. "The early 1850s shed a warm glow of hope and satisfaction over the American scene," wrote the historian Samuel Eliot Morison.[21] Industry prospered, railroads extended to the West, and immigrants continued to reach out to America's golden door of freedom and opportunity. During the second half of the century, concert and operatic life quickened, and noted European artists began to travel to the eastern seaboard and eventually venture out into the trans-Appalachian urban frontier. Sensational and eccentric entertainment appealed to Americans who demanded a real "show" for their money. The fine musicianship of conductor Louis Antoine Jullien was too often subjugated to his quest for the extravaganza, his love of the "monster" concert that exploded in volumes of instrumental forces and sound. Pleasurable humbug was offered the gullible public by master conjuror P. T. Barnum, and opera and concert stars were advertised as musical wonders of the world. Did it really matter whether or not the great De Begnis could sing 600 words and 300 bars of music in a minute, as claimed? The thrill lay in the anticipating, the daring—that emboldening promise that Americans took for granted as their undisputed right.

As the nation expanded westward, discussions about moving the capital to the geographical center of the new republic persisted. From 1840 to 1850, however, Congress showed a tendency to improve District conditions, and fear of relocation subsided. Large sums of money were appropriated for new public buildings and general civic development. By the mid-nineteenth century, moreover, the local population had increased to 40,000 (10,000 of whom were black), and while a full orchestral concert was still a rarity, touring grand opera companies began to allot the city seven or eight performances a year.

The excitement of the decade, however, had come with the arrival of Jenny Lind, who disembarked in New York on September 1, 1850, to begin a concert tour under the auspices of Barnum. Barely thirty at the time, she had reputedly sung in opera over 700 times and had just announced her retirement from its "immoral and evil roles." A contemporaneous young lawyer, George Templeton Strong, recounts her wild welcome by no less than 20,000 screaming spectators in New York harbor.[22] Lind's two concerts in Washington on December 16 and 18, 1850, were an enormous success. She was accompanied by an orchestra of sixty "professional men of New York and this city," directed by Julius Benedict. Arias and the ballad "Home Sweet Home" comprised the program, and on the December 18 playbill the final selection was the ever-popular "Hail Columbia."[23]

President Fillmore and his family occupied choice seats at both concerts held in the National Theater, its reconstruction barely finished after the fire of 1845. The audience, deemed "ill-mannered" by a local critic, disturbed the music with raucous applause at the late arrival of Daniel Webster and Henry Clay, since Washington society—southern and slave-holding in outlook but almost by definition committed to union—considered them heroes. After all, had they not been instrumental in halting a strong southern secessionist movement through their involvement in the Compromise of 1850 just two months prior to the concert? The president invited the diva to visit him and Abigail Fillmore, a great lover of music and literature, in the Executive Mansion. Jenny Lind's biographer C. G. Rosenberg describes her reaction: "She had sat and chatted with him, and with his wife and daughter—she had utterly forgotten his position for the time, and only when she retired did she recollect that she had been in the presence of the man who controlled the most powerful and vigorous government that had ever arisen in the short lapse of a single century."[24]

Millard Fillmore, who served as vice president under Zachary Taylor, had succeeded to the presidency upon Taylor's death in July 1850 and served until March 1853. Not long after the Fillmores took residency in the mansion, Mrs. Fillmore, the former Abigail Powers, began selecting books for the first White House library, and the "great room over the Blue Room" became a comfortable music room and library. The Fillmores' daughter, Mary Abigail ("Abbie"), was an accomplished linguist and pianist who also played the harp and guitar. She was eighteen when she first came to the White House, and the year after she left at age twenty-two, she died—one year after her mother. The upstairs oval room resembled the family music room of the Rutherford Hayeses several years later. Here, wrote a friend, Mrs. Fillmore "could enjoy the music she so loved."[25] Occasionally the president would join in the singing; a particular favorite of his was a new tune called "Old Folks at Home."[26] Composed in 1851, Stephen Foster's immortal song was popularized by the Christy Minstrels, but its nostalgic themes of longing for bygone days gave it universal appeal.

Government records show that there were three pianos tuned in the White House during Fillmore's term of office. One may have been the Tyler

Portrait of Mary Abigail Fillmore, daughter of Millard and Abigail Fillmore, is believed to be a daguerreotype from her White House years. Mary was a talented amateur performer who played the harp, piano, and guitar.

Scherr, the other Mrs. Fillmore's own piano brought from Buffalo, and the third a new piano purchased for the White House on March 22, 1852, from William Hall and Son. The voucher indicates that "one Rosewood, seven octave piano forte" was purchased for $475 and a "white printed india rubber piano cover" for $8.[27] The musical Fillmores, moreover, kept their piano tuner, Jacob Hilbus, busier than any previous first family. Not only were there three pianos to tune, but strings to repair, and "superintending the moving of pianos"—all to "Miss Fillmore's order."[28]

PIERCE AND BUCHANAN

The Franklin Pierce administration, from 1853 to 1857, while politically important, was socially quiet. There were the usual public receptions, levees, and dinners, but no brilliant entertainment of foreign dignitaries. With the administration of James Buchanan, however, the picture changed. Buchanan, whose term of office was overshadowed by that of his successor, Abraham Lincoln, was sixty-six years old when he reached the White House. A tired, once-brilliant lawyer, Buchanan spent four years trying to satisfy both North and South but failed to grasp the political realities of the stressful times. Buchanan was the only president who never married, and his niece and ward, Harriet Lane, served as White House hostess. Under her direction the Buchanan period saw some of the most brilliant receptions in the annals of the White House during the nineteenth century. As in earlier administrations, many were mobbed, however, and the president put police in charge to guard against theft. One visitor reported that he had the privilege of shaking hands with Miss Lane and having his pocket picked simultaneously in the presence of a strong force of Irish police, all to the tune of the "Star-Spangled Banner."

The outdoor concerts, too, continued to draw hundreds. One memorable event during this period was the visit of the Prince of Wales ("Baron Renfrew"), later King Edward VII. The young statesman arrived in Washington in early October 1860 and stayed about one week. Scala and the Marine Band played a special program for him featuring Scala's arrangement of "Listen to the Mocking Bird" by Richard Milburn, a Negro barber noted for his whistling and guitar playing. Milburn's jaunty song had been published five years earlier, but its spirited White House appearance set the piece firmly on its path to popularity.

Opera stars and concert artists occasionally came to the White House during this period as they did under Fillmore. We have no verification that they performed for the president, but their invitations to small gatherings and appearances at large public receptions show that their link with the president and his family was growing stronger as America's cultural life flourished.

In mid-February 1859 the Washington papers were full of the glitter of Ullman's Opera Troupe and its star, Mlle. Marietta Piccolomini. The twenty-year-old Italian diva, who had just sung in *Don Pasquale* in Washington, attended a reception at the White House on February 19, during which she shared the honors with a delegation of Potawatomie Indians. Several modern accounts have erroneously magnified her White House visit into a full-scale operatic production of *La traviata*. She may have sung a tune or two, but all we know of the incident is the following vignette:

> But who is this rising out of a cloud of pale yellow lace, a red rose in her bosom, a short budding vine drooping beneath her waist, her hair simply braided over her head, wearing no ornaments? Piccolomini for all the world, escorted by the Sardinian Minister. . . . Mr. Buchanan . . . made a gallant remark to the *prima donna* to the effect that he did not understand and could not speak French. . . . How the little coquette used her eyes and her smiles when this remark was translated to her only those who have seen her in *Traviata* can imagine. Mr. Buchanan would probably have stayed till daylight did appear, had not Mrs. Gwin intimated that it was time to go. Thereupon he shook hands with the several members of the family and disappeared.[29]

Thomas Greene Bethune ("Blind Tom"), an amazing idiot savant who toured Europe and America as a concert pianist and performed at the White House for President James Buchanan.

How she used her eyes! So did another—but his had no vision. He was blind. His distended "sightless eyeballs seemed to be searching in the stars and the great opera ear seemed to be catching harmony from the celestial spheres." He was labeled an idiot. "He claws the air with his hands, whistles through his teeth, capers about and see-saws up and down."[30] Yet at the age of ten he was playing the piano like Gottschalk, Mozart, or Beethoven. He was called "Blind Tom" and was presented at the White House to President Buchanan for whom he played a twenty-page piece of music shortly after hearing it for the first time.[31]

An excellent article by Geneva Southall discusses some of the inaccuracies written about Tom, a black musical genius whose strange antics may have been deliberately cultivated by his concert managers, who sent him on tours throughout America and Europe claiming his musical abilities derived from occult powers.[32] Thomas Green Bethune, born a slave in 1849, was perhaps the most exploited figure of this era of the American extravaganza. He was a sensitive, naturally gifted musician and composer, who was far more than a mere musical curiosity. Edgar Stillman Kelly, noted American composer, claimed his career diverted from painting to music after he heard Blind Tom perform Liszt's transcription of Mendelssohn's "Midsummer Night's Dream" Overture. And not long after Tom played for Buchanan, William Knabe, a well-known American piano manufacturer, gave the ten-year-old slave a grand piano, which bore the inscription "a tribute to genius."[33]

The piano Tom undoubtedly played at the White House, however, was a superb "full grand" made by Jonas Chickering, one of the first firms in America to make grand pianos. This style of piano was still quite rare in America, and it was considered a sign of great affluence and prestige for a home or concert hall to possess one. On June 22, 1857, John Blake, commissioner of Public Buildings and Grounds, wrote to Chickering: "Gentlemen—

I wish to purchase for the President's House a *first rate* grand piano of elegant appearance, but not elaborately carved or inlaid with pearl or paper maché nor in any other manner decorated so as to give a tinsel appearance." The firm replied, giving three choices, and Blake selected the medium-priced model for $800.[34] Harriet Lane enjoyed playing the piano, and a large album of her music, with her name tooled in gold, is property of the Wheatland home of Buchanan in Lancaster, Pennsylvania. (See Appendix A.)

ABRAHAM LINCOLN

But the 1850s saw hardship as well as prosperity. The North and South were moving in perilous directions that would one day collide. There set in "one of those terrifying, and rationally unaccountable, decades in American life when all the ingenuity, vigor, and hot blood of the country seem to concentrate into opposing channels of fear and self-righteousness," wrote Alistair Cooke.[35] In 1858 Abraham Lincoln, candidate for U.S. senator from Illinois, preached his vital testament of antislavery: "A house divided against itself cannot stand. I believe this government cannot endure, permanently half *slave* and half *free*"[36] Two years later at Cooper Union, New York City, Lincoln reiterated his views that no compromise with slavery was possible. When he was inaugurated on March 4, 1861, Lincoln became president of what was no longer the *United* States. The first gun of the fratricidal Civil War was fired against Fort Sumter the next month. As James P. Shenton noted, two brothers became separated by boundaries drawn in blood.[37]

The music that made its way to the White House during Lincoln's tenure from March 4, 1861, to April 14, 1965, reflected the spirit of the times more than it did during any other period of American history. For soldier or civilian, music's message was persuasive and powerful. Tones rang clear, thousands of songs captured the moment—tearful, tense, jubilant, courageous. Americans communicated through bands, songs, and choruses, at home by the fire, on the battlefield, and in churches, schools, and taverns. They told all through music; and music, in turn, sustained and diverted their spirits throughout the grim struggle. In his *Lincoln and the Music of the Civil War*, Kenneth Bernard writes: "Abraham Lincoln, like other Americans of that chaotic time, became absorbed in the music of the war that so well fitted every occasion, every mood. He heard it in the White House, throughout the city, and in many of the 'hundred circling camps.' He felt its strength and realized its power and influence. More than once he had been thrilled and moved to tears by it. Coming from the hearts of men and women whose lives were torn asunder by war, this music touched the heart of the wartime President time and again."[38]

Lincoln had been responsive to music from his early boyhood days in the wilderness frontier cabin. Friends recalled that certain sentimental ballads would "mist his eyes with tears and throw him into a fit of deep melancholy."[39] Among Lincoln's favorites were "Barbara Allen" (or "Barbary Ellen"), believed to have been sung by his mother Nancy Hanks in the Kentucky hill country of his youth, "Mary of Argyle," "Kathleen Mavourneen," "Old Rosin

This official portrait of Abraham Lincoln, painted by George P. A. Healy in 1869, was bequeathed to the White House in 1939 and hangs today in the State Dining Room. While not musically talented, Lincoln was deeply moved by patriotic songs, sentimental ballads, and grand opera.

the Beau," "Annie Laurie," and the spirited minstrel tune, "Blue Tail Fly" (or "Jim Crack Corn").[40]

But Lincoln's special musical passion was opera. As president he attended grand opera nineteen times, sometimes without Mrs. Lincoln, and he is the only president in history to have attended an inaugural opera when Flotow's *Martha* was staged for his second inauguration in 1865. Lincoln also enjoyed in Washington such productions as *The Magic Flute*, *La dame blanche*, *Norma*, *Der Freischütz*, and *Faust*, whose famous "Soldiers' Chorus" was a special favorite.[41] There were times when the president was criticized for attending the opera when the real life dramas of Bull Run and Harpers Ferry were raging, but he retorted, "The truth is I must have a change of some sort or die."[42]

On February 20, 1861, shortly before his inauguration, Lincoln witnessed at the Academy of Music in New York a chilling prophecy of his assassination. *A Masked Ball*, Lincoln's first opera and the American premier run of Verdi's dramatic masterpiece, is the story of a Swedish monarch's brutal murder. Four years later, Lincoln's own assassination was enacted in a theater—dramatically and with tragic realism. The president was fatally shot by John Wilkes Booth while attending a performance of *Our American Cousin*, a play with music starring Laura Keene, at Ford's Theater on April 14, 1865.

Whenever Lincoln could attend a concert by the popular pianist and composer Louis Moreau Gottschalk, he would do so. Born in New Orleans in 1829, the legendary matinee idol was touring at his typical pace of eighty-five recitals within a four- to five-month period when Lincoln heard him in Washington on March 24, 1864.[43] Gottschalk, an abolitionist whose sympathies were with the North, was America's first important pianist. His original compositions prophesied the coming of ragtime and jazz and the practice of musical quotation characteristic of Charles Ives.[44]

Neither Abraham nor Mary Todd Lincoln could read music, sing, or play an instrument. Shortly after moving into the White House, however, Mrs. Lincoln traded an older piano, "free of all expense for exchange, labor or transportation," for a fine new one made about 1860 by the Schomacker Company of Philadelphia.[45] The piano had a compass of seven octaves plus a minor third, a one-piece cast-iron frame, and was supported by three cyma-curved, scroll-carved legs. Its attractive top was edged in graceful leaf carving. Seated often at the "grand Schoomaker," as government records were prone to call it, were the two unruly Lincoln boys, Willie and Tad, with scholarly Professor Alexander Wolowski patiently guiding them.

If the president readily attended musical entertainment outside the White House, how he must have enjoyed the programs within the mansion! These events, while not numerous, were as varied as the president's own artistic preferences and as kaleidoscopic as American taste itself. The first guest artist to perform at the White House for the Lincolns was a young American opera singer, Meda Blanchard. Forgotten today, the aspiring diva also appears to be the first opera singer to have performed in the Executive Mansion. That the young soprano was a native of Washington attracted the attention of the press, which noted that she had sung in local churches, then went abroad to study with "the most eminent Italian masters."[46] When she returned to the city in 1861, her program took place on July 6 at Willard's Hall. But more important, she presented a preview a few days earlier at the White House:

Rosewood grand piano (#1,900) made by Schomacker and Company, Philadelphia, as it stands in the Chicago Historical Society today. The piano was placed in the White House by the firm of William H. Carryl in 1861 and remained in the Red Room until the beginning of Rutherford B. Hayes's administration (1877–81).

Urged to sing for Mrs. Lincoln's guests, she did so. Playing her own accompaniment, she sang in a manner that charmed everyone present. Just as she had finished and was about to leave, the President appeared. The music had reached his office upstairs, and he had now come down to listen. Mrs. Blanchard was recalled with the request that she sing for the President. She agreed, again went to the piano and, as one observer put it, ". . . having laid off the shawl from shoulders that no 'South' would ever have seceded from, (with its eyes open)," sang the "Casta diva" [from Bellini's *Norma*] and one or two ballads, and then, at the President's request, the "Marseillaise." The President was delighted and thanked her enthusiastically.[47]

If the president craved diversion from the increasing gloom of the war, he found it in three disparate entertainers whom he welcomed on different occasions at the Executive Mansion: an Indian songstress, a midget song-and-dance man, and a nine-year-old prodigy destined to become one of the century's finest pianists. Several months before Blanchard sang, another young woman presented a few numbers for the president and his guests at a White House reception in late March. Her name was Larooqua; she was an American Indian. There would not be another like her to fill the mansion with such "wood notes wild" nor "mellifluous voice," as the papers described her Washington program, until Princess Te Ata would sing for President Franklin Roosevelt in 1939. Larooqua was called the "aboriginal Jenny Lind," and her voice was described as "somewhat thin, but pleasant and of considerable cultivation."[48] Probably politics more than artistry brought her to the White House. She was in Washington assisting John Beeson, who was giving a series of lectures on the plight of the Indians in Oregon.

When Commodore Nutt entertained President and Mrs. Lincoln, the distressed chief of state had just witnessed his "darkest hour" through the disastrous carnage at Fredericksburg. On October 17, 1862, the great showman Phineas T. Barnum brought one of his $30,000 stars to the White House—a twenty-nine-inch-high midget that probably barely reached the president's knee. Advertised in the *National Republican* as the "smallest man in the world," George Washington Morrison Nutt was considered intelligent, enchanting, and a fine entertainer—"a most polite and refined gentleman."[49] The little performer delighted Lincoln and members of the cabinet by singing Thomas à Becket's popular "Columbia the Gem of the Ocean."

Another small artist was the amazing Venezuelan prodigy, Teresa Carreño, who was only nine when she was brought to the White House by her father in the fall of 1863. But she exhibited the temperament that was to become her hallmark. Recalling the event in her later years, she wrote:

> Without another word, I struck out into Gottschalk's funeral *Marche de Nuit*, and after I had finished modulated into *The Last Hope*, and ended with *The Dying Poet*. I knew my father was in despair and it stimulated me to extra effort. I think I never played with more sentiment. Then what do you think I did? I jumped off the piano stool and declared that I would play no more—that the piano was too badly out of tune to be used.
>
> My unhappy father looked as if he would swoon. But Mr. Lincoln patted me on the cheek and asked me if I could play *The Mocking Bird* with variations.[50]

Carreño was not the only artist to complain about the White House piano being out of tune. John Hutchinson did also. "We suffered a slight inconvenience in singing," wrote John, ". . . the piano was in shocking bad tune." In addition,

> No music stool could be found, and altogether it was evident that Mr. Lincoln and his family were thinking of something else than music in those days. . . . "There's nae luck aboot the house" might perhaps have

Commodore Nutt, a talented midget brought to the White House by Phineas T. Barnum in 1862, sang for President Abraham Lincoln and members of his cabinet.

been played upon the rattling old keys, but it would have been little less than treason to have attempted "Yankee Doodle" on such a rickety box of wires. At President Lincoln's request, I sent for my melodeon, and sang the "Ship on Fire," he having heard me sing it before at Springfield, Ill. I can seem to see our martyred President now as he stood only a few feet from me, holding his sweet boy, "Tad," by the hand. We were warmly applauded as our songs concluded. The room was as full as it could be.[51]

But the music closest to Lincoln were those tones bound most intimately with the people during their turbulent war years. Practically every familiar and lesser-known national tune encircled the White House in those days—melodies that revealed the soul of a people who knew the powers of both tragedy and joy, defeat and victory. One hundred years before Woodstock and the Rolling Stones, America's propensity for self-expression through song escalated to dramatic new heights: "We are coming, Father Abraham, Three hundred thousand more!" sang mobs of soldiers before the White House as they responded to the president's call; strong men cheéred, cried, and bellowed out George F. Root's immortal "Battle Cry of Freedom"—"Yes, we'll rally 'round the flag boys, we'll rally once again!" Thousands of black people gathered to sing spirituals on the White House lawn on July 4, 1864, in joint commemoration of Independence Day and the Emancipation Proclamation, five hundred members of the Christian Commission called on the president on January 27, 1865, singing "Your Mission," the "Soldiers' Chorus" from *Faust*, and various hymns; far into the night crowds gathered at the White House after the fall of Richmond, waving flags and serenading victory with Julia Ward Howe's "Battle Hymn of the Republic" and Dan Emmett's "Dixie." "Let's have it again!" cried the president, who had first heard "Dixie" at a minstrel show in Chicago. "It's our tune now!" he said, implying that both

North and South would find unity and fellowship in a common musical expression.[52]

How deeply the president was moved by these ubiquitous musical demonstrations has been recorded by those close to him. He was known to have called for certain pieces again and again. There were those special songs and singular incidents that drew mist to his eyes, such as Chaplain Charles C. McCabe's interpretation of the "Battle Hymn of the Republic," sung in the hall of the House of Representatives in February 1864, for the anniversary meeting of the Christian Commission. At the same meeting the following year, the president heard the talented Philip Phillips sing words that sent tears streaming down his face:

> If you can not in the conflict
>   Prove yourself a soldier true,
> If, where fire and smoke are thickest,
>   There's no work for you to do;
> When the battlefield is silent,
>   You can go with careful tread,
> You can bear away the wounded,
>   You can cover up the dead.

During the meeting Lincoln jotted off a quick note to Secretary of State William Seward: "Near the close let us have 'Your Mission' repeated by Mr. Philips [*sic*]. Don't say I called for it. Lincoln."[53]

War songs and patriotic music were performed often in the White House during the Lincoln receptions. The Marine Band, under Scala's direction, was on hand to play at all levees, described as "a curious mixture of fashion, elegance and the crudity of everyday frontier life."[54]

Lincoln was fond of the Marine Band and appreciated Scala's contribution to its excellence. On July 25, 1861, he established the first act to recognize the Marine Band by law. He attended the concerts whenever he could, and the following account only underlines what little peace the head of state had to pursue his own pleasures: "One Saturday afternoon when the lawn in front of the White House was crowded with people listening to the weekly concert of the Marine Band, the President appeared upon the portico. Instantly there was a clapping of hands and clamor for a speech. Bowing his thanks, and excusing himself he stepped back into the retirement of the circular parlor, remarking to me, with a disappointed air, as he reclined upon the sofa, 'I wish they would let me sit out there quietly, and enjoy the music.' "[55]

Did the president ever tire of hearing "Hail to the Chief"? It seemed to follow him around like a shadow during his entire presidency. It was the first piece of music he heard as he stepped into his carriage and started for the Capitol on the day of his first inauguration—and it was the last piece he heard before he died. The orchestra struck up the presidential march as Lincoln entered Ford's Theater on that fateful night of April 14, 1865. But the special feature of the evening, the "Patriotic Song and Chorus, Honor to Our Soldiers," was never played. Lincoln was assassinated by John Wilkes Booth; a stunned nation poured forth its grief through music—solemn hymns and dirges that numbered in the hundreds.

The funeral ceremony at the White House had no music, but the thirty-five-piece Marine Band played as the impressive cortege left the mansion for

The Marine Band performing in its bandstand on the White House grounds during the visit of Prince Napoleon of France. In the distance is the unfinished Washington Monument. *Frank Leslie's Illustrated Newspaper*, August 17, 1861.

the Capitol, led by a drum corps shrouded in quiet dignity. One thousand singers chanted as the martyred president lay in state in the Springfield City Hall, and when the funeral train arrived in Chicago, selections from Mendelssohn's *St. Paul* and *Elijah* were sung by a large choir. But the most impressive service of all was the quiet ceremony at Springfield's Oak Ridge Cemetery. George F. Root, composer of Lincoln's beloved "Battle Cry of Freedom," had composed an elegiac tribute, a simple song like those Lincoln loved:

> Farewell Father, Friend and guardian,
>   Thou has joined the martyr's band;
> But thy glorious work remaineth,
>   Our redeemed, beloved land.[56]

CHAPTER 3

THE WHITE HOUSE MUSICALE—
WHIMSICAL AND SUBLIME

Oh, it's really shameful! 'tis most scandalous,
The sorrows and hardships poor females must endure.
Those dreadful cabmen! swear, swear, grumbling!
. . . Or, if you hail an omnibus, conductors will deride,
With "Very sorry, ma'am we're full,—but won't you go outside?"

Mr. and Mrs. Howard Paul

ANDREW JOHNSON

Mary Todd Lincoln sat upstairs in the White House wringing her hands, half-demented, unable to pack her belongings and leave. There was no hurry, the new president assured her. Not long after the tormented Mrs. Lincoln had left for her lonely life ahead, Andrew Johnson moved into the mansion. It was June 9, 1865. The war was over, but the fires had left burning embers. Johnson faced some onerous tasks of his own—reconstruction of the devastated South and establishment of viable relationships between whites and newly freed slaves. There were at least four million of the latter, who had nowhere to go. Johnson adopted what he thought would have been Lincoln's program—faith in the South—but his policies clashed with those of Radical Republicans in Congress, and he was impeached, barely escaping removal from office.

The patriotic fervor, heartbreaks, and pride of Civil War music had little place in an America that wanted to forget. Even the songs of the Hutchinson Family carried a social message less urgent, less acidulous now. When they sang for Rutherford B. Hayes in the White House on April 18, 1878, the Hutchinsons featured such pieces as their "Lullabye Glee" and Henry Work's "Grandfather's Clock." Work's enduring song about the clock that "stopped short, never to run again" at the moment the old man died reflected the new postwar spirit: affectionate and nostalgic, rather than stirring or passionate—looking backward for solace, rather than forward for dramatic action. Charles Hamm summarizes this philosophy in his *Yesterdays: Popular Song in America*: "In deliberately turning away from contemporary issues, our songwriters made of popular song something it had never been before—escapism."[1]

Music at Johnson's White House often took the form of entertainment with a special appeal to children and youth. The mansion was described by staff members during Johnson's administration as "an old-fashioned, hospitable, home-like farm house," which rang with children's voices, games, good spirits—and most certainly, music. "We are plain people from the mountains of Tennessee," the Johnsons' daughter Martha once said. "I trust too much will not be expected of us."[2] The family was large. It comprised the President and Mrs. Johnson, their two sons, two daughters (the widowed Mary Stover and Martha Patterson with her husband), and five grandchildren, the oldest being about ten when Johnson became president.

All the Johnson grandchildren studied music and attended Marini's Dancing Academy during their more than three years in the White House. Mary Johnson Stover's children learned to play the violin and guitar, and many entries for strings are to be found in their mother's old account books.[3]

When Andrew Johnson took office on April 15, 1865, the Schomacker grand piano from the Lincoln administration was still in the Red Room. According to an inventory of February 18, 1867, it had been decked with a "new cloth covering with a rich silk fringe."[4] If the Hutchinsons could find no stool for their program for Lincoln, Johnson's household had the problem rectified. The inventory also stated that there were "two stools and one music rack," no doubt for the aspiring piano-duet players and violinists in the large family. Andrew Johnson also purchased identical Steinway square pianos for each of his daughters. While they were not part of the White House furnishings, they were enjoyed in the young women's Tennessee homes.[5]

As the war clouds gradually dispersed, the gala White House social life of prewar years returned. Martha Johnson, wife of Senator David Patterson, substituted for her chronically ill mother and proved to be an efficient, yet unpretentious hostess. For more than twenty years there had been no dancing at the White House. Now it was the younger crowd who set the pace with the rollicking "Juvenile Soiree" held on December 28, 1868. Four hundred members of Marini's Dancing Academy tripped to the measures of the Marine Band amid flowers, shimmering candles, and sumptuous repast. What did they dance? The small engraved program preserved in the White House Curator's Office tells us. Bound with a white satin ribbon, the little card is the earliest memento of White House entertaining to print a complete program. It lists the basket quadrille, the esmeralda, varsovienne, lancers, polka redowa, galop, and, of course, the waltz. But Dolley Madison's bequest to American society was given some precise guidelines by Thomas Hillgrove. Writing in 1863, Hillgrove observed that "it is improper for two gentlemen to dance together when ladies are present." He also noted that "in waltzing, a gentleman should exercise the utmost delicacy in touching the waist of his partner. Dance quietly," he added. "Do not jump, caper or sway your body."[6]

An abundance of capering took place earlier, however, when a gymnast exhibition was held on the South Lawn underpinned by some of the liveliest tunes of the Marine Band. What these selections were, however, we may never know. But it is assured that the popular *Turnverein*, brought to America by German immigrants, was often enlivened by music. And the gymnasts? One can only speculate. Women athletes, however, were not uncommon: "They do their contortions in slippers, striped stockings, loose pants, and other things. . . . The school mams are given to practice on the horizontal bar, while

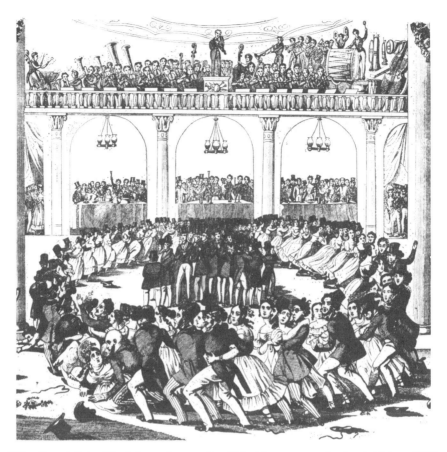

"The Grand Galop" by Johann Strauss (the Elder) in an engraving by A. Geiger, 1839. The rapid motion and lively spirit of the dance kept it popular at the White House until the end of the century.

it is noticed that the married women mostly devote their efforts to practice in swinging the heavy clubs."[7]

Another unique event was the performance of Mr. and Mrs. Howard Paul, who offered their "chaste and elegant divertisements" for the Johnsons and their guests on January 12, 1867. Forgotten today, this team came from England and apparently created quite a stir in America—albeit short-lived—during the 1860s and early 1870s.[8] Their six night run at Metzerott's Hall in Washington beginning Monday, January 7, 1867, was described by the *Evening Star* as a series of "concerts in costume, an entertainment which is by turns gay, serious, fanciful, grotesque and always amusing. Mrs. Paul is not only a great actress, but a singer of wonderful power, and Mr. Paul is an accomplished actor and vocalist. They have given great satisfaction wherever they have appeared." Their repertory included "The Ratcatcher's Daughter," "Mrs. & Mrs. Doubledot," and a frothy feminist ditty called "The Sorrows and Hardships Poor Females Must Endure."

While Mr. and Mrs. Howard Paul might be considered a British version of the American singing families who were at the height of their popularity during the 1840s and 1850s, they could also be considered the forerunners of modern popular duos such as Captain and Tennille, who would belt out their ballads and musical messages for Gerald Ford in the White House more than a hundred years later. By the 1860s and 1870s, however, families such as the Peakes, Alleghanians, Bakers, Bergers, and Barkers had joined forces with other entertainers to provide more variety and better "show." This was the type of program Johnson and his family heard on January 21, 1867, when the Peakes performed with the Swiss Bell Ringers. Undoubtedly the president brought along the grandchildren. There were special matinees for children and even children in the show itself.[9]

ULYSSES S. GRANT

By the time Ulysses S. Grant became president, the nation was ready for a grand celebration. The military hero of the North during the Civil War, General Grant was inaugurated on March 4, 1869, amid gala parades and the most brilliant inaugural ball to date, held in the just completed Treasury Department building. Visiting artists and guest entertainers at the White House during Grant's two terms were rare, however. Like another military president, General Dwight D. Eisenhower, Grant preferred military music and musicians, and his "in-house" court ensemble, the Marine Band, received a place of high accord. But the general had little eye for art and less ear for music. He openly avoided grand opera and theater and Gottschalk's quip that Grant knew only two tunes—"One is 'Yankee Doodle' and the other isn't"— may not have been too far off mark. Still the president must have enjoyed hearing the Hutchinson Family. According to the records of this famous singing family, the president attended several of their concerts.[10]

President Grant may also have enjoyed the rousing "songs of the father-land" on July 16, 1870, described by Esther Singleton: "There were numerous visitors today, however, to see the premises, among them a German society just returned from the Saengerfest who gave in the East Room, to the few listeners, a brief concert in chorus, including some of the loudest and most enthusiastic songs of [the] Fatherland."[11] The German society to which Singleton refers was most likely the Washington Sängerbund, who were participating in a local festival at the time and had sung at President Grant's inauguration. Reflecting the large influx of German immigrants between 1860 and 1890, the singing societies kept alive German musical traditions throughout many parts of the nation and shaped American cultural life for decades to come.

With the increase in both the frequency and importance of White House social events, the Marine Band's reputation as "The President's Own" became more visible than ever before. It played for all the galas, receptions, banquets, serenades, and holidays and added special luster to the wedding of the Grants' eighteen-year-old daughter Nellie to Algernon Sartoris on May 21, 1874. And while distinguished foreign guests had been entertained at the White House as early as Lafayette's visit in 1825, the first heads of state came to visit our nation during Grant's terms. King Kalakaua of Hawaii began his two week stay on December 12, 1874. Dom Pedro, emperor of Brazil, arrived on May 8, 1876. And there were other important guests during Grant's

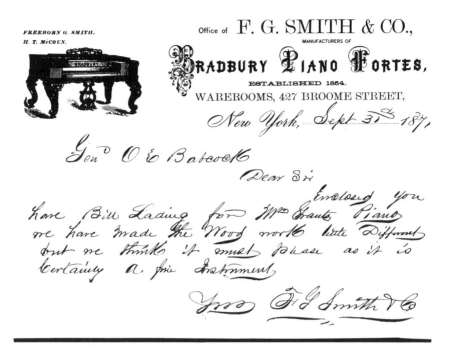

A bill for the Bradbury piano made for Julia Grant and delivered to the White House in September 1871. This was the first of nine Bradbury pianos to be placed in the White House before the turn of the century.

administrations: Prince Arthur of Connaught, Grand Duke Alexis of Russia, and the staff of the Japanese embassy. All were entertained with elegance and aplomb by the president and the festive airs of the Marine Band, now forty strong. King Kalakaua's historic entrance into Washington was heralded in due royal fashion with "Hail to the Chief." While today's ears may find this tribute surprising, it was perfectly natural to Americans who were honoring their first foreign chief.

On June 9, 1870, President Grant held a gala reception for Red Cloud and his Indian delegation of Ogallallas. They were shown through the White House and treated to a fine feast at which all the foreign ministers and many cabinet members with their wives were present. The Indians, delighted with what they saw, "expressed themselves as having a good heart toward the man who could have 'so much good eat and so much good squaw.' "[12] Many tried to get as close as possible to the Marine Band rendering the novel sounds of Verdi's *Attila*.

While some White House guests dined to the pleasant tunes of the Marine Band, others promanaded, jostled, elbowed, shoved and nearly suffocated to the melodious "soul-stirring airs" played during the large public receptions. Under Chester Arthur "the crush was so great," said one visitor, "that the Marine Band was swept from its moorings and could not continue playing because of the pressure of people. So famous a hero as General Phil Sheridan got in only by being helped through a portico window by two policemen."[13] By January 1, 1889, the crowds had reached nine thousand, and

Mrs. Grover Cleveland would have to have her aching arms massaged after shaking so many hands.

Almost as popular as the receptions were the public concerts presented by the Marine Band on the White House grounds every Saturday during summer and early fall. They usually alternated with the programs held at the Capitol each Wednesday. On May 1, 1872, the *Evening Star* announced that General Babcock, Commissioner of Public Buildings and Grounds, was preparing the South Lawn for the concerts. Now greatly enlarged, the lawn extended "throughout the entire space north of Executive Avenue." That the newspapers often listed the programs for these hour-long concerts indicates how attractive and important they now were to the public. For the open-air program on October 25, 1873, the *Star* gave the following: "1. March   2. Aria from the opera *I Masnadieri*, by Verdi   3. Overture *William Tell*, by Brossini [*sic* Rossini]   4. Waltz, Le Tourn [*sic*] du Monde, by Metra   5. Selection from *La Favorita* by Donizetti   6. Grand Galop, Battle of Inkermann, by Ed. van Buggenhout."

As an encore the band might have played a tune familiar to every U.S. Marine Corps member and all Americans as well—"The Marines' Hymn." At that time, however, it was known by a different name, "Couplets des Hommes d'Armes" (Duet of the Queen's Guards), sung by Pitou and Grabuge, two gendarmes in Jacques Offenbach's comic opera, *Geneviève de Brabant* of 1859. Like other songs that made their way into the American patriotic repertory via a folk tune transferred to opera (for example, "Hail to the Chief"), "The Marines' Hymn" is believed to have derived from a century-old Spanish folk song. A "Potpourri-Fantasie" from the opera containing this tune dated 1868 is in the Scala Collection at the Library of Congress, and John Philip Sousa's autograph appears on an early copy of the duet in the Marine Band Library. But while both duet and hymn share the same musical spirit and vigor, they differ dramatically in their texts. "The Marines' Hymn" closes with the confident lines: "We are proud to claim the title/Of United States Marine"; the jolly little *buffa* duet: "Ah, it's fine to be a gendarme, but it's such a grueling curse!"[14]

President and Mrs. Grant recognized the vital contribution of the Marine Band to the success of their entertaining and to the spirit of the people—but did Congress? These were rough years for the band. Problems mounted. Many players became disenchanted with the pay, which was considerably lower than civilian jobs in cities like New York and Philadelphia. A first-class musician in the Marine Band earned $34 per month with an additional $4 for his performances at the Capitol and on the White House grounds.[15] Along with his musical duties, the Marine Band player was required to "work on fortifications, surveys, roads, barracks, quarters, storehouses or hospitals, or as clerks at division or department headquarters and on constant labor."[16] When Congress refused to increase the pay of the band members, many submitted applications for discharge and left.

The Treasury Department also frowned upon the expensive instruments purchased by the band for President Grant's grand parties. Even the horse-drawn streetcar transportation that the band used weekly to travel from the Marine Corps Barracks to the White House came under attack by the fourth auditor. The secretary of the Navy, however, supported the request to continue each man's $4 allowance for this cause, and the streetcar stayed. The

Popular Marine band concerts on the White House lawn included works such as operatic excerpts by Verdi and Rossini and Van Buggenhout's "Grand Galop, Battle of Inkerman." *Harper's Weekly*, July 4, 1868.

biggest blow of all to the band, however, came with the bill during the last months of Grant's presidency to "reorganize" the time-honored institution. Section twelve of the bill expressed this desire bluntly: "The band known as the 'Marine Band' must be abolished at once, mustered out of service, the instruments sold, and the money turned into the Treasury of the United States." This time Congress rallied to the cause. On June 3, 1876, Charles Harrison of Illinois rose to defend what he called "the Athenian concept of music . . . which ennobled the heart and purified the soul":

Mr. Chairman, for fifteen long dreary years at the other end of Pennsylvania avenue the White House has been occupied by a Republican, and during the winter months, of evenings, the Marine Band has been up there at receptions to discourse sweet music for the delectation of a Republican President, and for the delectation of his friends. . . . For

Francis Maria Scala, born in Naples, Italy, was leader of the Marine Band from 1855 to 1871.

long years, of summer Saturday afternoons, twenty-four gentlemen in scarlet coats have caused twenty-four silvered instruments, on the green in front of the White House, to belch forth martial music for the delectation of a Republican President.

On the 4th of March next, sir, there will be a Democratic President in the White House. Sir, is the Democratic President to have no music? (Laughter). . . . And from deep down in my heart came a reply, "No! No!" . . . out there on that south portico I want to see a Democratic President sitting with his feet on the balustrade listening to the music poured forth by the Marine Band, and I hope to be one of his friends; and will sit there with my feet on the balustrade enjoying one of his Partagas [cigars]. But they wish to abolish the Marine Band. Think of this being done, Democrats, before the Democratic President goes into his position.[17]

Roars of laughter and applause from both sides of the house instantly brought defeat to the bill. Congressman Harrison won—and the Marine Band was saved. But there would be no Democratic chief executive with his feet on the balustrade enjoying the music. On March 4, 1877, Rutherford B. Hayes was inaugurated as the nineteenth president of the United States—a Republican!

RUTHERFORD B. HAYES

During the second half of the nineteenth century grand opera and that timeless cynosural delight, the diva, were becoming increasingly a part of the national artistic scene. And Washington, according to critics of the time, was turning into a "real center of culture." In the 1860s true opera seasons were evident in the nation's capital; John G. Nicolay, secretary to President Lincoln, found in opera "one of the most pleasant and useful auxiliaries to social pastime and enjoyment." By the final two decades of the century, Washington amusement pages were filled with notices of local and visiting opera companies, and reviews were emphasizing theaters packed with the wealth and beauty of the city. Divas and semi-divas frequently passed through the capital on the New York–Boston–Philadelphia–Chicago circuit, appearing in operatic productions as well as solo recitals. If one could manage a program at the White House, it was considered a coup. And many did.

Rutherford and Lucy Webb Hayes appeared to enjoy music and America's new cultural image more than any other first family of the century. If the Republicans wanted an upright president who would erase the taint of scandal lingering after Grant's administration, they found him in the conscientious, devout Hayes. One hundred years later President and Mrs. John F. Kennedy would reestablish the White House as a focal point for the performing arts in America. But the Hayeses were the pioneers. Nearly fifty musical programs were reported at the mansion during their one term in office, 1877–81. At least half of these were presented by guest artists: opera singers, instrumentalists, and choral groups that represented the finest in American taste in the latter part of the century.

The Hayeses entertained with elegance, grace, and conservatism (no liquor was served at the White House during their term). A fascinating replica of their taste is the beautiful hand-painted social register kept by O. L. Pruden, secretary to the president, now at the Hayes Presidential Center in Fremont, Ohio. While the concept of the 'musicale'—a term used in Europe to denote a private concert with social overtones—appears as early as John Tyler's administration, the Hayeses were the first to use the term at the White House. One way they incorporated music into their social scheme is recounted by opera singer Lillian Hegermann-Lindencrone, a former pupil of Gioachino Rossini:

Washington, March 1877

The question of annual diner diplomatique was cleverly managed by Mr. Evarts. Mr. Hayes wanted to suppress wine and give tea and mineral water, but Mr. Evarts put his foot down. He said that the diplomats would not understand an official dinner without wine, and proposed, instead, a *soirée musicale*—in other words, a rout. . . . The supper *ne laissait rien à désirer*, and there was a sumptuous buffet open the whole evening; punch-bowls filled with lemonade were placed in the different salons. On the whole, it was a great success.

I think that the teetotality of the White House displeases as much our country-people as it does the foreigners. At one of our musical parties Mr. Blaine came rather late, and, clapping his hands on John's shoulder, said, "My kingdom for a glass of whiskey; I have just dined at the White House." Others call the White House dinners "the life-saving station."

Mrs. Hayes was very nice to me. She sent me a magnificent basket of what she called "specimen flowers," which were superb orchids and begonias. On her card was written, "Thanking you again for the pleasure you gave me by your singing."[18]

President and Mrs. Hayes also enjoyed family gatherings. Lucy Hayes sang and played the piano frequently to pass an evening, and the president once wrote to her before they were married: "With no musical taste or cultivation myself, I am yet so fond of simple airs that I have often thought I could never love a woman who did not sing them." He also remarked to his daughter Fanny: "Music, you know, is the pet of both your mother and father."[19] For the Hayes administration, Sunday evenings at the White House had a character of their own. Often intimate friends were invited to participate in the dinner and family hymn singing sessions that followed. Little did it matter that President Hayes could not sing very well. The spirit was there. "Hayes can't sing any more than a canalboat," expounded the *Ohio State Journal* when Hayes was major general with the Ohio Volunteers during the Civil War. "He stampeded Averill's whole cavalry division once by trying to sing 'John Brown's Body.' They thought it was the long roll."[20]

With the family's love of hymns it is not surprising that an opera company visiting the White House should sing some of them for the president. Giuseppe Operti, "Celebrated Chef d'Orchestre," and other members of the C. D. Hess English Opera Company (more accurately, English-Language Opera Company) called on President and Mrs. Hayes on April 19, 1879. According to the *New York Times* the following day, they "sang a few hymn tunes to the delight of the Executive household in the library upstairs."

While the English translations of the Hess, Kellogg, and Abbott companies were significant in spreading the enjoyment of opera throughout the United States, the great Hungarian dramatic soprano, Etelka Gerster, specialized in singing Italian opera in the original language. At the age of twenty-three she made her highly successful American debut as Amina in *La sonnambula* at New York's Academy of Music on November 18, 1878. Three months later she sang selections from Bellini's opera at the White House.[21] But the most fascinating singer to entertain the Hayeses was a young black coloratura soprano, Marie Selika, who appears to be the earliest black artist to have presented a program at the White House. Selika pursued her remarkable career during the Reconstruction Era when America was barely willing to accept the black performer outside the confines of the minstrel show.

Before her program in the Green Room, Selika was introduced to President and Mrs. Hayes by Marshall Fred Douglass. She then sang Verdi's extraordinary showpiece for technical prowess, "Ernani, involami," with its

Secretary of the Interior Carl Schurz plays the piano for President Rutherford B. Hayes, Lucy Webb Hayes, and their guests during one of the weekly hymn-singing sessions in the family library upstairs (today's Yellow Oval Room). *Frank Leslie's Ilustrated Newspaper*, April 3, 1880.

two-octave range from high C to the B-flat below middle C. Following the aria she sang Thomas Moore's popular "The Last Rose of Summer" from his *Irish Melodies*, Harrison Millard's "Ave Maria," and Richard Mulder's "Staccato Polka," all accompanied by "Professor Richter." Selika's husband, baritone Sampson Williams, "sang by request the popular ballad 'Far Away' by Bliss"; the papers added, "The singers were warmly congratulated by President Hayes, Mrs. Hayes and their guests."[22] Called the "Queen of Staccato," Selika apparently became famous for a coloratura style characteristic of Mulder's "Staccato Polka"—a tricky little ditty whose frothy exterior belies the agility essential for putting across the song effectively. Perhaps the most interesting account of Selika is found in the memoirs of James Henry Mapleson. Writing at a time when blacks were hidden, segregated, or excluded from the concert hall, the English impresario tells about Selika's singing "in the extreme quarters" of Philadelphia.

> On entering, I was quite surprised to find an audience of some 1,500 or 2,000 who were all black, I being the only white man present. I must say I was amply repaid for the trouble I had taken, as the music was all of the first order.
>
> In the course of the concert, the prima donna appeared, gorgeously attired in a white satin dress, with feathers in her hair, and a magnificent diamond necklace and earrings. . . . She sang the Shadow Song from *Dinorah* delightfully, and in reply to a general encore, gave the valse from the *Romeo and Juliet* of Gounod. In fact, no better singing have I heard.[23]

Coloratura Marie ("Selika") Williams appears to be the earliest black artist to have presented a program at the White House. Photo from cover of "Selika, Grand Vocal Waltz of Magic" by Frederick G. Carnes, San Francisco: Sherman and Hyde, 1877.

This fascinating account raises some doubts about opera being purely an elitist art for white society. But, however impressed he was with Selika's singing, Mapleson did not offer the diva an engagement. Reviews mention only her concert performances, never an appearance in a fully staged opera.

There were other great singers who performed at the White House in those days: the American oratorio artist, Emma Thursby, accompanied by Silas Gamaliel Pratt (founder of Pittsburgh's Pratt Institute of Music and Art) on November 28, 1877; German soprano Teresina Singer on January 9, 1880; and the great Italian tenor, Italo Campanini of Her Majesty's Opera Company, on February 26 of that same year. Campanini had fought in Garibaldi's army in the Italian struggle for unification before his successful debut in 1871 in London. But in America his fame came when he sang the role of Faust in the inaugural production of the Metropolitan Opera Company in 1883.

As musicales at the White House became more frequent, they required more planning, finesse, and "connections" with the local artistic community. Someone was needed to assist the president and first lady, someone who knew the artists, was aware of who was in town, and could act as a sort of "White House impresario." A natural was black-bearded Professor Frederick Widdows, a virtuoso on the chimes of the Metropolitan Methodist Episcopal Church. The stately gentleman can well be considered the first in a long line of presidential impresarios, which included Henry Junge, Alexander Greiner, John Steinway, and even Frank Sinatra, who brought entertainers to the attention of the first family and arranged their appearances at the White House.

Widdows scored a triumph when he brought the famous Welsh harpist Thomas Aptommas to the White House on February 18, 1879. Six days earlier, he wrote to Mrs. Hayes:

> Mr. Aptommas the celebrated Harpist contemplates giving a harp recital in this city during Lent previous to his return to Europe. When here last year he expressed a great desire to have the honor of playing before the President and yourself and Friends, before returning to Europe, he having had the honor of playing before nearly all the Crowned Heads of Europe. I received a letter from him this morning stating that being in Baltimore he would visit this city on Saturday and if it was the pleasure of the President and yourself, would be pleased to arrange for some evening next week.[24]

A few months later Aptommas played again at the White House, but apparently he broke a string, and according to Donaldson's *Memoirs*, "became flushed, stopped and explained."[25]

The legendary Eduard (Ede) Remenyi appears to have been the first concert violinist to perform at the White House. A Hungarian with a particularly restless, romantic spirit, the great Remenyi had more adventure packed into his long life than all the historic violinists together. Born in 1828, he fought in the insurrection of 1848 and as a result was exiled and fled to the United States. He managed after bouts of poverty and depression to resume a reputable career as a virtuoso in America, and on December 6, 1878, entertained in the White House at Mrs. Hayes's request. While details of this historic program are lost, Remeny's reputation was undisputed by the time he

The fiery Hungarian violinist Eduard Remenyi entertained at the White House on December 6, 1878, for President Rutherford B. Hayes and his guests.

played for President Cleveland's inauguration in 1893. "He draws upon the instrument sounds the human ear never hears," wrote the *Washington Post.* "He has no rival, one of the meteors that flash at intervals across the sky."[26]

In addition to seasoned virtuosos, White House guest artists often included prodigies and youthful entertainers. Lulu Veling, a "remarkably skilled child pianist," played on January 16 and 17, 1880, for twelve-year-old Fanny Hayes, and the McGibeny Family performed their choicest selections before President and Mrs. Hayes on February 10 of this same year. The McGibenys comprised a father, mother, and eleven children; the oldest was sixteen and skilled in playing the violin, tuba, and cornet.[27] While solo pianists were infrequent at the White House, twenty-six-year-old Julie Rivé-King, one of America's finest women virtuosos, performed on March 17, 1880, for the women in Carl Schurz's family.[28] A few years earlier, Cincinnati-born Rivé-King had made her American debut with the New York Philharmonic. Her mother, Caroline Rivé, had been Lucy Webb Hayes's piano teacher, and it is possible the young artist was a family friend.

As to what piano Rivé-King might have played at the White House, her choices were excellent. Keeping up with the pianos coming in and out of the White House under the Hayeses, in fact, is like following a fast-moving shell game. There were at least four in the mansion at that time: a Bradbury upright in the oval library upstairs; a "cabinet piano" (possibly another

Bradbury) in twelve-year-old Fanny Hayes's room "so that she could practice undisturbed";[29] a Hallet and Davis "grand cabinet upright downstairs in the Red Room"; and in the Green Room a Knabe grand, the fine instrument that would have accompanied Etelka Gerster, Marie Selika, Eduard Remenyi, and others.

Pianos had always been an important part of White House furnishings as we have seen, but up until now they either had been brought to the mansion with the first families' personal possessions or were purchased for the White House with government funds. With the musical Hayeses—and possibly even with President Grant—a new trend began, coincident with the great boom in American piano production, structural development, and mass marketing techniques after mid-century. Some manufacturing firms realized that donating a piano to the president was a great honor: the carriage manufacturers had been doing it for years. One year after President Hayes took office, the Knabe Company, founded in 1837 and the leading piano maker for the southern states until the Civil War, made such an offer.

Gentlemen,

In reply to your communication of the 1st inst. I have to state that your firm will be allowed to place at your own risk, one of your Grand Pianos in the parlors of the Executive Mansion, subject to your future orders. It being distinctly understood that the said use and disposition of the piano shall in no way create or give rise to any claim of any description whatever against the United States.

Lt. Col. Thos. L. Casey

Dear Sir:

We beg to acknowledge receipt of your esteemed favor of 25th and to thank you for the privilege kindly accorded to us. We shall proceed at once to place the Grand Piano in the Parlors of the Executive Mansion on the Conditions stated by you in your letter.

Wm. Knabe and Co.[30]

Almost a year later this same piano was purchased for $800 with "appropriations available for furnishing the Executive Mansion" by Thomas Casey, on March 15, 1879.[31] Chester Arthur, however, felt that a new Knabe was in order when he decorated the White House to his elegant, sometimes extravagant tastes. On December 13, 1882, the three-year-old Hayes Knabe was removed, and a new seven-and-one-third octave, rosewood grand piano was delivered to the White House. This Knabe remained at the mansion for about twenty years—at least well into the early part of McKinley's administration.[32]

But one of the most fascinating White House piano tales concerns the great entrepreneur, Freeborn Garrettson Smith, who took over William Bradbury's flourishing piano firm in 1867.[33] Clever and resolute, Smith managed to place at least nine pianos in the White House before the century turned. On March 4, 1897, the day of McKinley's inauguration, an advertisement appeared in the *Washington Star* showing the likenesses of Presidents Grant, Hayes, Garfield, Arthur, Harrison, and Cleveland encircling an image of the White House. At the bottom of this laurel of luminaries was none other than Freeborn G. Smith himself. But for all his promotional drive, Smith did not lie. The Bradbury really *was* "The Administration Piano" as the ad claimed.

Smith's firm was not without competition, however. In 1877, he built the first piano to be especially designed for the White House, an upright decorated with an eagle made of a variety of different woods, which he had planned for the auspicious presidential lower parlor, or Red Room. When he learned that the Boston firm of Hallet and Davis had asked to place *its* upright in the same room, a veritable piano war broke out at the White House. The winner turned out to be Hallet and Davis, however, and Smith had to be content with placing his specially decorated Bradbury in the oval library upstairs.[34]

Under the musical Hayeses, even the polish of the Marine Band took on a new glow. In October 1880 Louis Schneider was replaced by one of the most distinguished band masters of all time—John Philip Sousa. Clearly the credit for building the modern repertory and reputation of the Marine Band goes to this famous showman who molded the somewhat mediocre unit into a superb marching and concert band. From the time he became leader during the last few months of the Hayes administration to the day he left to form his own world-famous touring band in 1892, he had raised the band's level of musicianship, modernized its instrumentation, and developed a repertory of almost symphonic proportions.

Sousa was only twenty-six when he became leader of the Marine Band, considerably younger than most of the players. To give himself an image of authority he grew a square-trimmed black beard and dressed impeccably, always with clean white gloves and a sword hitched to his belt. Born in Washington, D.C., in 1854, he was the first to break the long line of foreign-born Marine Band leaders whose nationalities had encompassed Italy, Germany, France, Spain, and England. Ten operettas, twelve suites, over fifty songs, several fantasies, waltzes, a cantata, and a symphonic poem all came from Sousa's prolific pen. But his forte was the march. He wrote more than one hundred. Some of his most popular marches enjoyed today are "Semper Fidelis" (1888), "The Washington Post March" (1889), and "The Stars and Stripes Forever" (1897), that irresistible proud and perky bit of Americana that Harold Schonberg claims has made more friends for the United States than any piece of music one can think of.[35]

Sousa's first concern as leader was to soften the sound that hit the guests as they entered the White House. He felt the limited repertory was "too robust" for the confines of the mansion during the state dinners and receptions, and he outlined some specific plans for President and Mrs. Hayes's first New Year's Day reception:

> The first to enter are the ambassadors, then the cabinet, then the supreme court, then the officers of the army, navy and marine corps stationed in Washington, the bureau chiefs of the departments, winding up with the general public. As the first-named arrived we played music of a subdued character, eliminating the percussion instruments, so that the drums, tympani and cymbals were largely squelched, all of which did not please the drummers, who had from long usage believed that they came not only to be seen, but to be heard. Then as the guests came in greater numbers, light operas were played, and when the general public

Photograph of the U. S. Marine Band taken in Albany, New York, in 1888. John Philip Sousa, the leader, appears second row, center. The Marine Band, America's oldest continuous musical ensemble, performed regularly throughout the nineteenth century for White House ceremonial and social events, as it does today.

arrived, I ran into marches, polkas, hornpipes and music of the liveliest character. I think my method gave the President a chance to shake hands with double the number of people he could have met had I played slow pieces. President Hayes's secretary told me it was a splendid idea, that the President was less fatigued than he had been after previous receptions. The President evidently appreciated the work I was doing.[36]

There was also a Marine Orchestra at this time, though no reference to string players or stringed instruments can be found in government inventories of the period. In his autobiography Sousa states that "as a band, we played in the ante-room which was an entrance to the Portico; as an orchestra, beside the staircase between the East Room and the reception rooms." What orchestral works were played? Twenty selections are listed under the category "Orchestral" in the catalogue compiled by Sousa in 1885.[37] Among them are Mendelssohn's "Wedding March" and Brahms's "Hungarian Dances." Since the orchestral versions of Brahms's popular four-hand piano pieces were first published in 1872 and 1874, Sousa was indeed a pioneer in bringing the music of the great German romanticist to America. President and Mrs. Benjamin Harrison, moreover, were probably the first in America to hear portions of Mascagni's *Cavalleria rusticana*, which was first produced in Rome in 1890. Sousa conducted selections from the opera at the Harrisons' New Year's reception in 1891, before the work had been given its American premiere.

But Sousa cannot take credit for forming the first Marine Orchestra. When President and Mrs. Hayes honored the Grand Duke Alexis at the White House on April 19, 1877, "dinner was announced; right off the grand Marine band commenced to play the Russian March; stringed instruments, fifty of them, played all through dinner; they were so far off the music was not deafening."[38] It is reasonable to assume, however, that a small Marine Orchestra existed from the earliest days of the White House. In both Europe and America the term "band" originally denoted almost any combination of instruments, just as it did under Lully, whose "24 violins du roy" was called "La Grande Bande" or Charles II, whose string ensemble comprised "The King's Private Band." For early White House dinners, and especially dances, wind players may have doubled on the strings, or supplementary musicians might have been borrowed from the local community, as is believed to have been the case during the Civil War.

While Sousa expanded the serious repertory of the Marine Band, it still comprised the works of mainly nineteenth-century European operatic composers, such as Offenbach, Rossini, Gounod, Glinka, Donizetti, Bellini, Halévy, Meyerbeer, Wagner, and Bizet, whose *Carmen* (1875) is represented by a medley. Eighteen operas of Giuseppe Verdi appear in Sousa's catalogue of 1885, as well as Haydn's "Surprise" and "Military" symphonies and Mozart's overture to *The Marriage of Figaro*. But while Sousa managed to enlarge the size of the band for its first national tour in 1891, its standard membership remained modest with thirty-eight players, less than Gilmore's band and other major concert bands in America at the time.

GARFIELD AND ARTHUR

James Garfield held office for only six months, from March 4 to September 19, 1881, when he died of an assassin's bullet. A devotee of literature, languages, and fine arts, the congenial Garfield liked to make up tunes for favorite poems by Tennyson and Longfellow and made certain his daughter Mollie and her four brothers all had music and dancing lessons.[39] Hal, aged seventeen when the close-knit family occupied the White House, was a gifted pianist, and the president often slipped upstairs to hear his eldest son play on the Bradbury upright still in the Oval Room. President Garfield's successor, Vice-President Chester Arthur, was, according to Colonel Crook, a long-time White House aide, "a different type of man from any who had preceded him during my experience there, and he was accustomed to light-heartedness and effervescence which has long distinguished social life in New York City. The new president was a large, heavy, tall man, strikingly handsome and possessing the Chesterfieldian manner. He delighted to entertain his friends; he wanted the best of everything, and wanted it served in the best manner."[40]

Arthur's wife, Ellen Lewis Herndon, had died only a year and one-half before Arthur took office, and Mary McElroy, the president's youngest sister, became the ranking lady of his administration. Arthur especially enjoyed music and must have had a special affinity with vocal music, particularly opera, judging from the number of noted singers who visited the White House during his administration. To Arthur opera was undoubtedly theater at its grandest, a true edification of the Gilded Age in which it was socially ensconced. Then, too, Arthur, like Lyndon Johnson who followed the arts-loving Kennedys, may have tried to keep alive some of the musical ambience that the Hayeses had brought to the White House.

It was Arthur and his desire for "the best" that reaped felicitous benefits for the White House—the first East Room concert for specially invited guests. Indeed, the program provided a prophetic glimpse of the dinner/musicale tradition of the twentieth-century White House. The gala event took place on February 23, 1883, in the newly renovated East Room that some thought resembled the Gold Salon of the Operá in Paris. More than one hundred guests heard the program, which comprised Mozart, Verdi and Wagner arias sung by Sofia Salchi and other members of Her Majesty's Opera Company. But the star of the evening was the famous Canadian soprano, Emma Albani, who had performed for Queen Victoria and Czar Alexander II. For the widower Arthur, Albani's final selection, "Robin Adair," had special meaning. His late wife Ellen had sung the popular Irish ballad often before they were married, and time and again he had asked her to sing the song. Albani's interpretation—with its long, sustained phrases, even tone quality, and well-executed ornaments—must have conjured up memories for the lonely president.[41]

The following month the East Room was opened to Swedish soprano Christine Nilsson, for whom the president held a dinner and reception especially in her honor. The exact date of her White House program is not certain, but between March 27 and 30, 1883, she was captivating Washington with her performance at Lincoln Hall. On the arm of the president, the graceful diva was escorted to the East Room for the large reception after the dinner. She then sat down at the Knabe grand piano moved in for the event and sang to her own accompaniment "The Last Rose of Summer" and Stephen Foster's "Way Down upon the Swanee River."[42] Whether or not the soprano included the great "Jewel Song" from Gounod's *Faust*, we do not know. But soon she would make operatic history. On October 22, 1883, Nilsson sang the role of Marguérite in *Faust* for the grand opening of the Metropolitan Opera in New York.

One of the most remarkable vocal programs of the century was held at the mansion during Arthur's term. The Jubilee Singers from Fisk University were the first in a long line of black choirs and ensembles to perform in the White House. Their hybrid art combined the lonely message of the blues, the rhythmic vitality of the minstrel song, and the diatonic harmonic structure of the European hymn. But the African roots and prejazz characteristics of the Jubilee Singers' style, such as syncopation and call-and-response patterns, must have created a distinctive sound for audiences of this time, and their program at the Congregational Church in Washington on February 16, 1882, was received with high acclaim. But with all their success, Rev. Dr. Rankin told the audience, the twelve-member group "were last night denied admission to

The Fisk Jubilee Singers during the 1880s, when they sang for President Chester Arthur at the White House.

every hotel in Washington and did not succeed until after midnight in finding a place to sleep. In most cases a want of room was assigned as a reason for refusing them hotel accommodations, but in three instances the refusal was put upon the ground of color and race."[43]

Yet the Jubilee Singers could sing for the president in the White House the next night and gently draw from him a response only the powers of music could elicit: "By appointment the colored Fisk Jubilee Singers accompanied by Rev. Dr. Rankin, called yesterday to pay their respects to President Arthur, and while there sang several melodies among them 'Safe in the Arms of Jesus,' which actually moved the President to tears. 'I never saw a man so deeply moved,' said Rev. Ranking, speaking of the incident last night, 'and I shall always believe President Arthur to be a truly good man.' The President frankly informed his visitors after hearing them that he had never before been guilty of so impulsive an exhibition of his feelings."[44]

Whether it was fine singing, the lively cachucha or a new presidential march, President Arthur made certain the White House halls reverberated with the music he wanted to hear. "What piece did you play when we went into dinner?" he once asked Sousa.

"Hail to the Chief, Mr. President."

"Do you consider it a suitable air?"

"No, sir," I answered. "It was selected long ago on account of its name, and not on account of its character. It is a boat song, and lacks modern military character either for reception or a parade."

"Then change it!" said he, and walked away.

I wrote the *Presidential Polonaise* for White House indoor affairs, and the *Semper Fidelis* march for review purposes outdoors. The latter became one of my most popular marches.[45]

But Sousa forgot to mention that "Hail to the Chief" remained, too.

During the 1880s and 1890s the banjo had assumed a role not unlike the parlor piano, but with an attraction for both sexes (the piano's appeal had been mainly to women). Chester Arthur played the banjo quite well. "President Arthur is no mean banjo player and can make the banjo do some lively humming when so disposed," said the *Star*. "His son is conceded to be an excellent player."[46] And Arthur and his son were not alone. "Washington players comprise some of our best people—Senator Bayard and his daughter Kate, Miss Beale, Miss Eustis, grand-daughter of W. W. Corcoran," and many others.[47]

Still for all of its new image within social circles, the banjo remained the spirit and heart of blacks. This was no doubt sensed when twenty-one-year-old Frances Folsom heard Sam Weston playing during her train trip to Washington: "The sweet strains reached her ear," noted the *Star*, "and she requested the porter to open the doors of the cars so that she might hear distinctly. Weston's wife sang two Negro tunes, which brought faint sounds of applause from the secluded car."[48] But soon Miss Folsom would hear music of quite a different kind, the marches and airs that would celebrate her marriage to Grover Cleveland—the only president in history to be married in the White House.

CHAPTER 4

FAMILIAR TUNES
WITH A NEW MESSAGE

> The President said a vacation he'd take;
> Said he to himself, said he. . . .
> And my friends who belong to the real estate ring
> Have promised a cottage to which I shall cling.
> Said he to himself, said he.
>
> Digby Bell (sung to the tune of the Lord
> Chancellor's song from *Iolanthe* by
> Gilbert and Sullivan)

GROVER CLEVELAND

If the first administration of Grover Cleveland opened in the midst of the great Gilbert and Sullivan rage, the second ended in the shadow of "Smoky Mokes" and "Goo-Goo Eyes," which were drawing the nation exuberantly toward ragtime and jazz. Cleveland seemed to pay little attention to America's bouncy musical mosaics. He was a serious man who frankly admitted a distaste for the glitter of White House social life. A prominent upstate New York lawyer, Cleveland was the only president to serve two terms nonconsecutively, from 1885 to 1889 and from 1893 to 1897. "When I left my breakfast table and went to my office, it used to seem that a yoke was placed around my neck from which I could not escape," he once said.[1]

Guest performers were rare at the White House under Cleveland, but there were times when music managed to lighten the load for the president. Occasionally he enjoyed the theater, "but I do not think he has seen a play since he has been in the White House," commented Washington journalist Frank Carpenter. "He is said to enjoy comedies and farces and to like a minstrel troupe or comic opera better than grand opera or an oratorio."[2] But like just about everyone else, Cleveland was caught up in the veritable mania then sweeping the nation—the Gilbert and Sullivan craze. The president did not have to leave the White House to hear these jaunty tunes, however. The Marine Band played them often—even at his wedding.

The marriage of long-time bachelor Grover Cleveland to the attractive young Frances Folsom on June 2, 1886, set tongues wagging. She was twenty-one, he forty-nine. The daughter of Cleveland's former law partner Oscar Folsom, Frances proved to be a charming first lady and a devoted wife and mother. The couple planned a quiet, private ceremony, despite the pleas of

The White House illuminated for a gala reception about the time of Grover Cleveland's first administration. Lithograph by C. Upham.

journalists who wanted to attend and cover the big event. Cleveland was the only president ever to be married in the White House. All Washington thronged outside the mansion, craning their necks to see and hear. Some even tried to bribe John Philip Sousa to let them in as members of the band. Sousa refused. But a detailed review of the big day hints that there might have been some who ignored the rules. With a modicum of drollery and charm, a *Star* reporter managed to capture the spirit of the occasion and music's powers of communication simultaneously.

The first visible evidence of the approaching ceremony was the arrival of some of the musicians of the Marine Band, gorgeous in their red uniforms. The members of the band came straggling along in such a manner that their number appeared much greater than it actually was. Some of the spectators declared that at least 150 men in red coats, with horns and trombones went into the mansion, and this gave rise to a report that the newspaper reporters had gone in disguise, like Nanki-Poo, as second trombones. . . . During all the evening the crowd kept account— or fancied they were keeping account of what was going on inside by noting the character of the music played and the intervals between the pieces. . . . As it grew dark the brilliantly illuminated mansion made a handsome spectacle. Light streamed from nearly every window. The band, which was stationed in the vestibule, played at frequent intervals during the evening and afforded very pleasant entertainment for the outsiders, several hundred of whom remained until the last musician had gone home.[3]

What music was selected for the wedding? As the guests assembled in the East Room the Marine Band played "And He's Going to Marry Yum Yum" and other airs from the *Mikado*. Gilbert and Sullivan tunes, however, had to share the wedding program with other selections, perhaps more appropriate: wedding marches by Mendelssohn and Wagner. Sousa and the Marine Band also played Mariana's "Io son la Rose," Weber's "Invitation to the Dance," Mendelssohn's "Spring Song," Robaudi's "Bright Star of Hope," and Sousa's "Student of Love" from his opera *Désirée*. This final selection gave the president problems. Could the bandmaster merely call this piece "Quartette," and eliminate the reference to "student of love"? Sousa complied.

The popularity of Gilbert and Sullivan at this time gave journalists, political cartoonists, and even performers themselves incentive to find new ways of satirizing current American politics. The *New York Times* featured a bit of froth on the front page called "A Joke of Digby Bell's Was Not Appreciated." Bell had been playing *Iolanthe* with the Duff Opera Company in Chicago to an audience that included "Prince" Russell Harrison, son of the incumbent of the White House. Apparently few in the theater new about the distinguished visitor, and Digby Bell, who was famous for his improvised gags and music within Gilbert and Sullivan's famous score, had his quiet shot at Harrison. An uncompromising Democrat, Bell managed to belt:

> The President said a vacation he'd take;
> Said he to himself, said he.
> Down by the blue sea, where the high breakers break,
> Said he to himself, said he.
> For the place needs the boom that my presence will bring
> And my friends who belong to the real estate ring
> Have promised a cottage to which I shall cling,
> Said he to himself, said he.

"Prince" Russell coughed and scratched his head behind his ear, and the Lord Chancellor on the stage continued his merrymaking oblivious to the fact that "Benny's own" was in the audience.[4]

But the classic of all Gilbert and Sullivan parodies is the cartoon showing Cleveland as "Grover Pooh-Bah" on the front page of the *Washington Post* of February 7, 1892, in "An Episode from the *Mikado*." He is singing ("with great effort") to three kimono-clad gentlemen, one of whom has "Hill" printed on his fan, words to the effect that he "can't talk to little girls like you"—an obvious take-off on the Tammany attempt to capture the Democratic convention in February.

When Grover and Frances Cleveland were married, they received a spectacular musical wedding gift. A fine Steinway grand piano was presented to them on June 23, 1886, by William Steinway, head of the firm. William Steinway first met Grover Cleveland in Buffalo when Cleveland, a young lawyer, was settling the estate of Steinway's mother-in-law. Cleveland became governor of New York and twice president, and Steinway remained a close personal friend. He served as a delegate to the Democratic convention in 1888 and kept active in politics all his life.[5] From photographs of the period,

AN EPISODE FROM "THE MIKADO."

GROVER POOH-BAH (with a great effort)—"How de do, how de do, little girls. Can't talk to little girls like you. Go away, there's dears.

President Grover Cleveland as "Grover Pooh-Bah" before his second term. The caricature also illustrates the wide popularity of Gilbert and Sullivan operas, frequent sources of political satire at this time. *Washington Post*, February 7, 1892.

the Steinway grand was situated in the family's quarters upstairs during Cleveland's second term.

Mrs. Cleveland's active interest in supporting young artists and aspiring musical organizations illustrates the important role that the performing arts were now playing in America. Both she and the president were honorary members of the Washington Choral Society, and they appear to be the first presidential couple to lend their names to the arts in this visible manner. From her correspondence in the Cleveland Papers, the young first lady showed a genuine concern for women who worked, and performing artists were no exception. She helped a struggling friend, who taught music to support herself, by obtaining several pupils for her. Through the sponsorship of Frances Cleveland, moreover, the young violinist Leonora Jackson went to Berlin to study with Joseph Joachim and walked off with the much-coveted Mendelssohn Stipendium—the first American to do so.[6]

One composer whose music the first lady especially enjoyed was Richard Wagner. Judging from the large Wagner repertory of the Marine Band at this time, the German giant must have been introduced to thousands of Americans via the popular "The President's Own." The rich orchestral scoring with prominent brass and wind passages offered fine possibilities for concert band transcriptions. John Philip Sousa once observed: "The President likes light music. . . . Mrs. Cleveland's favorite selection is the overture to Wagner's

Frances Cleveland in the upstairs Sitting Hall of the White House with the grand piano presented to her and the president as a wedding gift by William Steinway. Photograph by Pirie MacDonald, 1893.

Tannhäuser."[7] He recalled seeing the Clevelands at the window during a band concert on the White House lawn. "The President stood up and held on to the window as though he were afraid it would get away from him," he said. "His pretty young wife sat down facing him, enthralled." The concert closed with a mosaic from Wagner's *Lohengrin*, which had been given its Metropolitan Opera premiere only the year before. A reviewer of the White House concert had some comments of his own: "Those who weren't disciples of the 'music of the future' thought that King Ludwig was amply justified in going crazy, but there were many men who thought it was the best selection on the program."[8]

BENJAMIN HARRISON

President Benjamin Harrison's term in office fell between the two administrations of Grover Cleveland. He served from March 4, 1889, to March 3, 1893. Before she married "Ben," when she was twenty-one and he twenty, Caroline Scott had taught in the music department of the Oxford Female Institute, later part of Miami University, Ohio, and at a girls' school in Carrollton, Kentucky. Mrs. Harrison, and later Florence Harding, were the only presidential wives who had been professional musicians. The Harrisons' daughter, Mary McKee, was also musically inclined and played the piano often in the White House where she lived with her two children.

In 1889 the Harrisons' son Russell gave his mother a gilt-incised Fisher upright piano as a Christmas present during the family's first year in the White House.[9] The instrument stood in the private hall upstairs, its lid piled high with the family collection of musical favorites. Many were pieces Caroline Harrison had saved from her teaching days. One in particular—a well-worn, pencil-marked copy of Louis Moreau Gottschalk's "The Last Hope," now in the Benjamin Harrison Home, Indianapolis—was characteristic of the music both mother and daughter enjoyed. Composed in 1854, the piece became a sort of "religious meditation" as Gottschalk called it, and was very popular in the last half of the nineteenth century. And if the Harrisons were like everyone else, they would have been intrigued by that highly fashionable poetic image—death, the "commercial literary staple" of the era. "To be so full of feeling, that you lose control of yourself," Arthur Loesser notes, "that you tremble or weep or faint or drop dead, was wonderful, was a blessing, a thing to live for, to boast about, to pretend to." Loesser's description of this type of music summarizes the cultural age in which the Harrisons lived so marvelously that it deserves quoting at length. "*Last Hope* . . . consists of a sweet, slow, widely ranging melody; but this is decorated by a profusion of detached, rapid little tinkling twiddles in the high treble. Later on, longer ornamental runs and trills occur. To one of these the composer has appended the expression mark 'elegante,' to another 'scintillante,' and finally—toward the end—the word 'brilliante.' He cannot have intended these to represent the patient making a whirlwind finish; more likely they were a way of inducing the pianist to play those very high passages with great sparkle and thus to suggest the supernal refulgence of the heavenly next world."[10]

How "brilliante" or "scintillante" Caroline Harrison and her daughter played the piano, we do not know. But we do have records indicating that the president loved to dance and could kick up a pretty good "German." From the time of Nellie Grant's ball, only one dance was held in the White House before the turn of the century: Mrs. McKee's ball on April 23, 1890. Three hundred attended the brilliant event, and a canvas covering called "crash" was put down in the East Room to protect the floor. The *Post* entitled its review "Old Dreams Realized": "Such revelry by night has not been known at the White House for many a long year as filled the hearts of the elect brimful of joy last night."

One especially popular dance was the seemingly inelegant and controversial "German," which often fell under the designation waltz. Critics objected to this "depraved" dance. *The Inland* made no pretensions about its views regarding President and Mrs. Harrison's reception in the White House "in which 'The German' was the most popular amusement":

> "The German" is a dance in full party snobocratic dress, where the hugging process is the chief ingredient. Chaplain Milburn, who has been conversant of life at the White House for many years, says that no such ridiculous performance has occurred at the President's mansion since the days of President Tyler.
>
> The "German" today is tabooed even in the most worldly circles of society devotees. It is considered an offense to good taste, and the fringe or border on the cloak of lewd immorality. . . . Have the christian people

of the Nation been deceived in President Harrison or has he backslidden since he went to the "White House."[11]

One wonders what this reviewer would have said about the "Goo-Goo Eyes" two-step danced after the diplomatic dinner given by President and Mrs. William McKinley on Valentine's Day only a decade later.

But all was not mere social froth at the White House as the century drew to a close. The serious artists still came—the singers, flautists, child prodigies, string players, and chamber ensembles in oddly dichotomous combinations—all representing that wonderful potpourri that we might call "White House Musical Americana." For the president's home saw them all at one time or another. And this element of variety culminated in what appeared to be the first concert in the great mansion to use printed programs. "Mrs. Harrison's Musicale" was a kind of nineteenth-century mixed media that would become a prototype for many White House programs to the present. Indeed, variety has always been characteristic of the great mansion, where the curious melding of private and public, home and concert hall provides an endless source of fascination within the world of the performing arts.

While Chester Arthur was the first to hold concerts in the East Room, Caroline Harrison added her own special touch on April 18, 1890. Now the guests were given elegant commemorative programs. The selections were printed on nine-by-four inch, cream-colored satin ribbons with a gold presidential seal embossed at the top.[12] The whole affair was an ambitious undertaking: eleven selections performed by nine musicians for over one hundred distinguished guests who came specifically to hear the music. The performers, mainly from the Washington area, played a variety of selections. Did it matter if Verdi and Handel were interposed among Metra and Pinsuti? The press did not think so. The program was "most pleasing," the artists "most charming," and the guests "very lovely" in their gowns of white silk or pearl-colored brocade, and the reporter did not miss a single flower. But of special interest to this study was the description of the piano used for the big event—the newly fashionable "baby grand." "The East Room had been specially decked for the occasion. A semi-circle of chairs was made to converge about the door to the red corridore [*sic*]. A Bradbury 'baby grand' piano was drawn up on one side of the door and by the other were set a clump of palms and a velvet divan. Here the President and Mrs. Harrison stood to receive their friends."[13]

Two other significant concerts took place during the Harrison years, both presented by opera singers who were achieving fame in Europe and America. Prima donna Laura Schirmer-Mapleson offered her "soirée musicale" in the East Room on October 21, 1891. It was followed by a state dinner rather than light refreshments as the musicale the year before. After the dinner the newspapers indicated that the guests "returned to the East Room for more music." We do not have the details, but perhaps the Marine Band or Orchestra played while the guests had after-dinner coffee or cigars. Invited guests included members of the cabinet and diplomatic corps and their families, as well as some personal friends of Mrs. Harrison. The papers printed the entire program, and the Harrisons presented their guests with an elegant memento of the "soirée." While the original program is lost, a copy is preserved at the

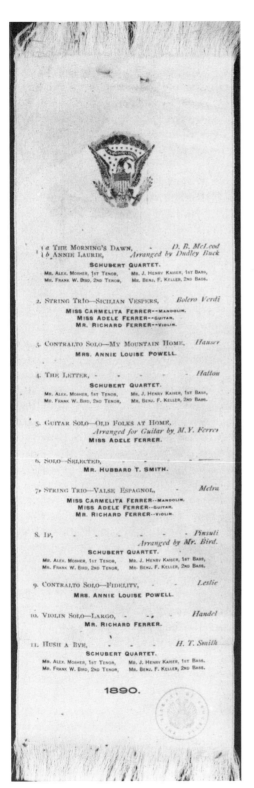

The earliest preserved White House musicale program 9 × 3½ inches, was printed on satin. The program on April 18, 1890, comprised the Schubert Quartet, contralto Annie Louise Powell, and a mandolin, guitar, violin trio.

Martin Luther King Memorial Library in Washington, D.C. It appears to have been printed on a fine fabric, possibly brocade or moreen silk.

One of the most interesting aspects of this program is the role President and Mrs. Harrison played in selecting the music. As the *Washington Post* observed: "A feature of the entertainment was that the pieces were selected by Mrs. Harrison (one of which was the mad scene from *Lucia*), with the exception of 'Old Folks at Home' which was the choice of the President."[14] The Donizetti and Gounod arias were complemented by a brilliant flute obligato played by Henry Jaeger. Undoubtedly he brought along his solid gold flute, then the only one in existence.

Even more remarkable than this fine "soirée musicale" was the less formal and pretentious program presented by Sissieretta Jones. Called the "Black Patti" after Adelina Patti, she also sang for William McKinley and Theodore Roosevelt, although we only have details for her program for the Harrisons. "Black Patti" was born Matilda S. Joyner in Portsmouth, Virginia, on January 5, 1869, the daughter of a former slave, and her early memories were those of a South burdened with social and economic problems. In 1876 she moved with her family to Rhode Island and began studies at the Providence Academy of Music at age fifteen, one year after her marriage to newspaper dealer and spendthrift David Richard Jones.

Like Marie Selika, sometimes called the "Brown Patti," who sang for President Hayes, Sissieretta Jones also went abroad to secure her reputation as a concert singer. In February 1892 President Harrison invited Jones to appear at a luncheon in the Blue Room of the White House, after which she sang Foster's "Swanee River," Bishop's "Home, Sweet Home," and the cavatina from Meyerbeer's *Robert le diable*. After the concert, Mrs. Harrison was so delighted that she presented her with a bouquet of White House orchids. Her voice, to judge from press accounts in her personal scrapbook, must have been extraordinary.[15] An undated *Washington Post* review is typical: "A Phenomenal Attraction . . . the upper notes of her voice are clear and bell-like, reminding one of Parepa Rosa, and her low notes are rich and sensuous with a tropical contralto quality. . . . In fact, the compass and quality of her registers surpass the usual limitations and seem to combine the height and depth of both soprano and contralto."

But for all the rave reviews and fame, Jones never realized her true ambition, to sing on the operatic stage. "I would like very much to sing in opera, but they tell me my color is against me," she told a *Detroit Tribune* reporter in 1893. Yielding to popular tastes of the time, from 1896 to 1916 Jones toured as the star of the Black Patti Troubadours, a company of about forty that combined elements of minstrel show, vaudeville, musical review, and grand opera. Amid this potpourri the singer managed to present her favorite operatic scenes from *Lucia, Il trovatore, Martha*, and Sousa's *El Capitan* with costumes and scenery. She died, largely forgotten, in 1933 at her home in Providence.

Before the time of the Harrisons, funeral ceremonies held inside the White House were brief and simple with no music. Two months before the Schubert Quartet sang for Mrs. Harrison's festive musicale in 1890, it had presented a program at the mansion for a much more solemn occasion—a double funeral. Early in February 1890 a fire broke out in the home of Benjamin F. Tracy, the secretary of the Navy, and his wife and daughter were

Matilda S. Joyner, called "Black Patti" after the phenomenal Adelina Patti, sang for Benjamin Harrison, William McKinley, and Theodore Roosevelt.

both killed. On February 5 their funeral took place in the East Room, and the Schubert Quartet and the choir of St. John's Church provided the music. After Secretary Tracy, his family and friends, President and Mrs. Harrison, and others had arrived,

> from out of the corridor, at its further end, came the sound of music. It came nearer and in a brief space of time the surpliced choir of St. John's Episcopal Church moved slowly into the room, singing "Lead, Kindly Light." . . . The boyish trebles and altos, the pure tones of the tenors and the organ-like quality of the basses mingled and balanced perfectly in the most pathetic prayer ever put to music. The effect as the voices died away in the distance was almost supernatural. Every one was controlled by its

influence and eyes that had hitherto been dry were moistened with lacrymal sympathy.

"I fear no foe, with Thee at hand to bless;
Ills have no weight and tears no bitterness."

sang the choir, and the Secretary's lips trembled beneath his grizzled mustache. The President was by his side in an instant and putting his right hand beneath the Secretary's left arm, supported his friend while tears rolled down his own cheeks as the two caskets were carried out.[16]

For all of its sentimental overtones, this poignant account is a moving reminder of the power of music upon the human spirit. For no matter who resides in or visits the White House—president, first lady, family, staff, kings, princes, diplomats, blacks, whites—music provides an essential bond, an image, a message like no other art form.

WILLIAM McKINLEY

"Administrations come and go, but the band plays on forever," said an account of the Marine Band concerts on the White House grounds in 1891.[17] During the final decades of the nineteenth century, America was caught up in a tremendous band craze. Hardly an event could be properly observed without a band, and every village or town seemed to have one. Like the parlor piano rage, which reached its peak, then tapered off just as the automobile, phonograph, movies, and radio began to take hold, amateur bands were springing up all over America. If the piano was the "family hearth," the bandstand was the town rallying point—an image of community spirit unknown to our era of COBOL and Concordes. The Marine Band during the second half of the nineteenth century was more than just "The President's Own." It was the people's as well. And it linked the presidential family with the nation like no other social or cultural phenomenon of the period.

The Marine Band under William McKinley was more vital to the spirit of the mansion than ever before. President McKinley took office on March 4, 1897, following Grover Cleveland's second term. A dignified lawyer from Canton, Ohio, McKinley provided strong leadership during the Spanish-American War, and his acquisition of overseas territories laid a stable foundation for the expansion of presidential power as the twentieth century opened. The modern presidency emerged with McKinley, as communication with the media and handling of news releases by the White House became systematized. Six months after the beginning of his second term in office, President McKinley was fatally shot by an anarchist at the Pan American Exposition in Buffalo. He died on September 14, 1901, and was succeeded by Vice-President Theodore Roosevelt.

By the beginning of McKinley's era, White House receptions had deteriorated to "vulgar mobs," as one reporter bluntly put it. If an officer had to raise his arm, he could not put it down again. "One officer had his arm over a lady's shoulder the better part of an hour and was simply unable to remove it. Another was so irresistibly pressed against a lady she nearly fainted, and he was powerless to relieve her. . . . Ladies have had their dresses torn off their backs." So described Col. T. A. Bingham, the president's fastidious blond, wax-mustachioed aide, who brought about sweeping, though simple reforms.[18] Instead of one invitation that covered the four official receptions—diplomatic, judiciary, congressional, and Army and Navy—separate invitations were sent for each function, thus reducing the number of guests and the bedlam.

The Marine Band concerts held outdoors on the White House lawn also took on new proportions under McKinley, as up to five thousand people attended. The tradition, begun by President Tyler, was so well established by the 1890s that one reviewer was convinced that people attended habitually, having been "inoculated with it in infancy," the babies in their carriages forming a "most entertaining part of these audiences."

> All kinds and conditions of men are apt to be found in the crowds, from clerks to millionaires, and there is music enough to stir all their souls. . . . There are oftentimes quite lively battles of words over who shall occupy a bench, and one afternoon last summer two reputable citizens got so excited over their respective rights that they almost came to blows, until a wary policeman whispered a word of warning.[19]

The only thing the Capitol concerts had that the White House lacked was the sound of thousands of feet as they pounded the asphalt in time to the infectious martial rhythms.

During McKinley's administration the band had the greatest reorganization of its history. On March 3, 1899, the president signed an act into law that doubled the band's membership and increased its salaries. Regular Marine Orchestra concerts were held as early as 1893 at the enlarged Marine Barracks music hall, but by 1900 under the leadership of William Santelmann, the orchestra received special focus at the White House as a concert, rather than merely a social ensemble. A Leipzig-trained violinist, Santelmann led the Marine Band for twenty-nine years, longer than any leader in the band's history; his son, also William, later served as leader for fifteen years. (See Appendix C.)

The repertory of both the orchestra and the band, however, was very similar. Chopin arrangements began to be included now as well as a variety of what were called "descriptives," a concept somewhere between a Richard Strauss tone poem and a D. W. Griffith silent film score. This was music that carried one to far away places. The audience loved it. Especially popular was Santelmann's creatively orchestrated "Voyage in a Troopship" and Francisco Fanciulli's "Voyage Comique—A Trip to Mars." Or if one wanted to stay closer to home there was the latter's "A Trip to Manhattan Beach," replete with daybreak, boat rides, gambling, dancing sea nymphs, fireworks, and an exhausted "Home, Sweet Home."[20]

Anyone who attends a White House state dinner today will watch the president and first lady come down the stairs and pause while "Ruffles and Flourishes" and "Hail to the Chief" are played by the Marine Band. While we know "Hail to the Chief" was formally associated with the president at the White House as far back as Tyler, there is no indication it was preceded by the short drum rolls (ruffles) and two-note bugle call (flourishes) until President McKinley's administration. The custom of announcing the arrival of royalty and heads of state with a fanfare of trumpets or drum rolls existed in England and was practiced by the colonists to honor high-ranking military officers during the Revolutionary War.[21]

In 1893 a regulation established that the chief executive would receive four ruffles and flourishes, but not until the state dinner for the president of Costa Rica on November 29, 1898, do we find that "four trumpeters were on hand to play the President's march, followed by 'Hail to the Chief' by the orchestra." In haste Bingham undoubtedly wrote the word "march" here when he meant bugle "call." Finally, in describing the dinner for Admiral George Dewey, hero of the Spanish-American War, Bingham offers an account that seems to indicate the presidential honors we know today: "The Presidential party proceeded down the main staircase in the usual manner, the Band playing 'The President's call' and 'Hail to the Chief.' "[22]

For most of the White House social events, the first lady received her guests while she was seated. Frail and infirm, Ida Saxton McKinley fought epilepsy and other illnesses most of her life. Santelmann's musical tribute to her offers a glimpse of the music she enjoyed. The maestro's "Timely Thoughts," first performed at the cabinet dinner on January 2, 1901, is a medley of her "beloved airs": the "Intermezzo" from Mascagni's *Cavalleria rusticana*, Stephen Foster's "Swanee River," and that indomitable symbol of Imperial Vienna, Strauss's "Blue Danube Waltz."[23] But the first lady also greatly enjoyed the few guest artists that came to perform at the White House during this period, especially the remarkable young black violinist, Joseph Douglass, who performed not only for McKinley but also later for President Taft.

Grandson of orator and statesman Frederick Douglass, Joseph was born in 1869 in Washington, D.C., and studied in that city and at Boston's New England Conservatory. Thereafter he went to Europe to further his career. Returning to Washington, his many recitals were reputed to have been an inspiration to other black youths to study the violin seriously. Douglass even performed in Washington with "Black Patti" on March 5, 1893, during the inaugural week of Grover Cleveland. He was also the first Negro violinist to make recordings for the Victor Talking Machine Company of Camden, New Jersey (now RCA Victor). Called "a thorough master of his instrument" by the Washington press, Douglass later taught at Howard University and at the Music Settlement School in New York City.[24]

But the most important string program of this period will be remembered not for the performers, but for the way in which their music became a vital part of the occasion. The McKinleys, drawing from past traditions, set the stage for the state dinner/musicale pattern that would become the focal point for modern entertaining at the White House. They had invited about seventy people for their Supreme Court dinner on February 8, 1898. After the elaborate meal with tables spread into the vestibule, the guests gathered in the East Room, where a grand piano had been placed, and enjoyed music by Mr. and Mrs. Ernest Lent, violinist and pianist, with Joseph O. Cadek, cellist.[25] The trio had been touring cities east of the Mississippi and, after their successful Baltimore appearance, received an invitation to play at the White House. For the Supreme Court dignitaries, the McKinleys chose a serious opener indeed: a piano trio, the first to be performed at the mansion. Chamber music concerts were still relatively rare in America, and rarer still in the nation's capital. Ernest Lent's Piano Trio in B Major was a lyrical four-movement work in the Schumann-Brahms tradition, not unlike the style Americans such as George Whitefield Chadwick were composing at this time, and for their White House appearance the performers selected the expressive finale. To commemorate the concert, the McKinleys printed the program on six-by-four inch cream-colored cards with blue lettering and a gold-scalloped border.[26]

A piano trio in the East Room, and still no piano regularly situated in the spacious parlor? Even so, the White House could now boast three grand pianos and an upright among its furnishings. The old Knabe of Arthur's time was still in the Green Room; the Bradbury baby grand from the Harrisons had been moved to the oval library upstairs; a fine A. B. Chase upright graced the other private family apartments;[27] but for the Supreme Court concert, the new Kimball grand most likely would have been the instrument chosen. The agent for the flourishing midwestern Kimball Company, Edwin S. Conway, was a great supporter of Ohio-born McKinley. As an inaugural gift he placed in the Blue Room a fine mahogany grand (#22091) with a blue-trimmed "scarf and stool to match."[28]

As the century drew to a close, the White House could count every variety of piano within its historic furnishings—small and wing-shaped pianofortes, massive squares, grands, uprights, and baby grands. One style was missing, however, that joyous icon of musical gadgetry—the player piano. But the mansion had had some offers. Hawlett Davis wanted to donate to the White House one of his "advanced electro-mechanical Pianophones," which was "built like a phonograph, has bearings like a bicycle and will last a lifetime."[29] And E. H. Droop, still on the White House musical scene as Washington dealer for Steinway and other makers, wrote to McKinley on April 24, 1901, with his bid. He asked if the president would like an upright piano and an "Angelus" (pneumatic attachment) placed in his private railroad car. Both offers were politely declined.[30] Apparently the White House had not yet succumbed to the persuasion of American advertisers that it was more enjoyable to pump pedals than to push keys.

The White House, however, did succumb to the fine art of dancing. Shortly after the turn of the century, before the president began his ill-starred second term, the McKinleys held a dance on Valentine's Day, 1901. It took place in the state dining room after a diplomatic dinner, and the Marine Band was moved into the conservatory with the plants and flowers. The program for the dancing was broken into two separate categories. Gone were the European designations varsovienne, esmeralda, polka redowa, and the like. In their place was a new category, the two-step—an American original. Like everywhere else in the nation, the White House was caught up in the great ragtime craze of the turn of the century. The McKinleys were right in style. Their choice of music reflects the synthesis of cakewalk, ragtime, march, and dance typical of an emerging new popular art.[31]

Included on the list of two-steps was Faust's "Galop St. Petersburg," appearing somewhat anomalous among the other titles. But while America may have "galoped" its way through the gay 1890s, it "trotted" through the early decades of the twentieth century to a new syncopated ragtime beat. For the fox-trot, "fish walk," and "bunny hug" heralded a new age. When the McKinley Legion rushed into the room carrying a pie six feet in diameter during the Gridiron Club Dinner on March 27, 1897, vaudeville star George O'Connor belted out his old-time minstrel songs for the president: "My Gal's a Highborn Lady" and "Mammy's Little Alabama Coon." A decade later he

Eleanor ("Nelly") Parke Custis, beloved granddaughter of Martha
Custis Washington, was adopted by the Washingtons as a small
child. Vivacious, charming, and musically gifted, Nelly was
eighteen when Washington left the presidency. Painting by James
Sharples, ca. 1796.

English guitar from Longman and Broderip, London, was a gift
to Nelly Custis from her stepgrandfather, George Washington.
The guitar's body contains six small hammers that, activated
by keys (right), rise up through the holes in the ivory rosette and strike the strings. The rosette bears Nelly's initials,
"E P C."

President's House in 1825. Aquatint by H. Stone, 1826.

Oil portrait of Louisa Catherine
Adams, wife of John Quincy Adams, by Charles Bird King, ca. 1824.

Fanny Elssler in her celebrated Spanish dance, the cachucha. Lithograph designed by N. Sarony.

"Swedish Nightingale" Jenny Lind presented concerts in Washington on December 16 and 18, 1850. Both were attended by President and Mrs. Millard Fillmore, who later received the celebrated soprano at the White House. Hand-tinted lithograph.

(Top) American soprano Clara Louise Kellogg was only twenty when Abraham Lincoln heard her in Donizetti's *La figlia del reggimento* in Washington. (Bottom) New York's Academy of Music where, as president-elect, Lincoln attended his first opera.

Title page of the 108-page, hand-tinted register: "Record of the Social Events at the Executive Mansion during the Administration of President Hayes. Executed with pen and pencil by Mr. O. L. Pruden, Assistant Secretary to the President."

Emma Abbott, an American soprano who sang for Presidents Hayes, Arthur, and Cleveland. Hand-tinted photograph, ca. 1880.

Caroline Scott Harrison was the earliest first lady to have been a professional musician. This posthumous portrait by Daniel Huntington, 1894, hangs in the White House.

This portrait of John Philip Sousa, painted by J. J. Capolino in the 1950s, hangs in the Sousa Band Hall at the Marine Barracks in Washington, D.C. The painting was inspired by a photograph of Sousa taken while he was leader of the U.S. Marine Band from 1880 to 1892.

"Goo-Goo Eyes" (1900), one of the popular new two-steps on the McKinleys' dance program for Valentine's Day, 1901, illustrates the merging of ragtime and social dance as the century turned.

would sing tunes from George M. Cohan's "45 Minutes from Broadway." Times were changing. An era was emerging. Presidential power was reactivating. Unlike a tired dancer from the Gilded Age, the enfeebled office of the late nineteenth-century presidency refused to "just sit this one out." Stature, strength, and dynamism lay just around the corner. And the new steps would be bellowed vigorously from the "bully pulpit."

PART TWO

1901—Present

CHAPTER 5

LYRICAL IMAGES
OF A GROWING NATION

> Paderewski outdid himself, though he
> was a little cold at first. By the time
> he got to the Polonaise . . . I think it
> may have been better than hearing Chopin himself.
>
> Cecilia Beaux
> The White House, April 3, 1902

THEODORE ROOSEVELT

The musical life of the White House during the energetic terms of Theodore Roosevelt was richer, more diversified, and more representative of the American cultural scene than any other previous era. It picked up the traditions and new concepts in musical entertainment enjoyed by the Harrisons and McKinleys, added its own special touch, then passed on this legacy to succeeding administrations, notably the Tafts and Wilsons. During President and Mrs. Roosevelt's two terms (1901–9), the White House blossomed as the nation's social center. The first lady now had her own private secretary, Isabella Hagner, and nine social aides instead of only three as in previous administrations.[1] For the first time, White House musical events became a major, regularly scheduled feature of the great mansion's social life. Music for "the home" was becoming music for "the people." And the presidential family became increasingly cognizant of the important role that this elusive, yet powerful, art form played in the life of the nation.

When President William McKinley died on September 14, 1901, Roosevelt assumed his new duties as chief executive with characteristic flamboyance and flair. The youngest man ever to reach the presidency, Roosevelt at forty-two captured public admiration with his vivid personality and multifaceted background as author, naturalist, explorer, soldier, and statesman.

Neither President nor Mrs. Roosevelt was especially musically inclined or talented, although they often enjoyed the Victor Herbert operettas at Washington theaters. According to Mabel P. Daggett, the president preferred ragtime to Chopin, but dutifully attended the musicales and supported Mrs. Roosevelt's endeavors. "Sometimes he gets to shifting uneasily in his seat, his gaze wanders, and before he knows it he is bowing his teeth to acquaintances across the room."[2] But the president, author of the multi-volume *Winning of*

the West, was especially attracted to the simple western ballad. As he wrote
on an opening page of John Lomax's *Cowboy Songs*:

> You have done a work emphatically worth doing and one which
> should appeal to the people of all our country, but particularly to the
> people of the west and southwest. . . . Under modern conditions however,
> the native ballad is speedily killed by competition with the music hall
> songs; the cowboy becoming ashamed to sing the crude homespun
> ballads in view of what Owen Winter calls the "ill-smelling saloon clever-
> ness" of the far less interesting composition of the music hall singers. It is
> therefore a work of real importance to preserve permanently the back
> country and the frontier.[3]

The most striking aspect of the music of the Theodore Roosevelt administration was the number of "firsts" brought to the White House: the first full
concert by a noted pianist; the first musicale devoted to a single opera; the
first performance on a clavichord; and the first East Room piano—a fine
concert grand from Steinway & Sons. Famous instrumental ensembles now
played complete Haydn and Schumann quartets. Fine singers programmed
Mozart arias, Brahms and Schubert lieder, and the songs of the modern
French composers André Messager, Cécile Chaminade, and Charles Koechlin. American-born artists performed John Alden Carpenter, George Chadwick, Arthur Foote, and Amy Cheney Beach. Probably more Edward Mac-
Dowell was played in the White House during the Roosevelt administration
than anywhere in America at this time, and the accent on American music
and artists was a conspicuous philosophy of both Mrs. Roosevelt and the
Steinway company, which assisted in the arrangements.[4]

But the event that dramatically changed the direction of White House
entertainment was the donation of the first concert grand piano to the
mansion—the famous 'Gold Steinway' presented in January 1903 on the
occasion of the Steinway firm's fiftieth anniversary. Its case, designed by R. D.
and J. H. Hunt, was covered with gold leaf and decorated with the coat of
arms of the thirteen original states. Under the lid, elegant, graceful figures
representing the nine Muses were painted by the noted American artist,
Thomas Wilmer Dewing. The Gold Steinway was not only the first piano to
become a regular part of the furnishings of the East Room, it established this
reception room as a focal point for the performing arts to the present day.

The Roosevelt administration also marked the beginning of Steinway's
assistance in arranging the musicales held at the White House. This indeed
was a natural for the firm: the first Steinway Hall, built in 1866, had
showcased so many world-renowned artists, it had become known as "America's first arts center." Thus Steinway served as a sort of clearinghouse for the
Executive Mansion—auditioning unknown performers, selecting the best,
and securing the famous for appearances before the president. Most of these
impresarial tasks were assigned to an intellectual, dapper gentleman with
droll wit and European charm, Henry Junge. Born in Germany, Junge was a
violinist trained at the Hanover Conservatory of Music, and his dedication to
the cause of fine music at the White House lasted until his death in 1939.[5]

With Steinway on the scene, the great pianists came—Busoni, Hofmann,
Samaroff, and the legendary Ignacy Jan Paderewski. A glamorous yet dignified showman, Paderewski played ten times for six presidents. But his first

(Below) Grand piano made by Steinway & Sons, New York, and presented to the White House in 1903. (Above) Inside the lid is a painting by noted American artist Thomas Wilmer Dewing showing the elegant female figures characteristic of his style. Josef Hofmann, Ferruccio Busoni, and Sergei Rachmaninoff were among the great pianists to play this instrument.

program at the White House on April 3, 1902, drew some observations from portrait painter Cecilia Beaux:

> The yellow head of the Lion shone gloriously against the satin of the Blue Room. . . . It is a thrilling moment when the Sovereigns come in, and we all rise, if we had been seated, an act which would turn the head of any ordinary civilian. . . . Paderewski outdid himself, though he was a little cold at first. By the time he got to the [Military] Polonaise . . . I think it may have been better than hearing Chopin himself.[6]

And Theodore Roosevelt's reaction? Paderewski himself summed it up: "The President listened with charming interest and applauded vociferously and always shouted out 'Bravo! Bravo! Fine! Splendid!—even during the performance."[7]

Another legendary artist who performed for the Roosevelts was the Italian Ferruccio Busoni, the first of the great modern pianists. A program by Busoni during his early years of touring America would have been considered avant-garde by most critics. For Busoni cherished the *idea*, rather than the technical display of his Romantic predecessors. "Mrs. Roosevelt has decided that it will be better to give Mr. Busoni the entire evening and will be glad to have him make up a program that will interest a very miscellaneous audience," the president's secretary wrote to Steinway.

> Of course she wishes the best music, classical music if necessary, but feels sure the pianist can from his repertoire make selections that will hold the attention of such an assembly as you have seen on these occasions.
>
> Would it not be well to include something from 'Parsifal,' now that the opera is so much talked of?[8]

While Busoni did not include Wagner on his program, German Romanticism was featured by one of the finest contraltos of the era, Mme. Ernestine Schumann-Heink. Possessing a rich voice of extraordinary warmth and beauty, Mme. Schumann-Heink retired in 1932 at the age of seventy-one, having just sung the demanding role of Erda in Wagner's *Siegfried*. Her program presented with the German Liederkranz and Arion Singing Societies of New York in the White House on February 24, 1903, was a milestone in the history of the presidential mansion. Alternating with the German choral works sung by the Liederkranz, she sang lieder of Schubert, Schumann, and Brahms. The printed invitations for this concert were among the most beautiful musical mementos ever issued from the White House. Measuring 7 × 9½ inches, they consisted of nine heavy cardboard pages bound with pink satin ribbon. The cover showed the White House with the West Wing as it was added in 1902, and page one bore cameolike images of President and Mrs. Roosevelt. But especially striking was the page showing portions of the music itself, artistically arranged and decorated with graceful boughs.

German cultural traditions continued to play a role at the White House when the Wiener Männergesangverein (Men's Singing Society) performed in a crowded East Room of five hundred guests and choristers. "Singers Capture City. Famed Austrian Society Gives White House Concert," flashed the *Washington Post* of May 7, 1906. And the stir created reveals the power this type of music still held in America. President Roosevelt was so fascinated with

Concert

Tendered by the

German Liederkranz and Arion

Singing Societies of New York

To the

President of the United States

And Mrs. Roosevelt

At the

White House, Washington, D. C.

February 24th, 1903

Above, two pages from the 8- × 9½-inch program for a concert presented by the German Liederkranz and Arion Singing Societies with Mme. Schumann-Heink at the White House. Images of President Roosevelt and Edith Kermit Roosevelt decorate the program.

the program, he asked to have some of the songs repeated. But the real key to the afternoon's success were the words of the society's president: "The German lied has been our steady companion as we left our old home across the water. As the most beautiful gift in our possession, we have proffered it to this, the land of our choice." A large crowd accompanied the singers to the station after the program, and as the train slowly pulled away, the American hosts ebulliently sang one of the tunes in English while the visitors sang the same song in German. Thus the "lied," the "song," became a binding force between two cultures long after the train moved out of sight.

While America was just beginning to recognize the genre of serious chamber music in the concert halls, it still viewed with suspicion the esoteric music of the Baroque and Renaissance periods. French-born Arnold Dolmetsch was a pioneer in the revival of early instrumental music, a fine scholar who built and performed on the viol, lute, recorder, harpsichord, clavichord, and related instruments within his large collection. Dolmetsch wrote to the president in 1908 and on December 14 received the following reply from Roosevelt: "Indeed it would give Mrs. Roosevelt and myself great pleasure if you could come to the White House on Wednesday, at 2:30, and let us hear the clavichord."[9] Apparently the president enjoyed the music of this intimate little keyboard instrument "with the voice of a mosquito," as Dolmetsch once described it.

Instrumental programs at the White House reached new heights during Roosevelt's administration with performances by the celebrated Kneisel Quartet, the Philadelphia Symphony Orchestra, the new Washington Symphony Orchestra and the forty-one member Marine Band Symphony Orchestra. The most distinctive program historically, however, was not an ensemble, but a solo recital. On January 15, 1904, twenty-eight-year-old cellist Pablo Casals shared a White House concert with Myron Whitney, Jr., a fine young baritone who traveled regularly with Nellie Melba and Lillian Nordica. Casals played a Boccherini sonata, Saint-Saëns's "Le Cygne," and "Spanish Dance" by the talented Czech cellist David Popper. Casals, who would later perform for John F. Kennedy, found President Roosevelt had an "infectious joviality. . . . He put his arm around my shoulder after the concert and led me around among the guests, introducing me to everyone and talking all the time. I felt that in a sense he personified the American nation, with all his energy, strength and confidence. It was not hard to picture him galloping on a horse or hunting big game, as he was so fond of doing."[10]

All of this music was undoubtedly heavy going for some White House guests—a point made blatantly by one member of the audience:

> Last year the president had some of his old hunter and trapper friends from Maine and the West at one of the musicales. One of these was Capt. Seth Bullock, a famous officer of Deadwood in the bad days of that town.
>
> At the close of the music programme performed by well-known artists, someone asked Bullock how he liked the music. "It's most too far up the gulch for me," answered Bullock in true Western style. The President overheard the remark and was immensely tickled. "All I've been afraid of," said Mr. Roosevelt, "was that Bullock might draw his guns and begin shooting the fiddlers."[11]

If Captain Bullock was looking for music which was a bit more "down home," melodies that would perhaps speak more directly to the American people, he would find it on many other occasions in the White House. Irish, Welsh, and Dutch folksongs were programmed by various artists, but American music, both art and folk varieties, was especially popular. On January 8, 1904, two American-born artists, Metropolitan Opera singer David Bispham and pianist Katherine Heyman, performed. Bispham, an ardent exponent of

Spanish cellist Pablo Casals, a few years after his performance for Theodore Roosevelt.

More than a half century after his Roosevelt concert, Pablo Casals played for President and Mrs. John Kennedy, Governor and Mrs. Luis Muñoz-Marín of Puerto Rico, and luminaries from the arts world.

American music, featured a group of songs by six living American composers, closing with the spirited "Danny Deever" with words by Rudyard Kipling. "Its conclusion," recalled Bispham, "brought the President upstanding to his feet, and with hands outstretched he came forward, saying, "By Jove, Mr. Bispham that was bully! With such a song as that you could lead a nation into battle!""[12]

But it was another form of American music that charmed the president's impetuous daughter, "Princess Alice," as she was called. When she asked the Marine Band to play Scott Joplin's daring new "Maple Leaf Rag" (1899), she "handed the genial bandmaster a wallop that staggered his musical ideals," recalled a member of the band.[13] The director complied, however, and Joplin's rag has never left the Marine Band repertory.

During the last years of this administration's distinguished and brilliant musical life, two dramatic events took place that brought the Roosevelt era to a close with a dash of creativity and charm. On April 23, 1907, the Indianist opera *Poia* by Arthur Nevin with libretto by Randolph Hartley was presented in an illustrated lecture at the piano. *Poia* reflected America's concern at the turn of the century for its native music. As Arthur Farwell claimed, America must "cease to see everything through German spectacles." Thus a number of Indianist composers, such as Nevin, Charles Wakefield

Cadman, and Charles Skilton, were attracted to an indigenous cultural form out of which they believed a truly representative American music could be built. Ironically, Nevin, who had spent many months on a Montana reservation studying Indian music, was unable to secure a performance for his *Poia*, in America; the opera was given its world premier at the Berlin State Opera in 1910.[14] Three years earlier, however, *Poia* had been presented at the White House, and by the president himself, who arranged to give it publicity.

Theodore Roosevelt's concern for the welfare of the American Indian is well known. When the Indian Bureau in Washington was directed to destroy all things pertaining to the civilization of the Indian people, Roosevelt did everything he could to preserve Indian music and art. "It fits in with all my policies of conservation," he said. "I don't know anything about Indian music, but the translation of Indian song poems shows them to be of rare value." When the president learned that government agents were punishing Indians who talked or sang in their native tongue, he set about to have all such legislation revoked. He even arranged to have a Cheyenne victory song performed during a cabinet luncheon during which the Indian question was being discussed. "These songs," he said, "cast a wholly new light on the depth and dignity of Indian thought—the strange charm, the charm of a vanished elder world of Indian poetry."[15]

But the triumph of this era was the elegant enterprise held on the White House lawn not long before the presidency passed into the hands of William Howard Taft. There were no famous concert artists, no gilded state piano, and the quaint musical score arranged and conducted by W. H. Humiston is forgotten today. But the impact of the two children's musical plays produced in costume on October 16 and 17, 1908, remains a segment of history all its own. The *Post* considered the event "one of the most notable performances ever seen in Washington." About four thousand people attended, having purchased tickets at $1 for adults and twenty-five cents for children beforehand to benefit the Washington Playgrounds Association.[16]

Under the direction of the Ben Greet Players—a noted Shakespearean group with whom Dolmetsch had worked—two tales of Nathanial Hawthorne were presented, *Pandora and the Mischief Box* and *Midas and the Golden Touch*. Local children joined the professional players in these gentle and tender reminiscences of Olympian days, which employed singing, dancing, and processions. As for the musical score, we know only that it consisted of harps, flutes, and cymbals. The Marine Band, conducted by William Santelmann, was divided into two sections—one as an ensemble furnishing music for the plays, the other as a band playing patriotic music before the performance, between the acts, and at the conclusion.[17]

WILLIAM H. TAFT

The Theodore Roosevelts placed primary importance on the White House musicale, but the Tafts and Wilsons molded it into a well-established tradition. The William Howard Taft administration, from 1909 to 1913, began the concept of the "Lenten Musicale" series that continued throughout the Franklin Roosevelt years. These programs, from four to six in number, featured classical artists and were held between February and April of each year. They were usually preceded by small dinner parties with the Marine Orchestra or newly formed Marine String Quartet playing in the background. The Lenten Musicales were organized as a double bill, such as the program of violinist Fritz Kreisler and pianist Fannie Bloomfield-Zeisler who appeared together on April 15, 1910. The artists for the Taft musicales were of high calibre and their musical selections were stylistically compatible and tastefully juxtaposed.

Helen Taft was known to have selected most of the artists for her musicales. A fine amateur pianist, she had studied music as a young girl in Cincinnati and retained a fondness for music all her life. She was the founder and first president of the Cincinnati Symphony Orchestra, and soon after she moved to the White House, the Baldwin Piano Company of Cincinnati gave her a style B parlor grand in empire design with ivory finish. The piano was trimmed in gold to match the motifs in the Blue Room, called at this time Mrs. Taft's "Music Room." When illness restricted her social activities, the first lady found time to practice in this room, which occupied a special place in her life. Even the president had his own corner of the new music room. He installed one of the "finest of the enclosed-horn or concealed-horn types of phonographs, with a liberal library of those records of grand operatic selections of which the President is so fond," said the papers.[18]

As a pianist, Mrs. Taft seemed to favor for her musicales the top women pianists of the day. In reviewing the list of major pianists who performed in the White House during the Taft years, nine of the eleven were women. There were the fiery, independent Olga Samaroff (née Olga Hickenlooper), who married Leopold Stokowski the year after her White House concert, and the twenty-three-year-old Hungarian-American Yolanda Merö, who played in the White House just four months after making her American debut in New York City. Fannie Bloomfield Zeisler was considered the most technically gifted woman pianist of her era with a staggering repertory. Others, important but less notable, were Augusta Cottlow, Estella Neuhaus, and Ellen Ballon. All came to the White House at a time when, according to Texas-born Olga Samaroff, "men pianists and women pianists were as rigorously separated in the managerial mind as the congregation of a Quaker meeting . . . and [women] received lower fees than a man with the same degree of success and reputation."[19]

The greatest pianist to appear at this time, however, was Josef Hofmann— a legendary figure and without a doubt one of the most remarkable talents in the annals of music. Hofmann represented the legacy of Busoni rather than of Paderewski: he fought the mannerisms of arch-Romanticism, perceived his music from a large-scale vantage point, and played with flawless elegance and purity.[20] On Friday, April 7, 1911, after an elegant state dinner, Hofmann played for President and Mrs. Taft, the Netherlands minister and his wife, and about four hundred guests. Gone now is the showy operatic paraphrase; preferred by Hofmann is a modern Russian group, which included Liadow's imaginative miniature, "Music Box" (Tabatière à musique), written in 1893 and Scriabin's "Poème," composed in either 1903 or 1905.[21]

When Steinway & Sons arranged the White House appearances of concert artists and singers, they usually paid their travel and other expenses, but the artists received no monetary remuneration for their performances. Appearing before the president was an honor and a highly sought-after experience—as it is today. Mrs. Hayes used to give women artists a bouquet of orchids from her conservatory. Theodore Roosevelt offered copies of his *Rough Riders* or an autographed photo in a silver frame. Mrs. Taft, however, initiated a gift of small gold medals bearing the presidential seal for the artists. Their first presentation was made on March 24, 1911, when Alexander Heinemann and Lilla Ormond sang. "After the classical numbers on the program," added a White House memo, "Miss Ormond, at the special request of the President, sang 'Home, Sweet Home,' 'Way Down upon the Swanee River' and 'Robin Adair.' "[22]

Does this last comment give us an idea of President Taft's tastes in music? Perhaps, but Ormond's encores seem somewhat sedate and old-fashioned compared with the new Tin Pan Alley songs coming from the president's graphanola at this time—Irving Berlin's "Alexander's Ragtime Band" (1911) and Lewis Muir's "Waitin' for the Robert E. Lee" (1912). Mrs. Taft bought all the latest records for the president, she said, to keep his mind off his troubles.[23]

The president also showed classical leanings, judging from his requests for encores during the musicales. He was fond of grand opera and once asked Fritz Kreisler to play the "Prize Song" from Wagner's *Die Meistersinger* after the famous violinist's concert at the White House on April 15, 1910. Three months earlier Taft heard the great Luisa Tetrazzini in Donizetti's *Daughter of the Regiment* at Washington's Belasco Theatre. "The only difference between us," he quipped, "is that she is on one stage and I on another." The president's favorite singer, however, was Enrico Caruso whom he heard for the first time in Baltimore in 1910. He liked to unwind to Caruso's recording of *La bohème* with its passionate "Che gelida manina."[24]

WOODROW WILSON

Performing artists were often prone to size up presidential tastes in music. One president, whom both David Bispham and Paderewski felt was especially musically inclined, was Woodrow Wilson. "President Wilson," said Bispham, "is devoted to music and something of a singer himself, with a tenor voice of considerable power and sweetness." Paderewski—who was so nervous when he played for President Wilson that he had to soak his hands in warm water beforehand—viewed the president as an "all-around, highly-educated man who recognized intellectually that music was a part of human progress . . . but he had little time for anything that was in the sphere of dreams."[25]

Woodrow Wilson's "sphere of dreams" had come earlier. Both he and his brother, Joseph, Jr., played the violin as boys, and Woodrow kept on playing, apparently casually, for many years as a young adult. Wilson sang tenor in the Princeton University Glee Club and later in the Johns Hopkins University Glee Club that he helped to organize. He also belonged to the College Chapel Choir and never really lost his interest in music. As president he had a way of thrilling his listeners by achieving and holding the high note at the end of "The Star-Spangled Banner" falsetto, à la John McCormack, some said.[26]

President Wilson made music a vital part of White House life, but he entertained only during the first of his two terms in office. The presidential years from 1913 to 1921 were beset with problems—the illness and death of Wilson's first wife, Ellen Louise Axon, on August 6, 1914; the four grim years of the war that began the same year; and finally the stroke that incapacitated him for the last seventeen months of his presidency.

Wilson's second wife, Edith Bolling Galt, was a handsome, strong-willed woman, accomplished in the field of music, and his daughter, Margaret, was a professional singer. It may have been Margaret's interest in vocal music that brought the exceptional Russian Cathedral Choir to the White House on a cold February evening in 1914. Comprising thirty-five men and boys from New York's St. Nicholas Cathedral, the choir was conducted by I. T. Gorokhoff, director of the Holy Synod Choir of Moscow. The music was described as "vocal without accompaniment and very remarkable in its Oriental character. . . . The musical genius of Russia has found fine inter-preters on American soil . . . but hitherto there has been no opportunity to hear the Russian church music, with examples of the complete range of its historical development."[27]

Other artists who performed for the Wilsons included the distinguished Spanish composer Enrique Granados and that indefatigable Australian, Percy Grainger, who played the piano with dash, vigor and effortless bril-liance.[28] But, while these programs captivated the guests, did they entertain the weary president? Indeed there must have been times when this music became a comforting sort of therapy—a calming way to forget, to capture, perhaps, that old "sphere of dreams," if only for a moment. Harpist Melville Clark recalled just this incident following the concert he shared with singer Margaret Wilson:

> A velvety soft moonlit night, May 27, 1914, stands forth, cameo-like, among my otherwise nebulous recollections of 4,000 harp recitals I have given. . . .
>
> The moonlight was so brilliant and all-pervading that night, out there on the portico at the rear of the White House, that I could distinctly see all the strings of my instrument. The historic pillars were sharply etched and wrapped in a phosphorescent glow; and from the shrubbery there peeped the secret service men—35 of them, I was later told—comprising the only audience for this extraordinary and, until now, unpublicized recital. . . .
>
> When the last distinguished guest had departed, the President asked me to take the harp and go with him to the rear portico of the White House. It afterward became plain that he was gravely worried over the possibilities of war between the United States and the countries of the diplomats he had just entertained; and sought to relieve the tension by singing. . . . He asked me if I could play "Drink to Me Only with Thine Eyes," and I bent eagerly over the harp and began softly the familiar melody. Then I was surprised, most pleasantly, when the President began to sing the song in a clear, lyric tenor voice.
>
> He suggested one song after another—Scotch and Irish songs, and those of Stephen Foster. He sang easily and with faultless diction, and it was nearly midnight when he stood up. And now, it pleased me to note, he was amazingly buoyant, relaxed, and unworried.[29]

The celebrated Australian pianist and composer Percy Grainger played several of his own compositions for Woodrow Wilson and his family on March 28, 1916.

But there was yet another White House "performer" that possessed an uncanny ability to distract and to soothe—the Victrola! Edith Wilson tells in her *Memoir* how the electric piano was turned on when she and the president were too tired to work: "We sat in the firelight and listened to some of the music from operas."[30] But for pure delight there was nothing like the Victrola. "Frequently at night we would go to the Oval Room upstairs after dinner," she wrote, "and he [the President] would put a record on the Victrola and say: 'Now, I'll show you how to do a jig step.' He was light on his feet and often said he envied Primrose the minstrel dancer and wished he could exchange jobs."[31]

HARDING, COOLIDGE, AND HOOVER

If the 1920s came in roaring "Yes, We Have No Bananas" from the seat of its madcap motor car, it left whimpering "Brother, Can You Spare a Dime?" in the throes of the Great Depression. The noisy, hot jazz of this decade seemed a musical counterpart to F. Scott Fitzgerald's dazzling lifestyle. But like no other decade, the 1920s could laugh—at least until late 1920. Music was rapidly becoming an industry, but the versatile stage show/motion picture combo managed to keep alive the vaudeville art, which was waning drastically in the face of competition from radio, movies, and electrical recordings. President Calvin Coolidge enjoyed several of these shows at Washington's Kieth Theater. Called "Silent Cal" for his quiet, remote ways, he surprised many by throwing back his head and laughing out loud. The president could even open a show directly from the White House now. In 1923, President Harding inaugurated the new Guild Theater on West 52nd Street in New York by pushing a button that, "over a specially leased wire," raised the curtain—and the show began.

Warren G. Harding took office on March 4, 1921, and served as president until his death in August 1923. Harding greatly enjoyed vaudeville, musical comedy, and especially the buoyant, brassy sounds of the concert band. He was also an avid fan of singer George O'Connor. But this was nothing new for a president. O'Connor entertained every chief executive from Cleveland to FDR. Called the "White House Jester," the red-faced, chunky little man had sung his way into the hearts of the administrations to such an extent that mail was addressed to him at the Executive Mansion. O'Connor was a prominent lawyer, but with his rare talent and generous spirit he managed to keep alive an outmoded art form until he died on September 28, 1946, at the age of seventy-two. His minstrel pieces, ragtime melodies, and dialect songs "brought tears of laughter even to the faces of men so dignified they could be suspected of wearing their silk hats under the shower bath," said the press.[32] "President Coolidge laughed so hard one night that he followed it up with an after-dinner speech that would have made Chauncey Depew envious."[33] The song that drew such attention was O'Connor's rendition of "Gasoline Gus in His Jitney Bus"—a ditty that celebrated the birth of the taxicab in 1915 and its ride for a nickel or a "jitney."

In the O'Connor Archives are several notes to the singer from President Franklin Roosevelt: "Dear George, Like special vintage wine, you improve with age. More years to you! FDR." FDR's favorite was "Saloon," an O'Connor staple written in 1921 by Ernest R. Ball under the name Roland E. Llab. Composer of such genteel parlor numbers as "Mother Machree" and "When Irish Eyes Are Smiling," Ernest Ball, in "Saloon," praises the glories of the old-fashioned bar that was supposed to have been killed by prohibition. The song was the joy of FDR, who had advocated prohibition repeal in his 1932 campaign, and also the hit of Coolidge and Hoover, who may have viewed its haunting tune as both an elegy of days gone by and a prayer for their return. Its lyrics by George Whiting run:

> Saloon, saloon, saloon . . . it runs through my brain like a tune.
> I don't like cafe, and I hate cabaret
> But just mention saloon and my cares fade away

Grace and Calvin Coolidge and various Hollywood stars at the White House in 1924. Immediately to the right of the president is Al Jolson.

> For it brings back a fond recollection of a little old low-ceiling room, with a
>   bar and a rail
> And a dime and a pail; saloon, saloon, saloon.[34]

Tin Pan Alley and the American musical theater were in a great state of verve and vitality in the period between the two world wars, and interest in this dynamic sphere of entertainment was reflected in the White House guest lists of this period. In 1924 Coolidge invited legendary showman Al Jolson to help him launch his election campaign at a White House pancake breakfast. A group of forty stage stars, including Jolson, John Drew, the Dolly Sisters, Hal Ford, Raymond Hitchcock, Charlotte Greenwood, and Ray Miller's Jazz Band, staged impromptu entertainment in the rear grounds.[35] And in 1931 the famous song and dance man, George M. Cohan, visited the White House to present the premier copy of his "Father of the Land We Love" to President Hoover.[36] While this patriotic song never sold a copy, another achieved immortality, when on March 3 of that same year, President Hoover signed the act making "The Star-Spangled Banner" America's official national anthem.

Among the numerous great artists who performed for President and Mrs. Herbert Hoover was twenty-seven-year-old Vladimir Horowitz.

The 1920s was also a dancing decade. The fox trot and its many derivatives were replacing the two-step and cakewalk, and the new Latin beat gave rise to such innovative steps as the tango, rumba, and Charleston. The older waltz was quite passé, but the ubiquitous "Blue Danube" was played by the Marine Band for White House dances well into the century. The noble waltz, however, fared no better with Harding than it did with Harrison. While some felt it was "not quite in accord with his high office for a President of the United States to waltz with other dancers in the East Room," others argued that it showed his "human" side. After all, noted the press, it was not the "jazz of the earlier hours" (at the White House Garden Party)—but "the 'Blue Danube' played by the Navy Yard Band which the President was unable to resist."[37]

But the age that could laugh and kick up its heels also saw major new developments in the sphere of serious composition and performance. Between the end of World War I and the economic collapse of 1929, youthful American symphonic composers moved ahead with the dynamic progressive currents, while older composers were gaining reputation as inheritors of the American cultivated tradition. It was a prosperous era and a time when the American people were growing increasingly aware of the potential of their own musical life. "Music is the art directly representative of democracy," wrote President Coolidge in a lengthy article for *The Musician* in September 1923. "If the best music is brought to the people, there need be no fear about their ability to appreciate it." Each administration of the decade—Harding, Coolidge, and Hoover—showed a special concern for the arts and a deepened interest in support, patronage, and responsibility within the field of music.

Each of the first ladies of this period was important in fostering and sustaining the nation's cultural life, and the unusually high quality of programs in the White House during this decade can be attributed mainly to their efforts. Of the three, Florence Kling Harding was the only professionally oriented musician, having studied at the Cincinnati Conservatory of Music. She was known to have practiced an hour daily while in the White

House. Shortly after she moved to the mansion, a mahogany Baldwin grand piano was shipped to her and appears in photographs of the second-floor oval room of this time.[38]

Florence Harding's support of the young pianist is reflected in eleven-year-old Shura Cherkassy's White House recital on May 17, 1923. The young Russian-born prodigy was a student of his mother, a protege of Sergei Rachmaninoff. Mrs. Harding was deeply impressed with the child's playing. Judging from his Washington recital at the time, her opinions were justified. The ambitious program included major works of Handel, J. S. Bach, Beethoven-Busoni, von Weber, Mendelssohn, Chopin, Grieg, Scriabin, Rachmaninoff, and the dazzling Strauss-Schutt "Fledermaus" paraphrase as a rousing finale.[39]

Grace Coolidge came from a background that fostered the love of music through what she called the "family orchestra." As first lady she attended concerts in Washington frequently and once evoked a comment from the president, "I don't see why you have to go out to get your music. There are four pianos in the White House."[40] Mrs. Coolidge was honorary chair of the World Fellowship through Music Convention, which featured the first Washington performance of J. S. Bach's B-Minor Mass on April 16, 1925. That same year, she brought to the White House the noted Dutch conductor Elizabeth Kuyper who came to the United States to found the Professional Woman's Symphony Orchestra of America. Mme. Kuyper was also the first woman to win the coveted Mendelssohn Prize for composition.

Lou Henry Hoover, who served as national president of the Girl Scouts, believed thoroughly in the value of music in the life of the young. At Christmas time she usually led a group of caroling Scouts carrying lighted candles through the darkened halls of the White House, and each Easter

Square pianoforte made by Astor and Company, London, 1799–1815. In 1932 Lou Henry Hoover borrowed the instrument for the White House from the Smithsonian Institution.

Monday they presented a program of national and international dances on the south grounds. Lou Hoover's interest in our nation's musical heritage also led her to furnish the White House with a pianoforte made by Astor and Company of London between 1799 and 1815, which she borrowed from the Smithsonian.[41] She also established a series of concerts at Stanford University when she left the White House and laid the groundwork for the Department of Music.

The Coolidges retained an entertainment plan similar to the Hardings' first year in office, but when the Hoovers took charge of the White House in 1929, they did away with the public band concerts and the old New Year's receptions, by now an assembly line of thousands. The population was growing too large, and there now were other ways for the public to see and hear the president—radio and motion picture. The social life of the Hoovers was remarkably elegant, despite the nation's suffering from a steadily worsening economic depression, but the Hoovers paid for their own small staff and used their own private funds for White House entertaining.

The entire period from Taft through Hoover can well be considered the "Golden Age" of the White House musicale. It was a time when the quality of artists and coordination of programming were finely tuned, and the seasons always had a classical aura about them. During the 1920s the White House became established as a performing arts center with the world's finest artists in a highly honored spotlight. Missing from these programs, however, were the newest currents of the 1920s and early 1930s—the music of Varèse, Cowell, Ives, and Stravinsky. Not even the new jazz-oriented sounds of Gershwin, Copland, or Berlin appear on the printed programs of this period. The selections artists chose to perform for the president often had an encore flavor, drawn from the more traditional, shorter nineteenth-century repertories. But there were some notable exceptions. On March 22, 1928, the Pro Arte Quartet, famous for its promotion of modern music, played Louis Gruenberg's "Two Indiscretions" composed in 1922. A founder of the important League of Composers, Gruenberg was one of the earliest American composers to incorporate jazz in large symphonic works.

During the month of March 1924, Sergei Rachmaninoff, Salzedo, Greta Torpadie, Marguerite D'Alvarez, John Barclay, John Charles Thomas, and the twenty-year-old violinist Erica Morini all appeared on the Coolidge Lenten musicale series.[42] Sergei Rachmaninoff played in the White House three times during the Coolidge administration, enough to make the papers comment that he had become a "White House tradition." Besides his 1924 program he played on January 16, 1925, and again on March 30, 1927.

Rachmaninoff toured frequently throughout the nation and formulated some candid views about America. In 1909 he wrote: "You know, in this accursed country, you're surrounded by nothing but Americans and the 'business, business,' they are forever doing, clutching you from all sides."[43] Twenty years later, his opinions were considerably mollified: "I have had ample opportunity of convincing myself of the great progress made by American audiences both in their power of assimilation and in their musical taste. . . . They have used every means in their power and have not spared any money in their effort to surpass Europe in this respect. They have succeeded. No man will dare to dispute the fact."[44] For certain the dour, unsmiling genius succeeded in captivating the friendship and respect of Mrs.

Mr. SERGEI RACHMANINOFF

———

PROGRAM

Rondo Capriccioso . . . . *Mendelssohn*

(*a*) Nocturne ⎱
(*b*) Valse   ⎬ . . . . *Chopin*
(*c*) Scherzo ⎰

(*a*) Prelude in C sharp minor . . . *Rachmaninoff*
(*b*) Minuet . . . . *Bizet-Rachmaninoff*
(*c*) Hopak . . . . . . *Moussorgsky-Rachmaninoff*

(*a*) Liebestraum . . . . *Liszt*
(*b*) Rhapsodie No. 2.
        (Cadenza by Rachmaninoff) . . . . . *Liszt*

Monday, March 10, 1924
THE WHITE HOUSE

The first of three programs Sergei Rachmaninoff, the great Russian pianist and composer, played in the White House during the Coolidge administration (original measurement: 4 × 6 inches).

Coolidge, who commented, "Dr. Rachmaninoff came and played again for me a week ago. I had about three hundred in for the music and tea. As Mrs. (Adolphus) Andrews, wife of the Captain of the *Mayflower* says, 'He looks like a convict and plays like an angel.'" Then the first lady added, "I do hear lots of wonderful music."[45] How right she was!

When they played after the Supreme Court dinner honoring Chief Justice

Dame Myra Hess, the great English pianist, played Brahms, Chopin, Albeniz, and De Falla for members of the Supreme Court at the White House.

Taft on January 26, 1928, pianist Myra Hess and violinist Joseph Szigeti formed a sensational double bill. Interestingly, Dame Hess's selections— Brahms waltzes, Chopin etudes, and pieces by Albeniz and De Falla— reflected her earlier programming tendencies. By the late 1920s the great English pianist preferred Beethoven, Schumann, and the sonatas of Schubert and Brahms—the "roast beef" as she said, rather than merely the "shrimp cocktail." Like Szigeti, she was admired for her classical precision and warm poetic imagination.

Perhaps the most elegant and unique program to appear in the White House at this time was given on December 15, 1927, after a diplomatic dinner. The Cappella, a stringed orchestra of fourteen players, presented important modern revivals of works by Thomas Tomkins (1572–1656), William Byrd (1543–1623), and Domenico Scarlatti (1685–1757) on rare Stradivarius, Amati, and Guadagnini instruments.[46] At a time when concerts of early music were uncommon in America, similar programs were offered by harpsichordist Lewis Richards in 1927, and by Paul Shirley, who, on January 7, 1932, gave for the Hoovers what is undoubtedly the only solo performance on the viola d'amore in White House history.

The roster of prominent artists who performed for President Herbert Hoover at the end of the 1920s and into the early 1930s reads like several seasons at Carnegie Hall. With the exception of the Aguilar Spanish Lute Quartet of Madrid and the Gordon String Quartet, the musicales presented mainly soloists, including Margaret Matzenauer, Claire Dux, Rosa Ponselle, Efrem Zimbalist, Gregor Piatigorsky, Grace Moore, Carlos Salzedo, Ossip Gabrilowitsch, Jascha Heifetz, and, of course, the perennial Paderewski.

Paderewski played his last concert at the White House on November 25, 1930; six weeks later the twenty-seven-year-old Vladimar Horowitz played his first. The young Russian pianist, who already possessed one of the most dazzling techniques of the century, had astounded audiences at his American debut four years earlier. Henry Junge had arranged for Horowitz to perform for President and Mrs. Hoover at a diplomatic dinner on January 8, 1931, and the pianist was more concerned about conversing with the guests in his broken English than about his program. Junge gave him some pointers on the train to Washington, Just say "I am delighted" and nothing more when passing through the receiving line, Junge advised. Horowitz took the suggestion to heart and voiced ebulliently to each of the solemn dignitaries in the line: "I am delightful, I am delightful!" No one seemed to mind the error. They probably agreed.[47] Horowitz had just played a superb program of Bach-Busoni, Hummel, Dohnanyi, a Chopin group, and closed with the sparkling vertiginous "Carmen" paraphrase that later became his signature piece. The selections were representative of his early concert fare, but the "Carmen" would reappear when the great Russian master played for President Jimmy Carter—and the world—in the first White House concert to be publicly telecast.

With the performance of the Hampton and Tuskegee choirs, President and Mrs. Hoover became the first to bring black choirs to the White House since the Fisk Jubilee Singers performed for Chester Arthur. The Hoovers were also the first to invite an artist to perform for a head of state: harpist Mildred Dilling played for King Phra Pok Klao Prajadhipok of Siam on April 29, 1931. Dilling was a close friend of Mrs. Hoover and the last artist she heard. She died suddenly of a heart attack after Dilling's concert in New York in January 1944.[48]

As the 1930s began, unemployment continued to be a grave national concern. Just before the stock market crash of 1929, 60 percent of U.S. citizens had annual incomes of less than $2,000, the bare minimum to supply the basic necessities of life. By January 7, 1931, unemployment was estimated at between four and five million, and while President Hoover tried desperately to stem the floodtide of the Depression, his programs were never realized. The voters insisted upon a change and elected Franklin D. Roosevelt. Hundreds of songs—many whose lyrics were depressingly moving—were composed by ordinary Americans in the early 1930s and sent to the president. It was as if the bread lines seemed shorter if one could sing, or perhaps political chaos was less unsettling if one hummed through its storms, as Jerome Kern once said.[49]

The marked increase in the number of offers to perform in the Executive

Mansion during the decade of the 1920s is noted in a memo indicating that "requests for artists to appear at the White House almost equals the request for appointments in this office."[50] Letters during the Hoover administration often reflected the sober moods of artists feeling the pinch of the Depression, as well as a characteristic view of Americana: dulcimer players, folk singers, "Peaceful Bear" who studied at Juilliard, and even a prize-winning billiard exhibition backed by a congressman's letter. Performers young and old wrote to the president asking to play in the White House for the prestige it would afford. Members of the Aeolian French Horn Quartet were earning money "to help their parents in hard times," they said. Some of these requests were referred to Henry Junge for auditioning and appraisal; others were turned down graciously.[51] Few made it to the White House.

The last formal musicales to be presented during the Hoover administration were held on February 11 and 21, 1933, after a somewhat curtailed winter social season due to President Coolidge's death. The concerts were prophetic. They seemed to foreshadow features of the Franklin Roosevelt programs with multiple artists in one evening, black choirs, Indian and ethnic music—a tendency to reach out to more varied aspects of the American musical spirit. President and Mrs. Hoover, while differing from the Roosevelts in their musical tastes, undoubtedly felt the need to link the White House programs to the American people more closely as the Depression intensified. Sometimes the "triple bill" resulted in some rather puzzling juxtapositions. The appearance of Mary Garden, a celebrated operatic singer, with Mildred Dilling at the diplomatic dinner on February 11, 1933, does not seem too incongruous—until an American Indian singer, Chief Yowlache of the Yakima Tribe of Washington, is added to the program.

Closer examination of this program, however, makes one wonder whether the individual selections are so widely disparate as they might seem. Nature—serene, contemplative, elegiac, and impressionistic—becomes a connecting link, bridging eras and nations, and elegant art music with humble chants. Thus, twentieth-century French composer Hahn's "The Boat" complements the American Indians' "Canoe Song"; Claude Debussy's "Clair de lune" idealizes moonlight while the Zuni Tribe's "Invocation" worships the Sun god. Russian steppes, Scotch highlands, and American eagles and hills are all part of the same world. For music, like nature, has the uncanny power of speaking directly to the people. And that is precisely what Franklin D. Roosevelt felt to be the special communicative power of this art form during the twelve years he served as president.

CHAPTER 6

MUSIC IN A WARTIME
WHITE HOUSE

You never know the people
Or what the people bring;
You never know the nation
Till you hear the people sing.

Angela Morgan
The People's Chorus of New York
The White House, March 18, 1936

FRANKLIN D. ROOSEVELT

Franklin Roosevelt heard his people sing. He heard balladist Joe Glazer sing, "When a fellow's out of a job," and a ragged Texan sharecropper cry, "Work all week,/Don't make enough,/To pay my board,/And buy my snuff." He heard massed choruses bellow "Onward Christian Soldiers" at the Atlantic Conference before the United States went to war, and the single, poignant voice of Marian Anderson in "My Country 'Tis of Thee" on the steps of the Lincoln Memorial, after she was denied an appearance in Constitution Hall because she was black. He heard the sounds of symphony orchestras from Brooklyn to Cedarburg, Wisconsin, playing to millions a form of music they had never heard before; and he felt the beat of "Rosie the Riveter" as 6.5 million women entered the labor force during World War II. From the Great Depression to the great war, America's musical voices were native, human, eager, and alive. Franklin Roosevelt heard them all—and listened.

He was known by many as the "people's president" because he seemed to reach the masses in a new, intimate way. He was the nation's first media president. His legendary Fireside Chats brought his voice directly to the American home via radio, a form of communication he claimed restored contact between the "masses and their chosen leaders." During Roosevelt's terms in office, from March 4, 1933, to April 13, 1945, the mass media came of age. Not only radio, but also motion pictures, newspapers, and picture magazines, wire service photographs, and even television transformed the way America viewed its presidency and the world. Speaking as a friend to listeners and viewers of all classes, FDR was "at the center of that era's great social dialogue."[1] It is not surprising, then, that music, with its dynamic powers of imagery, was also a form of communication to FDR—a vital artistic medium that should speak directly to the people. Through the New Deal's dedication to social values, the music world entered into a relationship with the public as never before in America. Stripped of its mysticism, music now found a new grassroots audience, reaching out to all—rich, poor, young, old, the man-on-the-street.

The FDR years began grimly. Sobered by the impact of the Great Depression, America's concert music in the 1930s was less innovative and exuberant than it had been during the 1920s. But with a new conservatism in musical attitudes came a trend toward historical and regional Americanism and a reaching out to broader audiences through the "simplest possible terms," as Aaron Copland admitted about his works of the 1930s. But America's musical moods during the Roosevelt era were also in a constant state of flux, shifting and melding like a kaleidoscope. The budding, brassy jazz sounds of the 1920s flowered into swing—and exploded into bop. Irving Berlin, Richard Rodgers, Cole Porter, Frank Loesser, and George Gershwin composed music reflecting a society not so much torn by war as buried in escapism. The Hollywood sound film and the New York musical stage became entertaining ways to forget the nation's problems.

President Roosevelt's concern for art was social, but behind this pragmatism lay a more intimate, personal vision. Roosevelt had always shown keen interest in Hollywood, the legitimate stage, and radio; there was always a touch of the showman in him, perhaps stemming from his youthful love of music and theater. From 1896 until his graduation in 1900, Franklin sang regularly in the choir and performed in various school plays at Groton. His letters to his mother during this period indicate an active interest in singing, first as soprano then tenor, finally baritone in college: "Today I got somewhat banged to pieces [at football] receiving a crack on the head, a wrench of the knee. . . . What do you think! I am going to take singing lessons! A Miss Reid comes up here once a week and gives lessons in either singing or declaiming. However, singing should come before speaking so I have decided to take one lesson a week, as they are not very expensive."[2]

As an adult FDR loved songs that conjured up images and feelings of America—unpaved country roads, the open West "where the skies are not cloudy all day," and always the sea. From his earliest childhood, Roosevelt loved the sea and considered water an emotional as well as physical therapy. "The water put me where I am," he once said of his paralysis, "and the water has to bring me back." He served as assistant secretary of the Navy under President Woodrow Wilson in 1913 and throughout World War I. His interesting collection of sheet music on nautical themes reflects not only a pastime but also an awareness of history told through song.

Opera for FDR had to reach out and touch everyone. Both he and Mrs. Roosevelt were honorary sponsors of the Metropolitan Opera Guild, formed in 1935. On January 31, 1940, the president wrote to David Sarnoff, chairman of the Met's Radio Division, a message that was read during Saturday afternoon's opera:

> I want you to count me among the thousands of radio listeners throughout the nation who wish the Metropolitan Opera to continue, and to go on to greater glory. Very often, on Saturday afternoons, when my work is done I have listened to the opera broadcasts and have enjoyed

the music which this modern miracle has brought into my study in Washington.

Grand opera has now become in a real sense, the people's opera rather than the possession of only a privileged few.[3]

Hymns, too, had their own personal message. For the memorable Thanksgiving Day service at the White House during Roosevelt's third term, the president chose "Onward Christian Soldiers," "Faith of Our Fathers," "Eternal Father Strong to Save," and "Battle Hymn of the Republic." While all the hymns, except the last, appear on the printed program in their entirety, only stanzas 1, 2, and 5 are given for "Battle Hymn." FDR admitted that the South still objected to some of the words of Julia Ward Howe's immortal hymn, and he wished that "somebody could eliminate those verses and substitute something else."[4]

Through her sensitivity to the needs of the underprivileged of all races, creeds, and nations, Anna Eleanor Roosevelt transformed the role of first lady when she came to the White House. She broke precedents by holding press conferences, traveling, lecturing, and expressing her opinions candidly in her daily syndicated newspaper column, "My Day." "She was an extraordinary woman," claimed contralto Marian Anderson. "She will never really be understood. She left an example behind her which influenced even those who have not yet lived." Her appearance? "To me she was beautiful, because in her one sees much more than just the physical. She radiated a beauty as big as life itself. And with all of this one was aware that she was shy—there was always a sadness in her eyes."[5]

To Mrs. Roosevelt music was an international language: "People," she said, "can get together and understand each other while making music in a way that would be impossible were they doing anything else in the world."[6] As first lady she brought to the White House a new touch of élan and informality. While operatic and concert artists still outnumbered other types of performers, the Roosevelts brought professional dancers to the mansion for the first time; a large percentage of black vocal artists; various WPA choruses; the first staged opera—*Hänsel und Gretel*; women's organizations, such as the New York Women's Trio with Antonio Brico and the National League of American Penwomen with Amy Marcy Beach; ethnic groups from Pan America, China, Russia, and Spain; and finally an array of American folk singers and players as never before seen in the White House.

How was all of this accomplished? Mainly through a voluminous amount of correspondence between Edith Helm, social secretary to Mrs. Roosevelt, and Henry Junge of Steinway & Sons in New York. Through his long association with Steinway, Junge knew just about every prominent artist in the world. John Steinway recalls: "Eleanor Roosevelt was an old friend of my parents [Theodore Steinway], and she and Henry Junge were great friends. He would spend a great deal of time discussing the entire season. He was almost blind shortly before he died—I remember helping him up and down the stairs. Eleanor kept him on just because she was so fond of him. They would sit upstairs and have tea together."[7] Mrs. Roosevelt kept actively involved, however, making suggestions, approving artists, and indicating the type of music she and the president preferred. Seasons' lists of performers

Eleanor Roosevelt with contralto Marian Anderson during Mrs. Roosevelt's visit to Japan in 1953.

often had scrawled across the top in Mrs. Helm's hand, "OKed by the President."[8]

Offers to perform at the White House came in at the rate of 250 per season during the 1930s. Aspiring artists felt a personal tie with the Roosevelts from hearing the president's voice on radio and reading Eleanor's "My Day" column. The latter, wrote Henry Junge to Mrs. Roosevelt, "seems to be devoured daily by your admirers, creating a unique interest in performing at the mansion not existing before."[9] People with dreams scratched their simple, polite notes on cheap writing paper: a woman whose husband earns $3.50 per week wants her little girl to dance for the president; a young baritone with infantile paralysis asks to sing in the White House; Hickey, the "Cowboy Caruso" sings "The Star-Spangled Banner"; a young man demonstrates the "Theremin Wave—a scientific musical mystery"; a woman plays the piano wearing mittens; a black mother's family of nine plays by ear, with baby of eighteen months directing in perfect time; a man and his little niece want to play "My Country 'Tis of Thee" on their violins for the president and at "every capital of the 48 states." None ever made his way to the White House.

Remarkably, each offer to perform was answered graciously by Edith Helm, who regularly referred the more promising unknowns to Henry Junge. The elderly impresario would then "placate these artists generally with a dose of ingenious platitudes where necessary, and encourage others who possess merits," as he wrote to Mrs. Helm in his usual prosaic manner. Auditions for the White House were sometimes very grueling. It was an all-day session at Steinway Hall when the program "Det Norske Folkedanselag" for the crown prince of Norway's visit to Hyde Park was approved. Twenty-four costumed dancers, six fiddlers, and three singers were found by Junge to be "attractive and gay, with dancing couples colorfully draped, their gestures most graceful and their singing in chorus of mellow quality and remarkably in unison." Another group recommended after a three-hour audition was Alexander Haas and his Budapest Gypsy Ensemble of eight to ten pieces, "who play ravishingly. They are dressed in scarlet coats and their Vienna Valses are so deucedly seductive that they would awaken Rip Van Winkle to dance the 'Blue Danube' all the way from 'Krum Elbow' to Washington, D.C."[10]

Combing the performers at the beginning of the season, worrying about which artists would come for dinner, who would need a stage and simple props, what selections were appropriate, and whether or not sufficient American artists were represented were some of the responsibilities facing Helm and Junge during the entertainment seasons of the busy early years. As Mrs. Helm wrote: "I have sorted out the infant prodigies, snake swallowers and others who have applied this year," and "Here is another of our rising young musicians. I sometimes wish they would stop rising and stay put."[11]

With the innovative features of White House musical entertainment—such as the large number of black performers and the dancers and the dramatic artists who required staging—came new concerns for those making the arrangements. To Mrs. Roosevelt music knew no racial or ethnic boundaries. Not all agreed with her. When word spread that Marian Anderson and the North Carolina Spiritual Singers were to sing in the East Room for the king and queen of England, "a staunch Democrat from Miami" protested: "It is an insult to the British King and Queen who are caucasians to present a negro vocalist for their entertainment. Do you want to engender racial hatred which might lead to serious consequences in the entire South?" Mrs. Helm calmly replied: "Mrs. Roosevelt asks me to acknowledge your telegram and to tell you that she is trying to give the King and Queen a picture of all American music. As the colored people are outstanding in a musical way, Mrs. Roosevelt feels that they should be presented with the others who will appear here."[12]

Thus the White House resounded with the rich, moving voices of black singers and choirs from all over America in a way that was never heard before in the mansion. The Sedalia Quartet from South Carolina sang on May 17, 1933; Arenia Mallory appeared with six black singers from the Industrial and Literary School of Lexington, Mississippi, on September 27, 1938. The Golden Gate Quartet, the Colored Group of Detroit, and the Hampton Choir sang, and the Spirituals Society of Charleston, South Carolina, sang in a modification of the Gullah tongue, a strange corruption of English spoken by the lowcountry Negroes and chanted by the slaves around their cabins.[13]

But there had been no black opera singer at the White House since Black Patti sang at the turn of the century. Lillian Evans Tibbs of Washington, D.C., was a young black lyric soprano who changed her name to Lillian Evanti and managed a successful career, even though her color created problems for her both abroad and at home. She was the first black to appear with an organized European opera company, the Nice Opera, in 1926. On February 9, 1934, Evanti sang for the Roosevelts, who were delighted with the brilliant young singer. The next year they invited Dorothy Maynor and baritone Todd Duncan, who sang on March 8, 1935.

That evening Duncan sang Cecil Cohen's "Death of an Old Seaman" because he knew the president loved the sea. "I can see him beaming right now," Duncan said. "How he loved that song! He beckoned me to come down and shake his hand after I sang it, and then I went back and sang the next song. All evening the President never stopped looking and never stopped listening. I never lost him for one minute."[14] Duncan sang at the White House three more times during the Roosevelt administration. He had created the role of Porgy in George Gershwin's *Porgy and Bess* when it first opened in Boston on September 30, 1935. When he sang "I Got Plenty of Nothin'" on March 31, 1937, and the dramatic "Buzzard Song" on May 6, 1940, he brought to the White House a totally new operatic experience—and a truly American one.

Marian Anderson, whose powerful, compelling, contralto voice Arturo Toscanini found "comes once in a hundred years," sang informally in the Monroe Room on February 19, 1936, one month after her Carnegie Hall debut. There were no printed programs. "I sensed a bit of fear—awe is a better word," she said, "even though there was such warmth in the atmosphere."[15] The charming Monroe Drawing Room, to the left of the oval room on the second floor, had been decorated with Monroe period furnishings by Lou Hoover. During FDR's time it became an intimate rendezvous for musical artists, such as Irving Berlin, who played and sang there after a Fireside Chat party in 1941.

During the 1930s, dancers of all varieties made their way to the White House—but the Roosevelts' eclectic tastes resulted in some anomalous juxtapositions at times: Carola Goya, in her galaxy of bright costumes, shared the program after a diplomatic dinner with the renowned cellist Gregor Piatigorsky and a Vienna State Opera contralto, Enid Szantho—"an aristocratic combination," claimed Junge, "which would appeal to the less musically-inclined." On another occasion La Argentina presented her fiery "impressions of a bull fight," followed by the Vienna Choir Boys' serene interpretation of "Silent Night." Perhaps the oddest combination of all was the program for Governor and Mrs. Herbert H. Lehman of New York on May 17, 1934. The brilliant young American, Paul Haakon, who had danced beside Pavlova, came after an old-timers' group that featured eighty-two-year-old Betty Smith fiddling away "Hell Broke Loose in Georgia."

But it was Martha Graham who made artistic history at the White House. Not only was she the most important dancer to appear there before the Kennedy era, but she also opened the door to fresh, artistic approaches at the mansion. Shortly before her program at the White House, Graham inquired about the space, lighting, and especially the floor surface of the East Room:

> Miss Hawkins, my manager, has just come back from Washington where she talked with Mr. Crim [the chief usher]. He showed her the room where the party for Mrs. Morgenthau is to be held. Miss Hawkins tells me that it has a highly polished parquet floor. Even though I have wanted very much to dance at the party and have been looking forward to it . . . I am afraid of slipping and injuring an ankle which was hurt last season . . . rosin is no solution because I dance barefoot.
>
> If when I return from the tour you would like me to dance, I should be delighted to have the opportunity.

Edith Helm wrote immediately that a stage could be put up and that Mrs. Roosevelt had not meant for her to dance on the floor itself. "It was simply an idea that the window would furnish a charming background for you." Frances

Martha Graham, noted innovator in modern dance, as the young bride in Aaron Copland's *Appalachian Spring*.

Hawkins wired: "Martha Graham delighted stage will make it possible for her to dance," and she listed the dancer's numbers as *Sarabande* (music by Lehman Engel), *Frontier* (music by Louis Horst), *Imperial Gesture* (music by Lehman Engel), and *Harlequinade* (music by Ernest Toch).[16]

Stages, props, and lighting were new aspects of entertaining with which the president's graceful home had to contend during this period. If the requests were too complicated and unreasonable, they were turned over to the chief usher, Howell Crim, who politely dealt with the situation. One monologist asked for six pieces of furniture "harmonious in design and color," an easily accessible dressing room with seven wall hooks, red, white and blue lights, a pink spot light, a "black-out" system to eliminate afternoon sun, and a stage curtain of neutral color.

"We do have a curtain which can be used before the stage," Crim noted. "However, it is made of discarded material, is extremely heavy and is not as beautiful as it probably should be. It requires about three or four men to run it back and forth between scenes."[17] The not-so-beautiful curtain did come in handy, though, when Humperdinck's *Hänsel und Gretel* was staged in the East Room by the National Music League on March 30, 1935. The three-act production had only six characters, ranging from eighteen to twenty-five years of age, and simple scenery, but it was the first opera to be staged in the White House.

One highly beneficial facility that allowed the musicales to run more smoothly ws the donation of a new state piano by Steinway & Sons. Presented to the nation on December 10, 1938, the new 9'7" instrument replaced the Gold Piano, which was donated to the Smithsonian Institution. It was designed by New York architect Eric Gugler. The case of Honduras mahogany was decorated in gold leaf by Dunbar Beck and the giant supporting eagles, also covered with gold leaf, were modeled by the sculptor Albert Stewart. The paintings on the case represented five forms of American music: the Virginia reel; the Indian ceremonial dance; the New England barn dance; black folk music; and the cowboy song, all forms of music close to the hearts of the president and first lady. Last renovated during the Carter administration, the historic piano remains in the East Room today.

President Roosevelt's keen interest in the new piano inspired a touch of whimsy that appeared in the *Philadelphia Inquirer* of February 15, 1937:

> The President.—The piano should have been thrown out years ago. It was all dented up from Theodore banging his fist on it to emphasize his points. What color is the new one?
>
> Mrs. Roosevelt.—Gold.
>
> The President (thoughtfully).—Silver would have been better. What did the Fine Arts Commission have to say about that?
>
> Mrs. Roosevelt.—They've approved the piano. It's the red draperies that bother them. They think the red's too red.
>
> The President.—Too red for what?
>
> Mrs. Roosevelt.—Oh, I suppose they see some political significance. One of the boys said something about Moscow.

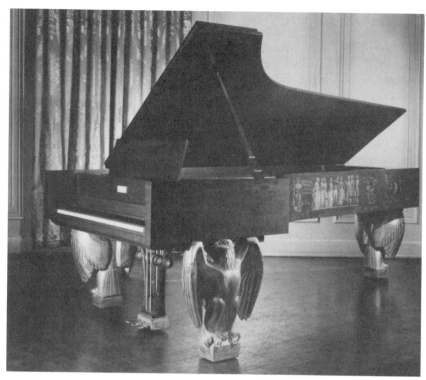

Mahogany Steinway concert grand piano, with supporting eagles of gold leaf, was presented to the White House by Steinway & Sons in 1938 and remains in the East Room today.

The President.—For goodness sake! Don't tell me there is still a commission left under my Administration with a Republican on it!

Often between Christmas and New Year's, the Roosevelts invited special entertainers for the younger children and their friends—a custom dating back at least to Theodore Roosevelt's terms. There were the usual magicians, puppeteers, and Lee Pearson with his wonder dog Grease Ball. But by far the most distinctive and creative performer was Wendy Marshall, "The Toy Lady," who entertained on December 26, 1933, Franklin Roosevelt's first Christmas as president. Having studied voice at Juilliard, Marshall was one of the first specialists in juvenile song and was among the first children's performers to appear on television.

Many brilliant concert and operatic artists performed for President and Mrs. Roosevelt: Percy Grainger, Josef Hofmann, Jascha Heifetz, Ruggiero Ricci (aged fifteen), Ray Lev, John Charles Thomas, the Curtis String Quartet, Kathryn Meisle, Frederick Jagel, Guiomar Novaes, Lotte Lehmann, Giovanni Martinelli, Antonia Brico, Lauritz Melchior, Bidu Sayao, Eugene List, Elizabeth Schumann, and Amy Marcy Beach, the first female composer to have a symphony performed in the United States. There was also the Russian princess, Dagmar Renina-Troubetskoi. And during this era duo-pianists appeared at the White House for the first time: Edwin and Bethany

Hughes, Guy Maier and Lee Pattison, Ethel Bartlett and Rae Robinson. Lily Pons sang Jerome Kern's "I Dream Too Much" from her recent RKO movie, bringing popular contemporary sounds to the formal White House musicale. On January 2, 1936, Pons closed the program with her legendary interpretation of the "Bell Song" from Delibe's *Lakmé*. Petite and glamorous, Pons was *the* coloratura of the era. Her revealing costume for the Met's *Lakmé* broke at the rib cage and resumed at the hips. Momentarily America forgot that these were the grim years of depression and war.

To FDR the music that spoke most directly to the people, however, was the folk music—"the voices of miners, farmers, lumberjacks, workers of all kinds, their wives and children . . . a tide of music rich and strange but vital and undeniably American," as the distinctive program notes for the June 8, 1939, White House concert read.[18] Presented in the East Room for Queen Elizabeth and King George VI, the first British monarchs to visit America, the concert was one of the most ambitious in the mansion's history. The logistics of amassing from various parts of the country square dancers, cowboys, black spiritual singers, and opera and popular singers into a coordinated whole for an "Evening of American Music" were staggering. They involved Edith Helm, the perennial Mr. Junge, Charles Seeger, pioneer ethnomusicologist and deputy director of the Federal Music Project, and Adrian Dornbush, head of the Special Skills Division of the Resettlement Administration, as well as President and Mrs. Roosevelt. Dornbush managed the folk portion in consultation with Seeger, Junge procured the concert artists and established the format of the program, while Mrs. Helm passed on all developments to the Roosevelts for their final approval.

While all managed to gel—ultimately—problems abounded. Mrs. Helm was concerned about the appearance of black and white performers on the same program; the president was worried about the cost of the "Cowboy Singers" ($1298.40),[19] and genteel old Mr. Junge remained baffled by the entire enterprise. He was especially worried about the twenty-one dancers who would be cramped for space. Since they wore heavy clogs, the platform would have to be reinforced "or I am afraid they might crash through the floor." He also noted that high jumps were dangerous and should be avoided "inasmuch as the chandelier leaves only a headroom of six feet one inch." And at the last minute Tibbett and Anderson—perhaps judiciously—omitted their operatic arias. "It was a hectic day," Junge admitted right before the big event—a rare admission from this devoted, patient servant.[20] Five weeks later, at the age of eighty-one, he was dead.

Heterogeneous as it was, the concert was a success. But like other innovative gestures, its message was not to be fully heard or appreciated until decades later. Its beautiful printed program booklet of eleven pages effectively described each folk selection and its significance with a note about the performers.[21] The North Carolina Spiritual Singers were a community activity group under the direction of the North Carolina Federal Music Project. Twenty-two-year-old Alan Lomax, assistant in charge of the Archive of American Folk Song at the Library of Congress, sang "Whoopee, Ti Yi Yo, Git Along Little Doggies" and "The Old Chisholm Trail." The Coon Creek Girls from Kentucky played and sang, among other tunes, "Cindy," and the Soco Gap Square-Dance Team were directed by Bascom Lamar Lunsford, a lawyer and farmer from Leicester known as "The Minstrel of the Appalachians."

Representing the popular and art music of America, Kate Smith chose "These Foolish Things," Macmurrough's "Macushla," and her own "When the Moon Comes over the Mountain." The last song became her trademark. Marian Anderson sang Schubert's "Ave Maria"—which had moved to tears the 75,000 at the Lincoln Memorial fourteen months earlier[22]—and the spiritual "My Soul's Been Anchored in the Lord." The young Metropolitan Opera baritone, Lawrence Tibbett, closed the program with "The Pilgrim's Song" by Tchaikovsky, Oley Speak's "Sylvia," and Marx's "If Love Hath Entered Thy Heart."

The concert spoke a direct language, in the precise spirit the Roosevelts wanted. But did it reach the king and queen? In just as direct and homespun a style, Coon Creek Girl Lily Ledford gave her answer:

> There were 89 guests, the cream of Washington society. Then I began to gather my wits about me, Lord! right there in the front row, about five feet from the stage, sat the King and Queen and the Roosevelts! I like to dropped a stitch or two on my banjo, but recovered and went on and tried not to stare, though I was able to size them up from the corner of my eye. Our spirits rose as we realized that the Queen and Mrs. Roosevelt were smiling as well as Mr. Roosevelt; but the King, with rather a long-faced, dour, dead-pan look, worried me a little. Then as I glanced down I caught him patting his foot, ever so little, and I knew we had him![23]

As the war in Europe cast its shadow over the capital's social life, White House entertaining diminished. But one event in particular stands out: "A Program of American Songs for American Soldiers," presented on February 17, 1941. Designed by Alan Lomax and Mrs. Roosevelt herself, the unusual program was printed on brown construction paper, creating a rough-hewn burlap effect. A reproduction of the 1846 *Crockett Almanac* frontispiece appeared on the cover with the words "arranged entirely on the Davy Crockett or Go Ahead Principle." Inside, the contents were described as: "Songs made by men who would rather hear a wild bull roar in a canyon than three choirs in a concert hall." The performers included folk, spiritual and ballad singers, such as J. M. Hunt, Wade Mainer, Burl Ives, and Joshua White, as well as enlisted men from posts nearby Washington. But the program was far more than an evening of "hillbilly" music. It was a new concept, a conscientious effort to relate American traditional music to the armed services at a critical period in the nation's history.

Even under wartime conditions the arts flourished, and symphonic societies, ballet groups, and opera houses sprang up all over the United States. Entertainment-hungry civilians and service personnel were offered romantic, escapist music, and the "dream" became all-pervasive with hits such as Irving Berlin's "White Christmas" of 1943. FDR had great rapport with the entertainment world and celebrities often wrote to him during the war years. Many performed for him and Mrs. Roosevelt at birthdays, inaugurals, and charitable functions. Their letters reflect the national political and cultural scene as well as the warm personal associations and high esteem in which the Roosevelts were held.[24]

On May 1, 1940, President Roosevelt presented George M. Cohan with a gold medal for his songs "You're a Grand Old Flag" (1906) and "Over There"

A PROGRAM OF AMERICAN SONGS FOR AMERICAN SOLDIERS

arranged entirely on
THE DAVY CROCKETT
or
go ahead PRINCIPLE

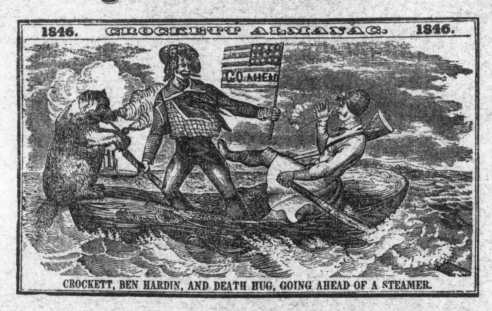

1846. CROCKETT ALMANAC. 1846.

CROCKETT, BEN HARDIN, AND DEATH HUG, GOING AHEAD OF A STEAMER.

The White House
Monday, February Seventeenth
Nine P. M.

Burl Ives and other folk singers participated in Eleanor Roosevelt's innovative program for the armed services at the White House in 1941. The program cover was designed by Mrs. Roosevelt and Alan Lomax.

(1917), two years before the famed vaudevillian died. In 1941 Mrs. Roosevelt honored Ignacy Jan Paderewski on the golden anniversary of his American debut. FDR was the last of seven presidents whom Paderewski knew or entertained. When Paderewski died on June 29, 1941, at eighty-two, the president ordered his state interment at the Arlington National Cemetery.

Perhaps the real "unsung hero" of the FDR White House was the ubiquitous Marine Band. It played for every important state dinner, reception, birthday, debut, anniversary, and holiday celebration at the White House and for numerous ceremonies within the capital and beyond. The basic ceremonial traditions established over the years were retained from one president to the next—so much so that the military aid at President Roosevelt's first reception at the White House announced blatantly, "The President and Mrs. Hoover!"—just as President and Mrs. Roosevelt had stopped at the established spot on the carpet and "Ruffles" was played. "I broke into 'Hail to the Chief' as fast as I could and tried to drown him out!" said the flustered Santelmann, who was second leader at the time. "I don't know what ever happened to that gentleman, but I know we never saw him at the White House again."[25]

The White House repertory of the band and orchestra at this time was generally conservative. Waltzes, marches, and the show tunes of Sigmund Romberg and Vincent Youmans served as pleasant background music for dining and conversation. But for dancing at the White House, the Roosevelts had to have an up-to-date swing orchestra. Ruby Newman reported, "The family members are all good dancers. . . . They do not particularly care whether it be sweet music or modern swing, but they enjoy the new styles."[26] Dance bands were brought to the White House for the first time during the FDR terms, mostly before 1941, whereas earlier administrations relied on the Marine or Navy bands for their dances. The new swing style was "terrible and disgusting," according to the band member who kept the logs in 1934 and must have watched Sidney Sideman's band playing the jitterbug for the Roosevelt boys. Other bands that appeared at this time in the president's home were those of Eddie Duchin, Joe Moses, Meyer Davis, and Eddie Peabody, who sometimes played the banjo during dinner.[27]

The Marine Band served to underpin nearly every mood at the White House—humorous, heroic, lyric, melancholy, exhilarating, poignant. But it also shared supreme moments of mourning. The band logs for April 14, 1945, show the word "cancelled" scrawled across all events for that day—except one: "Marine Band to head funeral procession for the late President Franklin Roosevelt. Leader, Second Leader and Drum Major with 81 men. Dress Blues with white caps. Band played at cadence of 100–110."

Franklin Roosevelt died on April 12 at Warm Springs, Georgia, on the eighty-third day of his fourth term. There was no music or dancing at New York's famous clubs the following day. A pall gripped Broadway as news of the president's death swept the great amusement belt. The burial service was simple and austere; the Army Band from West Point intoned Chopin's "Funeral March," "Nearer My God to Thee," and "Now the Laborer's Task is Done."[28] But FDR's legacy to Americans for decades to come would be found in the hymn he especially loved: "Shun not the struggle, face it. . . . Be strong!"

HARRY S. TRUMAN

"I don't dare think of facing the next two months let alone two years," Harry S. Truman wrote to his mother and sister shortly after he became president. He was spending an evening alone in the White House and seemed especially aware of the array of clocks all chiming the hour at once—the little one that, "like most small people, has a big voice"; the ship's clock with its "crazy sailor count of bells"; and the old grandpa clock in the hall, a high-pitched "fat tenor." "It is rather lonesome here in this old barn without anyone," admitted the new chief of state, ". . . but I get a lot of work done."[29]

From the time Truman was chosen as vice-presidential nominee on the ticket with Franklin Roosevelt in the summer of 1944, he knew that FDR was very ill. Nevertheless, the news of Roosevelt's death on April 12, 1945, was a shock, as Truman wrote: "When I arrived at the Pennsylvania entrance to the most famous house in America a couple of ushers met me, bowed and scraped and took my hat; . . . Mrs. Roosevelt put her arm on my shoulder and said, 'Harry, the president is dead.' It was the only time in my life, I think, that I ever felt like I'd had a real shock. I had hurried to the White House to see the President and when I arrived I found *I* was the President. No one in the history of our country ever had it happen to him just that way."[30]

Truman met the sudden, almost overwhelming, challenges of world leadership with courage, honesty, and a zestful, non-nonsense philosophy that he characteristically called "horse sense." His first year in office was monumental. Germany and Japan collapsed, and between the two surrenders Truman met with Joseph Stalin and Winston Churchill at Potsdam. On August 6 the first atomic bomb was dropped—a dramatic event that changed the entire world. "It was a terrible decision," Truman wrote to his sister Mary three years later. "But I made it. And I'd made it to save 250,000 boys from the United States, and I'd make it again under similar circumstances. It stopped the Jap war."[31] No one could say this as directly and effectively as Truman.

President Truman's intense love of music is legendary, and he admitted that his tastes were conservative. He preferred music with a recognizable melodic line to the more avant-garde sonorities ("I've heard the Enesco *Rhapsody* over the radio a couple of times. He's not a noise composer—thank goodness").[32] But even though Truman hoped and expected that his daughter Margaret would some day sing with the Metropolitan Opera, he never became an opera buff. When he was a young man, some friends took him to a performance of Wagner's *Parsifal* in Kansas City: "I haven't recovered from that siege of grand opera yet," he wrote to Bess Wallace before they were married.[33]

When he was president, Truman had a radio by his bedside and a piano by his desk. "It seemed hard for him to pass a piano anywhere without sitting down and playing, even for a minute or two," Rex Scouten recalls.[34] But Truman also played often and unabashedly in public. He played for world leaders (Stalin and Churchill), for U.S. presidents (John F. Kennedy), for concert artists (Eugene List), for movie stars (Lauren Bacall), for painters (Grandma Moses), and for some thirty million Americans during his televised tour of the newly remodeled White House in the spring of 1952. "He simply loved it," said Margaret, who performed herself as a professional singer.

NO ENCORE

This election-year cartoon by John Collins depicts the beleaguered Truman, score in hand, hurriedly abandoning the White House piano.

There was no attempt to provide the world with an image. He was just too candid for that. Perhaps "the fingers wouldn't work" on all the pieces he knew, but he would play them anyway. He was once asked if he sang tenor or baritone and replied, "I *Never* sing. I'm like Artemus Ward. 'I'm saddest when I sing and so are those that listen to me.'"[35]

Encouraged by his musical mother, Truman studied piano from age eight to about sixteen. He never had to be coerced to practice, which he always claimed was "pleasure and not work," adding that the only reason he missed being a musician was because he "was not good enough."[36] He loved the music of Mozart, Chopin, Liszt, Mendelssohn, and Debussy, and also enjoyed Strauss waltzes, Gershwin's *Rhapsody in Blue*, J. S. Bach's Preludes and Fugues from *The Well-Tempered Clavier*, and that musty old Broadway smash of the early years of the century, *Floradora*, by Owen Hall and Leslie Stuart. But the piece that most certainly bored him was the ubiquitous "Missouri Waltz": "I don't give a damn about it. But I can't say that out loud, because it's the song of Missouri."[37] He was also irked by that "peculiar American complex," which seems to want to know "what the President eats, how he sleeps, when he gets up," and so forth. "They want to know my favorite songs and when I say 'Pilgrim's Chorus' from *Parsifal* or 'Toreador' from *Carmen* or 'Hinky Dinky

Parlez Vous' or 'Dirty Gerty from Bizerte,' they are not sure whether I'm on the beam or not."[38]

During his years as president, Truman's "thirst for good music sometimes drew him out of the White House," as Margaret Truman observed in her book *Harry S. Truman*.[39] He attended outdoor concerts at Watergate and with Bess Truman heard Lauritz Melchior sing at Constitution Hall on the twenty-fifth anniversary of his American operatic debut. The Trumans also attended several musical plays in historic Gadsby's Tavern in Alexandria, Virginia, one of which was a production of the Gay/Pepusch *Beggar's Opera* of 1728. Both President and Mrs. Truman were great supporters of the National Symphony and good friends of the conductor, Howard Mitchell. "Just don't play that modern stuff," said Truman. But he went anyway, bringing along Prime Minister Ferenc Nagy of Hungary in June 1946 for a program of Bartok and Stravinsky. "I just couldn't believe it," said Mitchell.[40]

That Truman held only one series of concerts in the White House during his period in office may seem ironic, since he was the most musical of all U.S. presidents and had a daughter who was a professional singer. But the Trumans had to contend with the frugal postwar years, as well as a residence that was slowly crumbling and deteriorating. The upper floor of the White House had become so perilously weak that Margaret's Steinway grand, given to her by her father when she was a child, cracked through the surface. And when Eugene List played in the East Room on February 11, 1947, he noticed a large space left under the chandelier. The president explained that the house was just not safe and if the audience were to be seated under the giant crystal fixture, someone could be killed if it fell. In November 1948 the Truman family moved to Blair House where they lived for almost four years during the White House renovations.

The Truman musicales consisted of six programs held after the state dinners during the administration's only social season of 1946–47. These programs were arranged through the assistance of Steinway & Sons and Alexander Greiner, who succeeded Henry Junge as White House arts liaison in 1939. Because of the Trumans' classical tastes, their musicales had none of FDR's dichotomous mixtures of artists and styles. And as the president's letter to Margaret indicates, planning the programs was mainly a family affair:

> We are doing all sorts of things in the musical line while you are away—cat's away, you know! As you see, your father had first choice on the pianists; then your mother and I took over the violinists and they have been marked, leaving the vocalists for you. Would you mind marking your first, second, third, and so on, choice?[41]

From November 1946 to February 1947, Sylvia Zaremba, Lawrence Tibbett, Helen Traubel (Margaret's teacher), Oscar Levant, Frederick Jagel, Carroll Glenn and Eugene List entertained. "They all seem to get a fit of nerves when they perform in the East Room," said the president. "I don't know why. I'm not such a terrible person."[42]

Eugene List, who had played in the White House for FDR in 1941, was a great favorite and friend of the Truman family. A brilliant young pianist, at sixteen List had presented the American premier of Shostakovich's Piano Concert no. 1 with the Philadelphia Symphony Orchestra. Truman knew of

List's fame and not only brought the young Army sergeant to Potsdam to play for the Big Three on July 19, 1945, but even turned pages for him. Years later List recounted his impressions of the historic occasion:

> I played the theme of the Tchaikovsky Piano Concerto and Stalin sprang to his feet and said "I want to propose a toast to the sergeant." I couldn't believe it! I was about twenty-two years old. I didn't know what to do. I was rooted to the spot. The President beckoned to me to come forward to the center of the floor and somebody stuck a glass of Vodka in my hand—it was so unbelievable![43]

The next night List played again, and Stalin had sent to Moscow for some samplings of his version of Russian artistry. A quartet of two pianists and two violinists played Tchaikovsky, Liszt, and Ukrainian folk dances. "I never heard better," said Truman. "Since I'd had America's No. 1 pianist to play for Uncle Joe at my dinner, he had to go me one better. I had one and one—and he had two of each." Then he added, "They had dirty faces though, and the gals were rather fat."[44]

Unlike the other musical White House Margaret (President Wilson's daughter) Harry Truman's Margaret never presented a formal program in the White House. Her much publicized debut as a coloratura opera and concert singer took place on March 16, 1947, when she sang with the Detroit Symphony Orchestra for a radio audience of fifteen million. Following this concert she performed in the Hollywood Bowl, toured across the nation and appeared several times on television as a comedian with Jimmy Durante and other stars. But she was always the child of Harry Truman—talented, sensitive, resolute—and of Bess, a sincere, quietly charming first lady who seemed to leave the spotlight to her more politically and artistically inclined family. President Truman, who gave Margaret her first music lessons as a child, was a constant source of encouragement to his daughter. Her intense love of music mirrored his own. They were two of a kind. "Of course if that is what you want—that is what I want you to have," the president told her. "It seems to me you have gone about your career in the right way. . . . Your Daddy will support you to the end in whatever it takes to make these trials. But daughter don't fool yourself. You know what it takes."[45]

Many critics admired Margaret's warm presence and lithe, lyric voice that soared within a range of nearly three octaves. Others were less complimentary. After Margaret's Constitution Hall concert in December 1950, critic Paul Hume of the *Washington Post* wrote what became the most talked-about review in the annals of music criticism. "Miss Truman cannot sing very well. . . . She is flat a good deal of the time. . . . There are a few moments during her recital when one can relax and feel confident that she will make her goal, which is the end of the song." Bristling, the president dashed off a vitriolic note to Hume on White House memo paper calling the hostile critic "an eight-ulcer man on four-ulcer pay. . . . Some day I hope to meet you," lambasted Truman, "and when that happens you'll need a new nose, some beef steak for black eyes and perhaps a supporter below!"[46]

Two years later Truman had another run-in with the *Post*—this time over pianist Gina Bachauer's recital, which he and Bess attended at Lisner Auditorium. The next day the president wrote to Philip Graham of the *Post* suggesting that Graham "retire this frustrated old fuddy-duddy and hire a

Senator Harry S. Truman playing the piano with his daughter Margaret during the senatorial campaign of 1940.

reviewer . . . who knows what it's all about." Of course, the reference here was to none other than Paul Hume, whose review this time Truman called a "disgraceful piece of poppycock." Attached to the letter was Hume's review with the president's candid comments penciled in: "She depends upon the soft pedal more than custom and Haydn require . . . [Bunk!] . . . showed little knowledge of Bach, the adagios should remain quiet throughout . . . [How does he know? Bach is dead!] . . . the slow waltzes were badly misshapen . . . [More lousy bunk!]." Enclosed with Hume's review was a glowing one by Dillard Gunn of the *Star*. The president obviously was still convinced that Hume had no place in the world of music.[47]

Like earlier presidents, Truman was bombarded with mail from all over the country on topics consequential and frivolous, from people great and small. And entertainers were no exception. Pianists led the ranks. The "Liberettes" and every other Liberace fan club imaginable asked if their idol could play in the White House. There were scores of mothers with their child prodigies—and the unique phenomenon, Cirederf Nipohc, a sixty-four-year-old parking attendant from New York City who claimed he could *sing* all the Chopin Nocturnes, complete with turns and other ornamentation. Perhaps he could. After all, he claimed he was "The Ghost of Chopin."

Duo-pianists—father and daughter, teacher and pupil, identical twins—all wanted to appear in the East Room after the president's televised tour of the recently renovated White House on May 3, 1952. During the nation-wide broadcast, Truman played snatches of Mozart on each of the two fine concert grands in the East Room—the 1938 Steinway and, in the northwest corner, a sleek ebonized Baldwin, style D, which the firm donated to the White House on April 7, 1952.[48]

President Truman also received many fine musical gifts from major artists and great world leaders, such as autographed manuscripts and rare editions that are unique among presidential collections. Somehow they seem to symbolize and summarize his great love of music and keen attributes of leadership. Duke Ellington and Kate Smith presented personalized scores, and Irving Berlin sent his new song, "It Gets Lonely in the White House," composed in 1948 and used later in his Broadway show *Mr. President* (1962).

But for Truman the elegant gold medal that he received from the City of Salzburg, Austria, on October 4, 1951, meant more to him perhaps than anything else. About five years after he was presented with the medal, he made his first post-presidential trip to Europe. Salzburg, birthplace of Mozart, was part of the itinerary, and Truman was in his glory. He played part of Mozart's Sonata in A Major (K331) on the 250-year-old organ at the Salzburg Cathedral, visited Mozart's home, played his pianoforte, and was entertained at a concert of Mozart's music at the former palace of the archbishop of Salzburg. "I've never attended a happier or more pleasing musical event," wrote Truman in his diary.[49] Austria felt just as warmly toward Truman. On the plaque accompanying the gold medal he received in 1951 was inscribed:

Mr. President:

On April 19, 1951 the city of Salzburg unanimously passed the resolution to present to you, Mr. President, the

GREAT GOLDEN MOZART MEDAL OF THE CITY OF SALZBURG,

the highest award of the city for outstanding service in the field of music.

The great name of Mozart, son of our city and dear to us all is attached to this decoration, which is only presented to those who promote the cultural aims of the Mozart City, and who have furthered its good cause. It is with deepest gratitude, Mr. President, that we remember the good deeds of the citizens of the United States of America, whose representative you are. Without this help the cultural life of our country would not have grown again so soon.

CHAPTER 7

AMERICA'S MUSICAL SHOWCASE

I'm gettin' married in the mornin'!
Ding, dong! The bells are going to chime!
Pull out the stopper,
Let's have a whopper,
But get me to the church on time!

My Fair Lady
Alan Jay Lerner/Frederick Loewe

DWIGHT D. EISENHOWER

In 1952 Truman decided not to run for reelection and Dwight D. Eisenhower, hero of World War II, captured the nation with his prestige as commanding general of the victorious forces in Europe. Like Zachary Taylor and Ulysses Grant, Ike was a professional soldier who had never held a political office. The enormous popularity that carried Eisenhower into the White House on January 20, 1953, over his Democratic opponent, Adlai Stevenson, continued through his reelection in 1956.

Although the threat of Communism continued to trouble the world, Americans enjoyed unprecedented prosperity during the Eisenhower era. The arts were beginning to develop and thrive as never before, with increased sources of patronage, both public and private, and ever-expanding audiences. Arts centers, such as Lincoln Center in New York City, were being planned and built across the nation, providing fresh focus on musical performance and dance, while cultural exchange programs proved that the arts could also be a vital bridge between nations. With the new long-playing microgroove recording, the music industry was booming, but the latest innovative trends in American music at this time—bop, cool, jazz, and the new, explosive rock 'n' roll—had no place in the White House. This music made a social statement too strong, too controversial for after-dinner entertainment in the president's home. And electronic or other experimental music? There were segments of the American public who found political and subversive elements in *all* modern art, no matter what form it took.[1]

While President Truman preferred classical instrumental music, General Eisenhower and "Mamie," as the first lady was affectionately called, were fond of sentimental ballads and current show tunes—"Banks of the Wabash," "I Believe," "Stardust," "Oh, What a Beautiful Morning," and many old-time hymns. Once when the President had to give a speech in New York City, he went to a performance of *My Fair Lady* just because he was so fond of the song "Get Me to the Church on Time." He missed curtain time, but Mamie had saved a seat for him.[2] Both the Eisenhowers attended the National Symphony concerts on occasion, occupying the presidential box (number 13) at Constitution Hall. "Mr. President, what kind of music do you like?" Howard Mitchell asked, shortly after Eisenhower took office. "Do you know anything by Lawrence Welk?" Eisenhower responded, and then added, "I also like a good bass voice." Mitchell rallied to the request with the best American basso he could find—George London, who sang scenes from Musorgsky's *Boris Godunov* with the orchestra on October 21, 1953. "The President loved it," said Mitchell.[3]

While neither President nor Mrs. Eisenhower was especially knowledgeable in European classical music, they knew well the value of the music of their own nation and placed more emphasis than any of their predecessors on White House programs that reflected its kaleidoscopic variety. On May 8, 1958, they brought to the mansion that great, dynamic American art form—Broadway musical theater. Pat Stanley, Carol Lawrence, Eddie Hodges, and Salley Ann Howes were among the nine performers who sang hit tunes from *Pajama Game, West Side Story, Music Man, New Girl in Town,* and *My Fair Lady* for Chief Justice Earl Warren and about one hundred and fifty after-dinner guests.[4] The evening was a White House first—the celebration of an American musical form that would reappear at the mansion time and again to the present day.

Other vocal styles occupied a prime spot at the White House, too—from the large Mormon Tabernacle Choir to the many smaller vocal ensembles, such as the Carolers, the Trapp Family Singers, the Deep River Boys, and the Men of Song. And as military people, the Eisenhowers liked to feature the newly formed musical groups from the Army, Navy, and Air Force, as well as that perennial White House staple from the days of John Adams—the U.S. Marine Band. President Eisenhower also initiated the concept of the roving musicians, notably the three-year-old Air Force Strolling Strings who performed at the state dinner for the king of Saudi Arabia on January 30, 1957. This gracious concept, continued by the Kennedys, enhances many White House dinners even today.

But the Eisenhowers also brought to the White House noted popular orchestra leaders, many who were personal friends, such as Paul Whiteman and Lawrence Welk. Guy Lombardo's orchestra played for the king of Thailand, and his program illustrates how the concerts for heads of state were becoming more directly tailored to their interests. Sometimes this created problems. The king, for example, liked swing and other popular American styles, but not Rodgers and Hammerstein's current Broadway hit, *The King and I.* Lombardo had to eliminate his planned medley of songs from the show when he learned that the King felt the play treated his ancestors with too much frivolity. But of all the orchestra leaders, one moved the president more than any other: Fred Waring and his chorus of "Pennsylvanians." Waring performed three times in the White House during Eisenhower's terms in office. The most memorable to both the president and first lady was the program for Queen Elizabeth II and Prince Philip of Great Britain on October 17, 1957. Waring closed with his poignant arrangement of "Battle

The White House
Washington

October 17, 1957

This special cover for the program presented by Fred Waring and his Pennsylvanians for
Queen Elizabeth II and Prince Philip of England is decorated with an image of the White
House and a red/white/blue ribbon. Under the Eisenhowers, after-dinner musical entertain-
ment for visiting heads of state became an established tradition. Original measurement.

President Dwight D. Eisenhower and Mamie Dowd Eisenhower attending *My Fair Lady* at the Mark Hellinger Theater in New York.

Hymn of the Republic." When he put down his baton and looked over at the president, both he and Mamie were weeping.[5]

Toward the end of the Eisenhower presidency, significant changes in the frequency and content of the after-dinner musicales began to take place. As air transportation enabled more heads of state to visit the country, the demands for more world-renowned White House entertainers also increased. While President and Mrs. Hoover were the first to entertain a head of state with a guest performer in 1931, the Eisenhowers firmly established the practice. From January 1959 to October 1960, fourteen state dinners were held followed by musicales in the East Room. (See Appendix B.)

So musically active was the Eisenhower White House, in fact, that some newspaper reporters recommended that a special White House music committee be formed to plan the programs. Steinway, however, remained the mansion's artistic linchpin. When John Steinway learned that King Baudouin of Belgium would be arriving, he recommended to Mrs. Eisenhower that the brilliant young pianist, Leon Fleisher, perform for him.[6] At twenty-four, Fleisher had become the first American to win the coveted Queen Elisabeth International Competition held in Brussels—and his White House concert on May 11, 1959, was a prophetic glimpse of the famous Casals program that would take place under the Kennedys almost three years later. For the first time, music critics from major newspapers were invited to attend an after-dinner musical program at the White House. They applauded President Eisenhower's official recognition of America's standards of musical excellence, which they said marked a "turning point" for the White House.

The Eisenhowers also invited many great opera singers to perform—stars such as James Melton, Gladys Swarthout, Patrice Munsel, Jeanette MacDonald, Conrad Thibault, Todd Duncan, Rose Bampton, Marian Anderson, and Risë Stevens. But when the late pianist Artur Rubinstein played his brilliant program of Chopin, De Falla, and Debussy for the president of Vietnam, it was his first, and only, concert in the White House. "Mr. Rubinstein had made such an impression at his recital in Washington," commented the social secretary, Mary Jane McCaffree, "that the President and Mrs. Eisenhower expressed the desire to have him for a Musicale."[7] Because Rubinstein wanted to use his own Steinway, the nine-foot-seven-inch Steinway had to be removed from the East Room—no small task. As the chief usher remarked, "It is not on casters and is dreadfully heavy and takes a regiment of men to carry it."[8]

Highlighting the last concerts of the Eisenhowers in 1960 were the programs by Malcolm Frager, Gregor Piatigorsky[9] and finally the distinguished American conductor and composer, Leonard Bernstein, who made his White House debut on April 5. Bernstein not only conducted the forty-four-member New York Philharmonic in the East Room, he also performed as piano soloist in George Gershwin's enduring American classic, *Rhapsody in Blue*. A memo written to Major John Eisenhower, assistant to the president, from Mrs. McCaffree indicates how some of the larger groups of musicians made their way to the White House via military transport during this period: "Question: May we have the President's approval to transport musicians by plane from and to NY as we have done in the past for Fred Waring (always on state occasions of course)?" On the bottom of the memo is penciled in bold handwriting, "OK with DE."[10] After the concert the president wrote to Bernstein, "I am personally most grateful to you for contributing so much talent and time and effort to the affair. It was an occasion we shall all long remember."

Dwight David Eisenhower did more for America's artistic life in terms of support and legislation than any previous president. In 1954 the president sought $5 million for cultural exchange programs. "The exchange of artists is one of the most effective methods of strengthening world friendship," he said. The funds were promptly forthcoming. Thus, the *Porgy and Bess* company, the New York City Ballet, the Boston and Philadelphia Symphony Orchestras, Louis Armstrong, and other major artists toured Europe and the Soviet Union with the primary mission of easing tensions between the Free World and Communism.[11] And through the president's People-to-People Program, a twenty-three-year-old, strapping six-foot-four-inch Texan, Van Cliburn, was awarded first prize in the Soviet Union's International Tchaikovsky Competition by sixteen Moscow jurors—"an artistic bridge between the US and Russia," heralded the front page of the *New York Times*.

The president also signed a bill (H.R. 811) on August 1, 1956, granting a federal charter to the National Music Council, which represented all of the major voluntary musical organizations in the country. But his most significant achievement in the arts was the signing of the National Cultural Center Act

Pianist Artur Rubinstein played his only concert at the White House in 1957 for the president of Vietnam. His program comprised Chopin's Polonaise in A-flat, op. 53, and Nocturne in F-sharp Major; Debussy's "La plus que lente"; and De Falla's "Fire Dance."

on September 2, 1958. The giant complex—later to be renamed the John F. Kennedy Center for the Performing Arts—would radically alter the entire cultural life of Washington and provide a focal point for the finest performing arts groups from every corner of the nation.

The White House concerts during Eisenhower's second term, together with his visible encouragement of the nation's arts, link him more closely with his successor, John F. Kennedy, than with his predecessor, Harry Truman. In Eisenhower's ideology, "The development of American music, and the native development of any art, is the development of a national treasure." There is a prophetic ring to these words. Soon President John F. Kennedy and his artistic wife would add their own special flair to the American cultural scene. The nation was ready.

JOHN F. KENNEDY

He was a knight *extraordinaire*, possessing élan, courage, and wisdom; she was "Guinevere in a contentious Camelot," whose large eyes reflected an elegiac sophistication, sensitivity, and hint of shyness. John Fitzgerald Kennedy and

Jacqueline Lee Bouvier brought to the White House fresh images of youth and vitality that appealed immediately to America's pride and sense of self-confidence. "I feel that I'm a part of this man's hopes," said gospel super-star Mahalia Jackson when Kennedy was inaugurated in January 1961. "He lifts my spirit and makes me feel a part of the land I live in."[12]

Taking a vigorous stand in the cause for equal rights, Kennedy's administration saw the rise of new hopes and visions for an America that would be remembered, as he said, "not for our victories or defeats in battle or in politics, but for our contribution to the human spirit."[13] In an era of burgeoning commerciality, Kennedy looked forward to a nation that would not be afraid of grace and beauty. "I am determined that we begin to grow again, and that there will be an American renaissance in which imagination, daring and the creative arts point the way."[14] But he saw only the beginning. He was killed by an assassin's bullet at the close of his third year in office while riding in a motorcade through Dallas, Texas—the youngest man to be elected president, and the youngest to die in office.

John and Jacqueline Kennedy's arrival upon the national scene at this time was a felicitous and dramatic coincidence in American cultural history. The United States was experiencing a wave of city living, advances in mass communication, and an awareness of education that provided fertile soil for artistic pursuits. But without the Kennedys to give these pursuits a clearly defined focus, they might have fallen on barren ground and progressed less vigorously.

The real spotlight on the American cultural scene, however, fell on the White House itself—on the dramatic, cynosural array of musical entertainments that now had a positive mission: "to demonstrate that the White House could be an influence in encouraging public acceptance of the arts."[15] It was more than just a question of bringing the finest quality artists to the great mansion, however. Fine opera stars, dancers, and instrumentalists had performed there from the earliest years. It was the superb focus that the Kennedys managed to create. The White House became a deliberate showcase for America's leading performing arts organizations: the Metropolitan Opera Studio, Jerome Robbins Ballet, American Ballet Theater, Interlochen Arts Academy, American Shakespeare Festival, New York City Center Light Opera Company, Opera Society of Washington, Robert Joffrey Ballet, and others. Entire scenes were presented, tastefully staged with costumes and lighting. "My main concern," said Jacqueline Kennedy, "was to present the best in the arts, not necessarily what was popular at the time."[16]

New also were the youth concerts presented *by* young people and organized into a definite series. Chamber music programs included longer, more serious works, such as the complete forty-five-minute Schubert B-flat Trio performed as the evening's only selection by the famous Stern/Rose/Istomin Trio for French Cultural Minister André Malraux. Elizabethan music, elegantly underpinning poetry readings from this era, was played on authentic early instruments—viols, virginal, cittern, and lute.[17] Jazz, a long-time poor sister of the classical arts, was now listened to attentively for its own artistic merits rather than merely heard as a background for dancing. But the most significant innovation of the Kennedys involved the guest lists that included not only political and business leaders but also prominent performers, critics, composers, producers, and cultural luminaries from all over the nation. The

John Kennedy introduces the Greater Boston Youth Symphony and Breckenridge
Boys Choir, Texas, on the South Lawn of the White House before their performance
for the congressional children.

press capitalized on the "Kennedy Command Performance," and an en-
chanted America followed every nuance and interpretative detail of the
White House performing artists that the media offered.

Culture was by no means new to the Kennedys when they came to the
White House; their patronage was a natural extension of their accustomed
way of life. A Harvard graduate, John F. Kennedy won the Pulitzer Prize in
history for his *Profiles in Courage*, and his professional dealings with words and
images are legend. Music, however, was another matter, and his tastes ranged
from middlebrow to noncommittal. He studied piano as a child but, as one report indicated, "Anybody studying this boy's character when he was practicing scales would have said he'd never grow up to become President of the
United States."[18] "It was not only that he didn't particularly enjoy it [music],
but I think it was really painful," August Heckscher noted. "I don't mean
only painful for him to sit because of his back for any length of time, I think it
hurt his ears. I really don't think he liked music at all except a few things that
he knew."[19]

With Jacqueline Kennedy, the performing arts were quite a different
matter, and there can be no doubt that the White House programs reflected
her cultivated and intuitive tastes as well as her direct involvement in their
planning. "Mrs. Kennedy was White House impresario," asserted Chief
Usher Bernard West. "She knew all of the arts extremely well."[20] No better

overview of the Kennedy ambience and its engaging tribute to the nation's great artists can be found than that of Leonard Bernstein, who recalled:

> I'll never forget the end of that evening when there was dancing. The Marine Band was playing waltzes or something, and Roy Harris and Walter Piston and people like that were kicking up their heels in the White House, a little high, just so delighted to be there, so glad that they had been asked, feeling that they had finally been recognized as honored artists of the Republic. You know, I've never seen so many happy artists in my life.[21]

But with the historic Pablo Casals concert of November 13, 1961, the White House dramatically displayed the way in which it wished to participate in the cultural life of the nation. Without question the Casals event was the most publicized of all White House concerts—perhaps of any concert in America—and it drew press attention from all over the world. It harked back to the great musicale tradition of Taft, Coolidge, and Hoover, but with the important distinction of being opened now for the world to enjoy. It was broadcast nationally by NBC and ABC radio, and a recording was distributed commercially by Columbia with four pages of notes, critiques, and photographs.

The program was a serious one, lasting over an hour. To open, Casals chose Mendelssohn's flowing, virtuosic Trio in D Minor, op. 49, for which he was joined by pianist Mieczyslaw Horszowski and violinist Alexander Schneider. The remainder of the program consisted of Robert Schumann's Adagio and Allegro in A-flat Major, op. 70, for cello and piano, and a suite of five pieces by François Couperin. But it was a simple encore that expressed Casals's feelings most eloquently and powerfully. He closed his program with a piece from his birthplace, which he claimed depicted the people's longing for freedom. "You might know this song," he said almost weeping as he grasped the hand of Marine Band musician, John Bourgeois, after the concert. "It's a Catalan folk song, 'The Song of the Birds'—but to me, it's the song of the exile."[22]

Casals, who had played in the White House for Theodore Roosevelt in 1904, ceased his American appearances in 1938 because the United States recognized the Franco dictatorship that he despised. (see pictures pp. 93 & 94.) His long, self-imposed exile from his native Spain led him to establish residence in Puerto Rico, and when he received a letter from President Kennedy inviting him to play for a state dinner honoring Governor Luis Muñoz-Marín of Puerto Rico, he accepted because of his admiration for Kennedy.

Programs that involved only a single artist, such as twenty-five-year-old Grace Bumbry who made her American debut in the East Room in 1962, were relatively easy to produce. But the increasing number of large productions, both inside the White House and on the lawn, brought problems that would have chilled the marrow of Henry Junge and the modest White House staff of the early years. The Opera Society of Washington's *Magic Flute* had to be brought indoors because of drenching rains—"an operation very much like pouring two quarts of milk into a one pint bottle," wrote Irving Lowens in the *Star*.[23] Letitia ("Tish") Baldrige, the Kennedy social secretary, recalls the performance of the New York City Center Light Opera Company's *Brigadoon* for the king of Morocco:

Every fuse in our part of the mansion blew, plunging the East Room into total darkness. No lights, no music, no nothing. The Secret Servicemen sprang to all exits, guns drawn, fearing the worst.

The audience was shocked into silence, but I heard the President from the first row, saying in embarrassment, "Your Majesty, it's part of the show, you know."

It was the longest minute and a half I ever spent in my life. I half prayed in English, half swore in Italian, for those fuses to be fixed. Then the lights went on again, and the tape began to revolve. The dancers on stage had frozen in their stances, without a word, when the electricity failed. They began again exactly in step; they had not missed one beat.[24]

One of the most important tasks the social secretary faces is communicating with the president about matters of taste and protocol. The Kennedy years were no exception. According to Baldrige:

The President had always had a little problem with classical music. He had been caught in the East Room on several occasions clapping at the wrong time and not being sure when the concert was finally over. Even following a program, the number of different movements within one composition confused him—as it does many people. We therefore worked out a code system for the Stern concert. As the last piece was almost finished, I was to open the central door of the East Room from the outside about two inches—enough for him to glimpse the prominent Baldrige nose structure in the crack. It worked beautifully that night and for all future concerts. When the President noticed the door slightly ajar, that meant the last piece was in progress. He would await the applause; then, clapping heartily, he would take Mrs. Kennedy by the arm, and escort the honored guests to the stage, to congratulate the musicians. Both Kennedys thought I was brilliantly sophisticated in music to be able to do this. What they did not know was that I knew less than they did about serious music. I simply made one of the Social Aides stay by me. He happened to be an accomplished musician who was familiar with all major classical compositions.[25]

The Kennedys expanded traditions in the area of military musical practices, both ceremonial and social. They added more dignity to the arrival ceremony for a state visitor by holding it now on the White House grounds rather than at the railroad station or airport where it had taken place formerly. Under the Kennedys, moreover, the current practice of alternating the four service bands (Marine, Army, Navy, Air Force) for White House arrivals was established. The Kennedys also added pomp and historical flair in greeting their foreign dignitaries through both the Fife and Drum Corps in their Continental Army dress red uniforms and the U.S. Army's Herald Trumpets created under Eisenhower in 1959. Inside the White House, however, the Marine Band held firmly to its tradition as "The President's Own." But it now fell more directly under the thumb of Mrs. Kennedy, who wanted "constant music—no dull moments."[26] As a consequence, the band formed more units and ensembles.

On November 13, 1963, the famous Royal Highland Regiment, The Black Watch, presented a special program of piping, marching, and spirited dancing on the South Lawn. Guests for the afternoon were 1,700 children

Members of American Ballet Theater, who had performed Aaron Copland's *Billy the Kid* in the East Room for the president of the Ivory Coast, are congratulated by President and Mrs. Kennedy.

from childcare agencies served by the United Givers Fund, and they managed to devour over 10,000 cookies. "I don't know when I have seen the President enjoy himself more," wrote Mrs. Kennedy to Major W. M. Wingate-Gray. "The ceremony was one of the most stirring we have ever had at the White House."[27] Soon she would hear the pipers again. Jack would not. Ten days later the president was assassinated by Lee Harvey Oswald. At the White House nine pipers played once again "The Barren Rocks of Aden." But this time the hauntingly poignant march was rendered for the statesman's funeral cortege—and the whole world mourned.[28]

Musical artists, great and small, paid tribute in ways they knew best: a young Bosnian in Sarajevo, Yugoslavia, sang to his own accompaniment on the ancient single-stringed *gusla*, his lyrical epic:

> They knew for certain John was gone.
> The caisson carries him
> With a white horse from the White House
> To the soldiers' grave of heroes.[29]

In New York Isaac Stern, Leonard Rose, and Eugene Istomin played on television the expressive slow movement from Schubert's B-flat Trio, which they had performed at the White House for André Malraux. Symphony orchestras all over the land paid their last respects with commemorative programs. One of the most hauntingly moving was the National Symphony's post-midnight performance to a completely empty Constitution Hall, a few blocks from the White House. "The orchestra of the presidents," as it had come to be called, was conducted by Howard Mitchell and played Debussy's *La mer* in memory of the president's love of the ocean and his valor as a naval officer; the "Adagio for Strings" by the American composer Samuel Barber, the last distinguished representative of the arts to be invited to the White House before the president's death; and the overture to Beethoven's *Fidelio*, a tribute to Mrs. Kennedy, described by Mitchell as a "true heroine" who "walked in tragic beauty" during her days of sorrow.[30]

In memory of the assassination, Igor Stravinsky composed a miniature for baritone (later revised for mezzo-soprano) and three clarinets called simply "Elegy for JFK" (1964). The text by W. H. Auden consists of four stanzas of free haiku, and the atonal, transparent textures seem to feature an interplay between the diabolical tri-tone (G#-D) and the eternally hopeful perfect fifth (D#-A#)—the "oneness," perhaps, of both "sorrow and joy." Thus music, a vital part of the Kennedy White House years, offered its own special tribute to the new image, the fresh promises, and the bleak dawn.

> When a just man dies
> Lamentation and praise,
> Sorrow and joy are one.
>
> Why then? Why there?
> Why thus, we cry, did he die?
> The Heavens are silent.
>
> What he was, he was:
> What he is fated to become
> Depends on us.
>
> Remembering his death
> How we choose to live
> Will decide its meaning.[31]

LYNDON B. JOHNSON

On November 22, 1963, Vice-President Lyndon Baines Johnson became the nation's thirty-sixth president. He took the oath of office standing in the crowded presidential plane with his wife Claudia Taylor (Lady Bird) Johnson at his right side and Mrs. John F. Kennedy (her pink suit still stained with the blood of the assassinated president) at his left. Johnson was a man of great complexity. He was sensitive and ruthless, devious and candid, commanding and compassionate. In the words of Jack Valenti, Johnson's White House advisor and confidant, he was "a very human President."[32] The poverty of the Texas hill country, where Johnson was born, could not be easily forgotten as he grew up, and this link with the human spirit in its humblest as well as proudest form permeated his thinking on the arts. "Lyndon felt that the arts belonged to and came from all over the country," Mrs. Johnson once said, "and that they should not be concentrated in just the big cities."[33]

Johnson's commitment to art as our "nation's most precious heritage" was more than mere words drafted by an astute speech writer. His administration gave major impetus to numerous cultural programs, including the authorization of the John F. Kennedy Center in January 1964; the National Museum Act of 1966; the federal acquisition of the Joseph H. Hirshhorn collection of 6,000 paintings, drawings, and sculpture; and the establishment of the National Foundation for the Arts and Humanities in 1965.[34] "One of the things that people don't realize about Johnson is . . . his extraordinary aesthetic sensibility," said Abe Fortas, one of the president's most intimate advisors and an enthusiastic music lover and amateur violinist. "It's untrained as far as music and art are concerned . . . he just has a kind of natural appreciation."[35]

The Johnsons claimed they did not consciously try to continue the type of musical programs held at the White House by the Kennedys, but there is no way they could have escaped their influence. Like the Kennedys, the Johnsons strove for the highest quality of talent, superb productions, and fresh ways in which the White House could publicly honor the performing arts of America. And they succeeded. During their five-plus years in office, November 22, 1963, to January 19, 1969, they arranged some of the most outstanding programs ever presented at the White House, especially in the areas of musical theater, youth programs, jazz, and the dance. The Johnsons, it seemed, went a step further than the Kennedys in their aim to reach out to all of America. They reached also to the west, not just as a geographic area, but to what it stood for—freedom, the wide-open spaces, the common man, sunshine and soil, the human side of the arts.

Coming right after the Kennedys' sophisticated tastes, these philosophies were not immediately grasped by the nation—and less so by the music critics. In retrospect, however, it was just as logical to hold the first state dinner, in this case for Chancellor Ludwig Erhard of Germany, at the Johnsons' Texas ranch in the hill country, settled by German families in the 1840s, as it was for the Kennedys to entertain the president of Pakistan at historic Mt. Vernon— perhaps even more logical. Mid barbecue, red-checkered tablecloths, and bales of hay, Van Cliburn, who was born in East Texas, performed on his elegant Steinway concert grand while Cactus Pryor courageously and masterfully held together the diverse program. This incongruous practice of mixing and melding national spirit, sensibilities, and styles was characteristic of the White House as it related to its honored guests. But it can become problematic aesthetically when the musical styles themselves are too disparate. Where else, for example, but at the White House (western or otherwise) would one find a world-famous concert pianist playing Beethoven after a nun had conducted her choir singing "Deep in the Heart of Texas"? The chancellor, nevertheless, was delighted, and after this touch of western froth he turned to Lady Bird and said, "We know that song in Germany too."[36] Another bridge between two nations had been built.

The new currents in American music were picked up by the Johnsons with caution, but those that did make their way to the White House were significant. Jazz occupied a prime place in the mansion now. Dave Brubeck,

AGE OF PERICLES?

ARTS BILL

PAINTING
SCULPTURE
ARCHITECTURE
LITERATURE
MUSIC
DRAMA
DANCE

AMERICA THE BEAUTIFUL

A caricature of President Lyndon Baines Johnson, who established the National Foundation for the Arts and Humanities in 1965.

Charlie Byrd, the North Texas State University Lab Jazz Band, and the Gerry Mulligan Trio each performed on different occasions for various heads of state. (See Appendix B.) Occasionally folk, pop-folk, Baroque-pop, and night-club styles (Tony Bennett, Tammy Grimes) had their place at the White House. "I remember Robert Goulet getting down on the floor with his microphone singing intimately into the rather flushed faces of the guests," Luci Johnson confided. "They weren't used to this in the White House."[37]

The Johnsons showed their commitment to the arts by several programs at the White House that honored talent and achievement, but also seemed to underscore how American attitudes had changed. On July 4, 1964, composer Aaron Copland and soprano Leontyne Price became the first musicians to receive the Presidential Medal of Freedom, created by John Kennedy shortly before he died to honor distinguished Americans from the fields of science, business, journalism, theology, and the arts.[38] Ironically, only a decade earlier, Copland's *A Lincoln Portrait* had been hastily removed from Dwight Eisenhower's inaugural concert program in 1953 because a member of Congress considered the composer a "Communist sympathizer."

World-renowned concert and operatic artists also performed during this period: Leontyne Price, Walter Trampler, André Watts, Richard Tucker, Patricia Brooks, Isaac Stern, Rudolf Serkin, and Jaime Laredo. Two artists especially, Van Cliburn and Robert Merrill, had become close friends with the Johnsons. "We had a sort of parochial pride in Van Cliburn from Texas," admitted Mrs. Johnson. "And there was no more congenial, obliging, amusing person than Robert Merrill. He would pinch-hit whenever we needed him," she added.[39]

But Merrill had a near miss when he selected his program for Prime Minister Harold Wilson of Great Britain. The famous opera singer gave his list to Liz Carpenter, Mrs. Johnson's press secretary (the "merry warrior," according to Valenti), who promptly put out a press release. The reaction was instantaneous. "You must be out of your minds," exclaimed Walt Rostow, who, among others, did not see how Merrill could sing "On the Road to Mandalay" when Great Britain had just pulled all their troops out of Suez. And he thought "I Got Plenty of Nothin'" was totally inappropriate since Great Britain had just devalued the pound. According to Carpenter, Merrill was allowed to sing the songs, but he added another number, "It Ain't Necessarily So," as a musical disclaimer.[40]

The most striking feature of the musical programs presented at the White House by Lyndon and Lady Bird Johnson was the sheer magnitude of their scope. Most of the concerts combined several performers and groups, and many were staged with costumes, lighting, props, and sound amplification. The intensity, informality, and thorough attention to detail surpassed any previous administration. Many of the parties were held on the South Lawn for which a specially constructed sixty-four-foot stage was built. One of the most spectacular evenings was the first "Salute to Congress" on August 19, 1964. "You of the 88th Congress have made many of his [JFK's] hopes a reality," said the narrators. "Tonight a song is dedicated to YOU, the 88th! And hereby begins a tradition. As far as we know, no one before has ever sung a song to Congress—certainly not from the White House lawn."[41]

With Lincoln Center opening its new theaters during the Johnson years—and the Kennedy Center not yet completed—New York was the source for many of the big musical shows that came to the White House. For the Vice-President/Chief Justice/Speaker's parties, the Johnsons chose musical comedy and Broadway hits. On January 17, 1967, Carol Channing and a cast of twenty-five presented a thirty-minute segment from Act II of *Hello, Dolly*, the smash success that closed in 1970 after 2,844 performances.

Other musical shows at the mansion were equally effective: scenes from Rodgers and Hammerstein's *Oklahoma!*; Carol Lawrence and Gordon Mac-Rae in portions of *I Do, I Do*; the New York City Opera Company's *Guys and Dolls* in 1967 and *Fiorello* in 1968; and the American Light Opera Company's scenes from *Peter Pan*. Only one opera was presented during LBJ's terms—portions of Jacques Offenbach's fantasy, *Voyage to the Moon*. Presented by the Boston Opera Company and directed by Sarah Caldwell, the opera was replete with rocketships, a girl-in-the-moon, a "Dr. Blastoff," and all the whimsical science fiction of a bygone era. It was staged in the East Room on December 9, 1968, for 140 guests, who included the Apollo 7 and 8 astronauts. Some nearly got into the cast. "A man from NASA called," observed Bess Abell, "and suggested that some of the astronauts appear in one of the scenes."[42] But the idea fell rather flat.

The 1960s saw a great increase in the dance as an important national artistic medium, and the White House recognized these exciting new ventures by inviting the most prominent companies of the day: the Joffrey Ballet, American Ballet Theater, Harkness Ballet, National Ballet, Martha Graham Dance Company, and the Alvin Ailey Dancers. "I especially loved the whole range of ballet performances we had," reminisces Mrs. Johnson. "The appreciation for that form of dance really entered my life during our White House years."[43] But the major event that ultimately made dance more sophisticated and comfortable at the White House was the donation of a portable stage by the Rebekah Harkness Foundation. The historic presentation took place on September 29, 1965.[44]

There were many social dances held at the White House during this period. The Johnson daughters enjoyed the new rock-inspired gyrations of the early 1960s—the frug, watusi, twist, freddy, swim, and the mashed potato. Lyndon Johnson, who genuinely loved to dance, preferred "Alexander's Ragtime Band," and the rating given him by his dancing partners ranged from "not bad" to "very good." Johnson once danced with the great blues singer, Sarah Vaughan; Bess Abell later found her sobbing in the dressing room after the party for the prime minister of Japan. "What's the matter?" Bess asked her, distressed. "Nothing is the matter," Miss Vaughan said. "It's just that 20 years ago when I came to Washington, I couldn't even get a hotel room, and tonight I sang for the President of the United States in the White House—and then, he asked me to dance with him. It is more than I can stand."[45]

Black night-club singer Eartha Kitt, however, was less complimentary. When she rose at Lady Bird's Woman Doer's Luncheon on January 18, 1968, it was to lash out angrily against the war in Vietnam and Johnson's policies as the cause of ghetto crime. The subject of the luncheon was "Crime and What the Average Citizen Can Do to Stop It," and Kitt's diatribe came through as abrasive, ill-mannered, and rude. The stunned first lady, her voice trembling and eyes welling with tears, answered, "Because there is a war on . . . that still doesn't give us a free ticket *not* to try to work for better things, such as less crime in the streets, better education and better health for our people."[46] For days the nation let Mrs. Johnson know its feelings about the incident in a deluge of mail that poured into the White House. One sample follows.

Dear Mrs. Johnson:
    Please know that the majority of the Negro race is ashamed of the way in which Mrs. Eartha Kitt conducted herself at your dinner. . . . Mr. Johnson has done more for the Negros than any other President. . . . Why would one *bite the hand that feeds them?*

Respectfully submitted,
A GROUP OF INTERESTED CITIZENS
IN NORTH CAROLINA[47]

Another *scena* took place when poet Robert Lowell refused an invitation to an all-day "White House Festival of the Arts" because of his distrust of the president's actions concerning U.S. foreign policy. The festival, held on June 14, 1965, was an ambitious extravaganza that presented exhibitions of paintings, sculpture, and photography; prose and poetry readings, music and ballet, both inside the White House and on the lawn. But as Liz Carpenter reported, instead of poetry, Lowell produced for this occasion "some blistering prose." By sending his telegram refusing the invitation to the press, a felicitous artistic event immediately became a political travesty. Twenty artists and writers backed Lowell publicly—eighteen of whom had not even been invited to the festival. One who had, Dwight MacDonald, disrupted the festival's ambience by circulating a petition that was, in effect, pro-Lowell and anti-Vietnam war. "I think most of the guests were embarrassed and confused by what occurred," said Barbaralee Diamonstein.

> . . . no one stopped him from what he planned to do. He wore a widely striped shirt, as I recall, and a sport coat. He was quite obese and extremely untidy. The thing that I remember is that in his frenzy, the lower buttons of his shirt were open. The shirt was tucked into his trousers, and his bare stomach was exposed and no one even chose to point that out to him, let alone deter him from circulating this petition.[48]

The tragedy of the event lay not in its content, which was expertly planned and presented, but in the way it was perceived. Buried among all the political rubble and the confusion over what the President and Mrs. Johnson were trying to accomplish was an extraordinary cultural occasion—one of the most striking ever to be held at the White House. No one bothered to consider the adventuresome, creative touches: Duke Ellington, at age sixty-six, was making his long-overdue debut at the White House;[49] with an introductory narration by Gene Kelly, the Joffrey Ballet presented the American premier of *Gamelon* to the music of Lou Harrison; scenes from five motion pictures recognized the U.S. film industry as an important art form. And not since Louis Gruenberg's "Two Indiscretions" was performed for Calvin Coolidge was an instrumental work of a serious contemporary American composer featured in a concert at the White House. At the festival Ned Rorem's *Studies for Eleven Players* (1959), which treats each of the players as virtuoso soloists, was presented by members of the Louisville Symphony Orchestra.

"All the afternoon will be American," wrote Bess Abell to Eric Goldman who coordinated the festival.[50] Grass-roots philosophies? Perhaps. For over the entire day loomed the imposing figure of LBJ. The president had scrawled his approval earlier across a memo from Goldman describing the ideology of the festival: "I like this. Ask Bill M. and Jack to see me about it before I take final action."[51] It was, after all, a Texas-size event for the White House, in keeping with his thinking. As he told the artists during the festival, "Your art is not a political weapon. Yet much of what you do is profoundly political. For you seek out the common pleasures and visions, terrors and cruelties of man's day on this planet. You help dissolve the barriers of hatred and ignorance which are the source of so much pain and danger. In this way you work toward peace—not the peace which is simply the absence of war—but the peace which liberates man to reach for the finest fulfillment of his spirit."[52]

RICHARD NIXON

On August 8, 1974, facing almost certain impeachment, Richard Nixon became the first president to resign from office, leaving an administration embattled over the political scandal known as Watergate. There was something Wagnerian about the whole drama—the rivalry between truth and power, dignity and corruption. President Nixon, although he denied any personal involvement, left office to end the scandal; one month after Nixon resigned, his successor, Gerald Ford, granted him an unqualified pardon.

Ceremonial flourishes proliferated during Nixon's administration. The chief of state clearly enjoyed the pageantry that went with his office, causing some press people to call his administration "The Imperial Presidency." "I think," said Paul Miller, director of ceremonies for the Military District of Washington, "that this 'Imperial Presidency' business came about because Nixon was trying to upgrade the White House ceremonial guards. He gave them new uniforms with 'student prince' caps that some thought rather foolish-looking. I think this is why the media gave him a hard time about the Imperial Presidency. In reality, he was no more ceremonial than his predecessors."[53]

President Nixon did add an extra ruffle or two to the basic flourish, however. He continued the Kennedy and Johnson traditions for state arrival ceremonies, stationing on the south balcony the fourteen trumpeters, two drummers, and leader, known as the U.S Army Herald Trumpets. But he also took the Herald Trumpet concept a step further by bringing it indoors. He used four trumpeters from the U.S. Marine Band to herald his arrival as he walked into the East Room to greet his guests at receptions. They played a specially composed "Presidential Fanfare" that lasted fifteen to twenty seconds, sounding a majestic, or at least an attention-getting, entry.[54]

Like Harry Truman, Richard Nixon gravitated toward the piano whenever he had a chance. "Playing the piano is a way of expressing oneself that is perhaps even more fulfilling than writing or speaking," he wrote in his memoirs. "In fact, I have always had two great—and still unfulfilled—ambitions: to direct a symphony orchestra and to play an organ in a cathedral. I think that to create great music is one of the highest aspirations man can set for himself."[55]

Throughout Nixon's years as president, the media repeatedly criticized his "mundane" artistic tastes and his attitude of "benevolent indifference" toward the arts. Frank Getlein of *The New York Times* charged: "The Nixon taste is, in a word, deplorable. Or in a couple of words, there isn't any."[56] But there was no "benevolent indifference" when Nancy Hanks, chairman of the National Endowment for the Arts, received the president's approval for a big increase—almost double—in the annual budget for the endowment in 1971, and double again for 1972, bringing the total arts and humanities money to $61.2 million.

The media lashed out against the Nixon White House entertainment, too. It was either too "bland" ("Writing about the Nixon Administration," said Art Buchwald, "is about as exciting as covering the Prudential Life Insurance Company");[57] or it was too filled with Hollywood entertainers and night club acts. But an overview of the state entertainment from March 24, 1969, to March 7, 1974, reveals a variety of styles, overlooked by a press perhaps still

Grand Duchess Charlotte of Luxembourg compliments Basil Rathbone and members of the Consort Players, who presented an evening of Elizabethan poetry and music for the Kennedys and their guests.

Violinist Isaac Stern chats with the Kennedys after his program with cellist Leonard Rose and pianist Eugene Istomin. The trio entertained President André Malraux of France on May 11, 1962.

In the main foyer of the White House Carol Channing dances with President Lyndon Johnson after portions of *Hello, Dolly!* were performed in the East Room. Among those watching are House Minority Leader Gerald Ford and his wife, Betty.

On the new portable stage given to the White House by the Rebekah Harkness Foundation, dancers from the Harkness Ballet perform Prokofiev's *Classical Symphony*. The stage, cleverly designed to match the decor of the East Room, was presented on September 29, 1965.

Four trumpeters from the Marine Band herald the arrival of President Richard M. Nixon before the state dinner for President Josip Broz Tito of Yugoslavia, October 28, 1971.

Special presidential accompaniment is provided for Pearl Bailey, as she sings for the Governors Reception, March 7, 1974.

President Gerald R. Ford awards the Medal of Freedom to pianist Artur Rubinstein, April 1, 1976.

Van Cliburn performs Chopin, Debussy, and Schumann for the emperor and empress of Japan on October 2, 1975.

Betty Ford, Martha Graham, and Cliburn converse after the pianist's concert.

President Jimmy Carter enjoys the Marine Band String Quartet in the foyer of the White House while a Secret Service man watches.

Agnes DeMille is a special guest of Jimmy and Rosalynn Carter during the American Dance Machine's performance on February 6, 1979. The program followed a state dinner for Prime Minister Khunyinng Virat Chomanan of Thailand (right) and his wife.

Ronald Reagan introduces his long-time friends, Frank Sinatra and Perry Como, before they sing for President Alessandro Pertini of Italy after a state dinner on March 25, 1982.

Nancy Reagan helps a small White House visitor explore the trumpet as guest conductor Keith Brion looks on. Brion, a Sousa scholar, dressed like the legendary bandmaster for the Marine Band concert for congressional children on the White House Lawn in July 1982.

The Reagans' first Christmas in the White House was celebrated by a concert in the foyer on December 17, 1981, presented by one of the many choirs that serenade the first family at Christmastime.

charmed by the spectacular Kennedy/Johnson decade: twenty-four popular and night club performers; nineteen classical artists; six jazz programs; three dance; three country music; one musical theater. With its special focus on American styles—jazz, country, and popular—the Nixon White House repertory was broader than any of its predecessors. But unlike the Johnsons, the Nixons avoided big productions. "The logistics are just very difficult," said Connie Stuart, Mrs. Nixon's staff director. "It takes twelve hours to put up the stage. This is not just a theater," she added. "It's a house. A very alive, vital house. Everything does not come to a grinding halt because we're producing a show."[58]

President and Mrs. Nixon still managed to bring to the White House a stellar array of entertainers. Eleven different concerts composed their "Evenings at the White House" series and included programs by Sammy Davis, Jr., Merle Haggard, Beverly Sills, Billy Taylor, Richard Tucker, and Frank Sinatra, who worked his ineffable magic on April 17, 1973, for President Giulio Andreotti of Italy and two hundred other distinguished guests.[59] During these years, the president's picture often appeared with one of his performers on the front page of the newspapers, reflecting the importance he attached to the entertainment. Even the printed White House programs were enlarged and realized in brilliant colors, rather than the traditional plain white of previous administrations.

Music was so vital to the Nixons that hardly a national holiday, family birthday, White House church service, or important world event went by without some form of musical expression at the mansion.[60] Pat Nixon's birthday party on March 16 often included Irish ballads. Another famous birthday celebration was the dinner for Duke Ellington, who turned seventy on April 29, 1969. The impressive guest list included Dizzy Gillespie, Benny Goodman, Cab Calloway, Earl Hines, Mahalia Jackson, and an array of other jazz luminaries. After Ellington's program at the Steinway, a massive jam session took place, but the surprise of the evening was the Duke's improvisations. "I shall pick a name—gentle, graceful—something like Patricia," he said. "And when he started to play," recalled the president, "it was lyrical, delicate, and beautiful—like Pat."[61]

Richard Nixon was the first president to acknowledge important world events with major commemorative musical tributes—and gala indeed they were. Even the White House was not large enough to accommodate the fifteen hundred invited guests for the state dinner to honor the Apollo 11 astronauts, so the event took place in the ballroom of the Century Plaza Hotel in Los Angeles. Music provided by more than a hundred members of the various armed forces musical organizations kept the president "clasping and unclasping his hands in cadence" all evening.[62]

The Nixons also held a state dinner at the White House to celebrate the twenty-fifth anniversary of the United Nations. Later in the evening Metropolitan Opera stars James McCracken and Sandra Warfield sang arias from *Fidelio, Turandot*, and *Carmen*. But when Bob Hope, Phyllis Diller, John Wayne, Irving Berlin and others entertained the six hundred former Vietnam prisoners of war in May 1973, special outdoor facilities had to be built on the South Lawn. "We constructed a large stage with built-in lighting, a huge tent for the dinner, another for the dressing rooms and a third where the performers could relax and have a cup of coffee," Rex Scouten said. Then it

Duke Ellington at the White House birthday dinner given in his honor by President Nixon on April 29, 1969.

rained. "It was the only time in my life that I had ever seen them mopping the grass at the White House with a regular floor mop."[63]

Great opera singers and pianists also performed at the White House for the Nixons. Among them were Roberta Peters, Anno Moffo, Birgit Nilsson, Rudolf Serkin, André Watts, and Van Cliburn. Isaac Stern performed Mozart and Bloch with Leonard Bernstein during the state visit of Israeli Prime Minister Golda Meir. Israeli Foreign Minister Abba Eban told President Nixon that Stern had once played Bloch's *Nigun* (which has heavily religious overtones for Jews) in Russia—"a courageous thing to do."[64] The hauntingly expressive piece moved the seventy-one-year-old leader of embattled Israel to tears. But then the great violinist had a way of making the Bloch an emotional experience for everyone who heard it.

Music at the Nixon White House reflected the music of the late 1960s and early 1970s all over America. Magnified by explosive tones, provocative lyrics, and the all-pervasive power of the mass media, popular music made a social statement so intense that there were times when not even the presidential estate could escape its message. We were a nation suffering from a massive ego trip, from rebellion and unrest manifest in nearly every aspect of American life from hippies to hemlines. Gigantic rock festivals and other musical trends vividly told the story, while the lone hip-gyrating balladeer, Elvis Presley, became a nostalgic hero. But all had their messages—sometimes oddly poignant ones.

> We don't smoke marijuana in Muskogee
> We don't take our trips on LSD
> We don't burn our draft cards down on Main Street
> We like living right and being free

Thus sang Merle Haggard, legendary country and western singer on March 16, 1973, as part of the "Evenings at the White House" series. Along with "Okie from Muskogee," he sang "Walkin' on the Fightin' Side of Me." "Okie" and "Welfare Cadilac" (spelled with one l) were Nixon favorites that the president had requested Johnny Cash to sing in his 1970 White House appearance. Cash told the White House staff that he would prefer not to sing

President Richard Nixon chats with rock 'n' roll balladeer Elvis Presley in the Oval Office in 1970.

these songs and substituted "A Boy Named Sue," another Nixon favorite, and "What Is Truth?"

Some singers were not as concerned abut offensive lyrics as Cash. White House or not, they belted out their messages. During her White House performance, Carol Feraci unfurled a blue banner from her bosom that read "Stop the killing." Staged as a protest against the Vietnam War, the act shocked the Nixons' distinguished audience. "Stop bombing human beings, animals and vegetation," cried Feraci in the middle of a choral number directed by Ray Coniff. "If Jesus Christ were here tonight, you would not dare to drop another bomb." How to prevent such incidents? "I don't know," said Lucy Winchester. She recalled a cartoon that Bess Abell had placed on her desk along with a vase of flowers when she first took over as social secretary. It showed a concert pianist in his white tie and tails with a piano in the background. He was saying, "Before I begin my concert, I would like to make a foreign policy statement."[65]

The appearance and dress of some of the White House performers during these years raised eyebrows. The press, perennially prone to latch on to an unbuttoned shirt (Tony Bennett's "strip tease" act for LBJ), or a "cleavage down to here" (Metropolitan Opera singer Anna Moffo's "slipped moorings"), or just the crass headline, "Topless at the White House," which referred to opera star Beverly Sills's gown that came unzipped (luckily, in back) while she was singing Donizetti. "I threw my velvet evening coat over my shoulders just in the nick of time," she said.[66] Male performers fared no better. A young, long-haired violinist and member of the faculty of the Chicago Musical College was led away by a White House guard until the social secretary rescued him and verified that he was part of the program inside.

There were performers who refused to come to the White House as Watergate became more intense. Yale's famous Whiffenpoofs turned down an invitation to sing Christmas carols. "We were afraid our appearance might imply we support President Nixon—and we don't."[67] The last few months of 1973 and the first ones of 1974 were grim socially—"White House Tomb" the press called the president's home. "I really don't know how Nixon stood up," said pianist Eugene List, who played at the summit meeting in Moscow a few weeks before Nixon left the White House. "Everybody knew it was the end. And Mrs. Nixon must have been under terrible pressure. She was such a lovely, noble lady. I remember her wearing a very beautiful gown that day."[68]

There was no way to escape Watergate. But there was a way to hide momentarily. "Mrs. Nixon disclosed that the President has taken to playing the piano late at night in the family quarters of the White House," the *New York Times* reported. Then on March 7, 1974, the nation's governors were treated to one of the liveliest White House after-dinner shows in years when Pearl Bailey and the president collaborated in an impromptu performance. The great blues singer coaxed the president into playing, pointing out that he could choose anything he wanted. But when he began "Home on the Range," Bailey smiled and complained, "Mr. President, I want to sing a song, not ride a horse." And then they had problems finding the same key at the same time. "I don't know whether I'm finding him, or he's finding me," Bailey quipped. Vice-President Gerald Ford said he had never laughed so hard in his life. The president added, "I just want to say to our distinguished guests that this piano will never be the same again, and neither will I."[69]

Shortly before Nixon resigned from office, mobs lined the White House gates chanting their eerie permutation of a time-honored tune—"Jail to the Chief!" On August 9, 1974, Vice-President Ford was sworn in as the nation's new leader. The curtain descended on the final scene. The drama was over.

GERALD R. FORD

Gerald and Betty Ford continued the diversity of entertainment that the Nixons had enjoyed, but their tastes leaned even more toward the popular and night-club styles. While President Nixon had been the overseer of White House programming, the weight shifted back to the first lady under the brief years of the Ford administration. President Ford was not particularly fond of music. "I'm so envious of talent," he said. "Betty says I can't even listen on key."[70] With First Lady Betty Ford, however, the arts were quite a different matter. She loved the theater, especially all forms of dance. "I think she's got every book ever written on ballet," said Nancy Howe, Mrs. Ford's close confidant and personal assistant at the White House.[71] Betty Bloomer Ford studied dance at Bennington College in Vermont. Deciding to make her career in dance, she then became a member of Martha Graham's company in New York City.

The Ford White House entertainment was marked by relaxation and spontaneity. President and Mrs. Ford seemed to enjoy their parties. Of the thirty-four state dinners, twenty-eight featured light entertainment, and, unlike the Nixons, dancing was often a focal point of the evening. "Jerry likes to dance to old Glenn Miller-style numbers like 'In the Mood'," Mrs. Ford related in her book, *The Times of My Life*. "Some members of the press have written that he does the same two-step no matter what the music is."[72]

President and Mrs. Ford were especially successful in matching the musical programs to the interests of the state visitors, by this period a major factor in selecting the entertainment. (See Appendix B.) It is a study in itself to peruse the artistic preferences of foreign heads of state while they are guests in this country. For example, Betty Ford learned that Chancellor Helmut Schmidt of West Germany loved opera, so she invited Phyllis Curtin to sing; for France's blues-loving, piano-playing Giscard d'Estaing, Earl Hines performed; and the extraordinary blind jazz genius George Shearing satisfied the request of President Kekkonen of Finland. Ann-Margret sang and danced for the shah of Iran "because the shah likes pretty girls," according to the president. As her costume grew briefer while her act grew longer, there were undoubtedly others who felt the same way. For President Giovanni Leone of Italy, the White House offered its first ragtime evening on September 25, 1974. Composer and jazz historian Gunther Schuller brought his New England Conservatory Ragtime Ensemble for a program of the music of Scott Joplin, harking back to the time "The Maple Leaf Rag" was played by the Marine Band in Theodore Roosevelt's White House.

But there were certain very special moments at the White House when music became a powerful binding force, linking people, feelings and cultures. When Pearl Bailey sang for President Anwar Sadat of Egypt, her characteristic warm informality "had helped bring our two nations together," said President Ford. So did Van Cliburn's sweeping interpretation of Chopin,

Schumann, and Debussy during the first White House entertainment for a reigning Japanese emperor. The great American pianist opened his concert with a majestic interpretation of the Japanese national anthem. But Billy Taylor's program for Prime Minister Begum Bhutto of Pakistan offered yet another touch. "I'd like to show you how much we admire the music of your country," Taylor said to Bhutto, and brilliantly he improvised on a raga. "It was a smash," recalled the pianist. "They loved it!"[73]

On three occasions President Ford bestowed the Medal of Freedom on distinguished Americans in the fields of science, humanities, and the arts. Artur Rubinstein was the first recipient, on April 1, 1976. The eighty-nine-year-old pianist had played only once in the White House, for Dwight Eisenhower in 1957, and although he had been decorated by fifteen other countries, the United States had never recognized him. "Artur Rubinstein has given something more than the joy of music—he has given the joy of life itself," remarked Ford at the opening of the ceremony. "His country, the United States of America, is proud to proclaim him as a giant among artists and men."[74] Later that year eighty-two-year-old iconoclastic dancer and choreographer Martha Graham also received the distinguished Medal of Freedom. Betty Ford's former teacher became the first to be honored in the field of dance on October 14, 1976.[75]

The White House, with its unique melding of music, politics, and protocol, has been perennially prone to mishaps and infelicities of coordination. The Captain and Tennille's big hit "Love Will Keep Us Together" was an appropriate theme song for the two nations, England and America, during their program for Queen Elizabeth II and Prince Philip on July 7, 1976. Their "Muskrat Love Song" was not, however. According to some guests, the gentle little song's cutesy, suggestive lyrics—punctuated with animal love gurgles from the ARP synthesizer—were unsuitable fare for royalty. The applause was unusually weak for lyrics like:

> Now he's ticklin' her fancy, rubbin' her toes
> Muzzle to muzzle now anything goes
> As they wiggle, Sue starts to giggle
> They whirl and they twirl and they tangle.[76]

Queen Elizabeth II received another ill-timed tribute when, purely by accident, the Marine Band struck up "The Lady Is a Tramp" just as she started to dance. "We took the piece immediately out of our repertoire," said Marine Band Leader Colonel John Bourgeois, recalling the incident.

The press was particularly critical of entertainment during the Nixon and Ford years. White House tastes were either too "dismal" (George Will) or "establishment" (Charlie McCollum) or just plain "lowbrow" (Betty Beale). "Indeed," continued Beale, "any singer who won't perform without clutching a mike shouldn't be there."[77] Other critics recommended more exploration of the riches of our culture by bringing to the White House segments of the current Folk Life Festival in Washington; performances from the John F. Kennedy Center (which opened in 1971 with Bernstein's controversial *Mass*); artist groups from across the country encouraged by grants from the National Council on the Arts; and, for the first time, that wayward son of American socio-musical life—rock, "distinguished" rock, that is.

How about Paul Simon in the White House, recommended Charlie

McCollum of the *Star*, or Linda Ronstadt, The Eagles, Bobby Short (who, McCollum forgot, *did* play for the Nixons in 1970), folk singer Woodie Guthrie and "such 'outlaws'" as Bob Dylan?[78] McCollum may have had a point. But the mere fact that rock groups were now considered respectable at the White House tells us something about American tastes of the later 1970s—a time less innovative than inventive, less radical than romantic. It was a period for reworking, reconsidering, and the drive to protest society's ills unabashedly in song was less urgent. "I just wonder what establishment Washington is going to think if Jimmy Carter gets elected and has Bob Dylan and the Allman Brothers play his first state dinner?" mused McCollum. He was in for some surprises.

CHAPTER 8

MUSIC, MASS MEDIA, AND THE MODERN WHITE HOUSE

> We are trying to do at the White House
> what Leontyne Price has always done:
> to prove that opera is not just a luxury
> for the few, but a thing of beauty for all.
>
> Jimmy Carter
> PBS Telecast, October 8, 1978

JIMMY CARTER

There was little warmth in the filtered sun, and the wind whipped unmercifully about President James Earl Carter, Jr., as he smiled and waved to the throngs nearby. Dramatically departing from tradition, the new president and his family walked from the Capitol to the White House following the inauguration on January 20, 1977. During his vigorous campaign to capture the Democratic nomination and the presidency, Jimmy Carter promised to remain close to the people. Through the art of music, especially, he kept his promise.

Few presidential families have enjoyed classical music as much as the Carters. "I hope you'll play the Prelude to the third act of *Tristan and Isolde* sometime," President Carter told the surprised leader of the Marine Band. "I enjoy that very much."[1] This was not the usual background music for White House receptions. But then neither were the Bach Brandenburg Concertos. For the Tito state dinner a harpsichord was brought in, and an entire program of J. S. Bach was played in the foyer of the mansion. The press, usually reporters of social, not musical, affairs, did not always understand. One reporter claimed Mozart's *Eine kleine Nachtmusik* was played "over and over again," when it was actually played only once. The reporter failed to recognize the thematic repetitions characteristic of Viennese classicism.[2]

The Carters enjoyed their White House concerts so much, they often attended even the rehearsals. Almost three-quarters of their programs consisted of classical artists and repertory, notably pianist Rudolf Serkin; Metropolitan Opera's Shirley Verrett; the Dallas Symphony Orchestra Brass Quartet; Tchaikovsky Competition winners Elmar Oliveira and Nathaniel Rose; Isaac Stern, Andre Previn, and Martina Arroyo—all three for the signing of the Panama Treaty on September 7, 1977; and the New York City Ballet for

Leontyne Price presented a nationally televised concert in the East Room for the Carters and their guests on October 8, 1978. The American soprano has sung several times in the White House, including for the Carters' Israeli-Egyptian Peace Treaty Signing, for the welcoming ceremonies of Pope John Paul II, and during the Johnson and Reagan administrations.

the North Atlantic Alliance summit on May 30, 1978. But the most exciting innovation during the Carter administration was the Sunday afternoon PBS series of five hour-long programs broadcast nationally and throughout Europe from the East Room. "Jimmy and I wanted all of America to enjoy the White House like we did," Rosalynn Carter explained.[3] Via the medium of television, they had their wish.

The first concert, presented by pianist Vladimir Horowitz on February 26, 1978, set the tone and pattern for the succeeding programs. The audience of about three hundred at Horowitz's request consisted mainly of musicians and arts celebrities ("not politicians who look at their watches to see when I will finish"), and included Samuel Barber, William Warfield, Isaac Stern, Alice Tully, John Steinway and many others.[4] A problem arose when the East Room proved too live acoustically for Horowitz. President Carter, dressed in blue jeans, sweater, and suede shoes, ran upstairs and with the chief usher's help found an oriental rug on the third floor that he brought down and placed before the platform.[5] The concert was a huge success; the critics were ecstatic. But the primary critic was the president himself, who came onstage at the close of the concert clearly moved. "The White House has been host to a lot of great people," he said, "but never a greater man or greater performance."[6]

On October 8, Leontyne Price presented her program in the PBS series. The famous soprano sang works by Handel, Richard Strauss, and Puccini, closing with a group of American art songs and spirituals. For the third telecast, on February 25, 1979, the special portable stage donated by the Harkness Ballet under Lyndon Johnson was erected, and Mikhail Baryshnikov and Patricia McBride dazzled the 130 guests with spins that soared a mere hair's breadth beneath the East Room crystal chandelier. Because of the Egyptian Israeli peace negotiations, President Carter had to miss the final two concerts. In one, noted cellist and artistic director of the National Symphony Orchestra, Mstislav Rostropovich, played works by Bach, Weber, Schumann, and Shostakovich. For the final telecast, Andrés Segovia performed the colorful Spanish guitar music that had endeared him to the world.

On March 25, 1979, two weeks after Segovia's telecast, sixteen hundred White House guests, five thousand spectators, and a global television audience of millions watched the signing of the Egyptian–Israeli peace treaty. It was a time of "filtered joy," as one report stated, for wars and tortuous months of negotiations had left their scars, and the difficulties that lay ahead were on the faces of the three participants, Egypt's Anwar Sadat, Israel's Menachem Begin, and Jimmy Carter. But it was the music of the evening that underpinned the renewed spirit of peace and hope in a manner like no other. For the largest dinner in White House history, held under a forty-five-foot-high tent, the musical entertainment was sheer genius. "Normally we have six to eight weeks to plan the entertainment for a state dinner," Gretchen Poston, the Carters' social secretary, said. "For the peace celebration, we had five days. We didn't know how one artist could represent all three countries, so we asked each nation to bring its own performer. Sadat provided a popular Egyptian trio of guitar, tabla drum and electronic organ; for Israel we had violinists Itzhak Perlman and Pinchas Zukerman (both native Israelis); and to represent our own country, we invited Leontyne Price."[7] The great diva sang the powerful "Pace, pace, mio Dio," from Verdi's *La forza del destino.*

Musical units from all four branches of the service performed, and an especially beautiful touch was provided by the U.S. Army Chorus conducted by Major Allen Crowell. Within the course of a few days, Army arranger James Kessler researched a Hebrew song Sadat would have known and came up with "Salma ya Salma," a very old chant from the Egyptian leader's native village. Kessler, who holds a bachelor of music degree in composition from Eastman School of Music, then found a popular Israeli song of the 1960s, "Machar" by Naomi Shemer, with the help of the embassy of Israel and cleverly combined the two tunes in a moving commemoration of the historic event. Both songs had as their subject peace, their modal lines interweaving in simple counterpoint, overlapping on the word "peace" to emphasize the song's poignant message: "Peace will arrive with the morning sun. This is more than the proverb of a dreamer." "As the chorus sang, both Sadat and Begin recognized their tunes," Kessler recalled. "They were obviously delighted."[8]

But there was another side to Carter. He felt that it was important to recognize the ethnic and folk traditions in America, and he did this effectively by dedicating entire programs to one style of American popular or indigenous music. These programs were held on the South Lawn as eight

Ninety-five-year-old jazz pianist Eubie Blake plays during a program honoring the Newport Jazz Festival on the White House Lawn to the delight of the Carters and their guests.

hundred guests picnicked on paper plates and enjoyed the music in a relaxed setting. Honoring the twenty-fifth anniversary of the Newport Jazz Festival, the White House Jazz Concert, held on June 18, 1978, featured nine decades of this art form with performances by ninety-five-year-old Eubie Blake, Katherine Handy Lewis, Mary Lou Williams, Jo Jones, Clark Terry, Sonny Rollins, Max Roach, Herbie Hancock, Dizzy Gillespie, Ornette Coleman, Lionel Hampton, Stan Getz, and other luminaries. Sitting on the lawn in his shirtsleeves, President Carter asked Dizzy Gillespie to play "Salt Peanuts" and joined the great bop artist with repeated exclamations of "salt peanuts!" during breaks. Someone made the comment that this must have been the "first presidential hot chorus in history."[9] In the fall the Carters held an "Old Fashioned Gospel Singin'" festival, a remarkable program that underscored

Colonel John R. Bourgeois, U.S. Marine Corps, was appointed the twenty-fifth director of the U.S. Marine Band in May 1979. The Marine Band performs more than 150 programs a year at the White House.

the president's remarks that gospel was "a music of pain, a music of longing and a music of faith."[10]

Music had a powerful message for the president, but what effect did the president have on the artists? White House Social Secretary Gretchen Poston recalls the reaction of Andre Kostelanetz when he conducted his "Promenade at the White House" on May 20, 1978. "Kostelanetz had been given just about every award by this time," said Poston, "but when he met the president, tears just streamed down his face. He said that at no time in his life did he have anything more exciting happen to him than this. It was always impressive to see how people felt when performing at the White House. And Baryshnikov felt this same way when he danced. I noticed that the artists were almost overwhelmed. The bigger the artist, the humbler they seemed."[11]

But great or humble, artists can experience mishaps at the White House—and they can be especially funny. Soprano Clamma Dale, Poston recalls, was rehearsing in a room below the state dining room during a dinner given for Premier Nicolae Ceausescu of Romania:

Just as President Carter lifted his glass and opened his mouth to begin the after-dinner toasts we heard 'ah-ah-ah-ah-ah'—scales going up and down. Everybody looked around. The President tried again, and as he lifted his glass once more and opened his mouth to speak, out came the scales again. I was just dumfounded. So I ran upstairs and finally discovered Miss Dale back in the corner of the linen closet, where she thought she was not disturbing anyone. She was, in fact, at the base of the shaft going up to the fireplace directly behind the President as he stood in the state dining room. For a while we thought we had lost our soprano in a fireplace.[12]

RONALD REAGAN

As the 1970s came to a close and the 1980s began, mass communication seemed to hold every American in its portentous grasp. The airways were congested with citizen-band radios, video games, stereos, and cordless phones. Television, with its abilities to reach millions, told most of the stories to most of the people most of the time. Soap operas, full-scale ballets, and political debates moved with equal ease into the American living room. And for Ronald Reagan television was the natural vehicle to share with the nation his inauguration as president in January 1981—a gigantic four day celebration that was viewed throughout America and abroad. "It's great having an actor in the White House," quipped Bob Hope. "We went from peanuts to popcorn. It's the greatest thing to happen to Hollywood since George Burns played God."

As a former actor and actress, Ronald and Nancy Reagan came to the White House with extensive knowledge of the entertainment world. Poised, petite, with an aura of graceful informality about her, the new first lady proved to be far from fragile. She used the media and the entertainment world to campaign for a better America, and her clever song-and-dance routine—"Second Hand Rose" at the 1982 Gridiron Dinner—convinced the nation that she was a first lady with wit and spunk. Nancy Reagan's most impressive performance, however, took place after the death of her friend, Princess Grace of Monaco. Mrs. Reagan substituted for her as the narrator in the National Symphony's performance of *Carnival of the Animals* by Saint Saëns. As a result, Sultan Quboos Said of Oman presented the symphony with a $300,000 endowment to establish The Nancy Reagan Chair of Narrative Music.

Shortly after the Reagans came to the White House, they began plans for a series of televised concerts that would originate for the most part from the East Room. Called "In Performance at the White House," the various series of PBS concerts have been among the most visible, imaginative, and wholly successful arts ventures to come from the White House. While the Carters' televised programs were formal and classical, the Reagans added their own special mark by broadening the musical styles to include Broadway, country, jazz, and gospel. "We try to create programs that salute distinguished American performers as well as brilliant young talent which has not yet received recognition in this country," Mabel ("Muffie") Brandon, the Reagans' social secretary, emphasized.[13] Thus older, established artists per

Beverly Sills, Ida Levin, and Rudolf Serkin open the young artists' "In Performance at the White House" televised series on November 22, 1981.

formed with younger talent on these telecasts, which included biographical documentary film. The opening theme music, the joyous finale from Aaron Copland's *The Red Pony*, set the tone for each of the programs, which reverberated with a spirit of youth, grace, and the vibrant musical images of America.

Mrs. Reagan's opening remarks at the first concert seemed to bring the long skein of White House musical history to a brilliant and vital focal point. And all the musical styles so important to the great mansion's traditions came alive again. "Good evening and a warm welcome to the White House," she began.

> Ever since this wonderful house was built, it's been filled with music. Thomas Jefferson played his violin and Harry Truman played his piano in this room. The Marine Band has serenaded countless foreign dignitaries at state dinners and some of the world's most dazzling performers have appeared beneath these chandeliers. . . . Tonight with the participation of public television, the East Room becomes a concert hall for the entire nation.[14]

The first series was introduced by Beverly Sills, who served as mistress of ceremonies for each of the programs. The opening concert on November 22,

President and Mrs. Reagan enjoy the country music of Merle Haggard with mistress of ceremonies Beverly Sills at a ranch near the Western White House.

1981, featured veteran pianist Rudolf Serkin and the brilliant eighteen-year-old Ida Levin, a 1980 Leventritt Artist, who had studied with Serkin at Vermont's Marlboro School of Music. The two artists communicated vividly together, despite almost sixty years difference in their ages. Serkin played Beethoven's "Moonlight Sonata," Levin continued with one of the most challenging works in the violin repertory, Ysaÿe's "Ballad," and both artists collaborated in Schubert's spirited Rondo Brilliant.

The next month, eight singers from the New York City Opera performed various arias, and the following spring, several young dancers from the San Francisco Ballet, Martha Graham Dance Company, and the cast of *Sophisticated Ladies* tapped, shuffled, leaped, and swirled on the small East Room stage. Gene Kelly, a long-time friend of the Reagans, introduced the dancers, and eighty-seven-year-old Martha Graham was the honored guest. But the season's surprise had yet to come. The 1981–82 series ended with a lively program broadcast from a California ranch near President Reagan's Western White House. It featured country music star Merle Haggard and twenty-year-old champion fiddler Mark O'Connor. Seated on bales of hay in Western attire, President and Mrs. Reagan and their guests enjoyed Haggard's rendition of "Pennies from Heaven" and other songs. But nothing drew laughs from the president quite like "Rainbow Stew." "When a President goes through a White House door and does what he says he'll do," sang Haggard, "We'll all be drinkin' free bubble up and eatin' that rainbow stew."

The success of the first four televised programs encouraged the Reagans to continue the series. Between 1982 and 1984 all areas of America's performing arts traditions were featured—from classical to jazz, from Broadway to opera. Among the artists who performed in these series were Itzhak Perlman,

On the occasion of its 100th anniversary, the Boston Pops Orchestra performed at the White House on July 15, 1985. Nancy Reagan is seated with Vice-President and Mrs. George Bush, front row, right.

Ken Noda, Dizzy Gillespie, Diane Schuur, the Juilliard String Quartet, Mary Martin, and Leontyne Price with six stellar members of the Metropolitan Opera's Young Artist Development Program. The president himself topped off the last broadcast with a wry reference to the old film *Night at the Opera*: "For years I didn't think you could give *Il trovatore* without the Marx Brothers." Then he added: "From talent like we've just heard here, drawn from the Met's wonderful training program, opera lovers can be confident of this inspirational art form in the future in America. Again, we can't thank you enough. God bless you all."

With Marvin Hamlisch as emcee, the last "In Performance at the White House" series took place between October 1986 and August 1988 and comprised five programs that were entitled "A Tribute to American Music." The first four were devoted to the music of George Gershwin, Rodgers and Hart, Cole Porter, and Jerome Kern, respectively, but the fifth program was the capstone—a lively, colorful show that highlighted America's great singing and dancing choruses from well-known Broadway musicals. Held at night on the South Lawn, the show was aired on August 10, 1988, and featured Shirley Jones, Stubby Kaye, Lee Roy Reams, the Morgan State University Choir, and the cast from the long-running hit, *A Chorus Line*. The program also included the Marine Band, Army Band, Navy Sea Chanters, and the Air Force Singing Sergeants, creating a colorful array of blue, red, gold and white. But most impressive of all was the backdrop—the White House itself, gleaming softly in the evening light—another dimension of a great American musical tradition that brought the Reagan era to a spirited and joyous close.

The Reagans held several other outdoor musical programs throughout their administration. Some celebrated America's orchestras, such as the Boston Pops Orchestra and New York's Mostly Mozart Festival Orchestra that played the U.S. premier of a newly discovered Mozart symphony.[15] Others were musical parties for children, holiday fêtes, or congressional picnics. To help raise money for young mentally retarded athletes in the Special Olympics, the Beach Boys performed on the South Lawn on June 12, 1983. Missing from the audience was Secretary of the Interior James Watt, who had said two months earlier that "rock groups attracted the wrong element" and could not play on the Washington mall. But the president intervened.[16]

Less common were the large extravaganzas of the Kennedy, Johnson and Nixon years. With the John F. Kennedy Center for the Performing Arts nearby, the first family can now attend elaborate productions with ease, and through the nationally televised Kennedy Center Honors, they are able to salute America's greatest performers with elegance and visibility. Then too, explains the Reagans' chief usher, Rex Scouten, "the White House is not a concert hall, and everything we do here involves some compromise." When Zubin Mehta and the New York Philharmonic came to perform for Indira Gandhi's visit, they had to rehearse on the South Lawn in the 95 degree heat in order to prevent disturbance of the president's cabinet meeting. "Luckily," Scouten added, "we found a lot of volunteers who held umbrellas over the musicians while they played to protect the instruments from the blazing sun."[17] And then there is the problem of security—a never ending concern at the White House. Until President Carter took office, every instrument and case had to be checked by hand, and when large groups of artists performed, this could take almost an hour. Today security has been facilitated by metal detectors, and dogs sniff routinely for suspicious materials.

GEORGE BUSH

Under the administration of George Bush, who became our nation's fortieth president in 1989, the concept of the White House as home—both public and private—becomes a powerful and engaging symbol. And there is no better manifestation of this symbol than Barbara Bush's own words:

> One of the great privileges of living in the White House is meeting the best and brightest America has to offer, especially in the field of music. So many great performers have brought their magic here. Leontyne Price captivated a state dinner audience. Country group Alabama had hundreds of congressmen tapping their toes during a South Lawn barbecue. The President and I were spellbound simply watching the rehearsal of *Phantom of the Opera*. All of these musicians have greatly enriched life here at the White House and have been wonderfully representative of all that our American culture has to offer.[18]

Judy Kaye and Barry Bostwick sing for President and Mrs. Bush and their guests during the nationally televised "In Performance at the White House," July 5, 1989.

Through the simplicity, warmth and candid style of their musical programs, President and Mrs. Bush have expressed what the White House signifies to them. Perhaps this comes as no surprise. As Donnie Radcliffe commented in her biography of Mrs. Bush: "George's affable nature and Barbara's folksy hospitality that could put anybody at ease had made them the quintessential couple long before their return address was the White House."[19] A true signature of this charming social ambience is the title of the Bushes' first PBS "In Performance at the White House" series: "The House I Live In." For through these nationally televised programs, brought into our own living rooms, we can relive those rare and wonderful early years of White House musical life—when there was a special intimacy between the president, the artist, and the audience.

President and Mrs. Bush have held three "In Performance" telecasts, which were aired on July 5, 1989, October 4, 1989, and February 14, 1990. Each celebrated a different national holiday: Independence Day, Columbus Day, and President's Day. The series opened with Earl Robinson's moving symbol of the nation, "The House I Live In," powerfully sung by the black opera singer Simon Estes. It was effectively balanced by Judy Kaye's final number from the musical show, *1600 Pennsylvania Avenue*. "Take care of this

Cellist Mstislav Rostropovich greets President Bush after his concert in the East Room.

house," she sang, "it's the hope of us all." Others on the program were Joshua Rifkin, John Denver, and Barry Bostwick, but the president summed up the meaning of the evening when he said: "American music, like America itself, is a song of many voices . . . America is indeed the house we live in, and we'll take good care of our house."

The remaining two telecasts presented a variety of artists, notably Teresa Stratas, Ray Price, Benny Carter, Patti LuPone, Jeffrey Osborne, and the Dick Hyman Jazz Trio. But it was Marilyn Horne's interpretation of "Make a Rainbow," a song written for her by Portia Nelson, that closed the series with a touch of warmth and charm. "One of the tenderest moments I recall, Mr. President," noted Horne, "was when you said that you held your twelfth grandchild." Then she sang, "Make a rainbow, let the colors dance and sparkle . . . the colors of children will shine everywhere in a world of love." Visibly moved, the president offered his own brief message at the end of the program. "That song spoke of a special promise," he said, "the promise that lies in the children of the world."

George and Barbara Bush find in music a means of relaxation which they often share with their family. Fans of country music, they enjoy Nashville's Grand Old Opry, but also the musical revue *Forever Plaid*, which they attended at Ford's Theatre, and Andrew Lloyd Webber's *Phantom of the Opera* produced at Kennedy Center. When Webber's roller-skating extravaganza, *Starlight Express*, came to the Center, the president took his grandchildren to see it. In October 1991 President and Mrs. Bush and their Mexican-born daughter-in-law, Columba Bush, joined the First Lady of Mexico at a performance of the Ballet Folklorico de Mexico at Lisner Auditorium. Earlier that year, the Bushes attended the Houston Ballet as part of Kennedy Center's Texas Festival. One reviewer wished they would come to the ballet more often. The president's attendance, he said, had a "tonic effect" on the dancers, who looked stronger than ever before and "understandably danced their hearts out."[20]

With their dedication to improving the quality of life through education, George and Barbara Bush value the arts and humanities as vital facets in shaping the whole human being. On her ABC Radio Network series, "Mrs. Bush's Storytime," the first lady introduced children to literature and the joys of literacy by reading several stories and books to them. She also has attended the National Symphony Youth Concerts and serves as honorary chair or cochair of several major arts organizations, such as the American Ballet Theater, Dance Theater of Harlem, and the Choral Arts Society. The president and first lady not only host annual receptions at the White House for the Kennedy Center honorees, but also attend their galas at the Center afterwards, occupying the special presidential box. Recent honorees have included Robert Shaw, Risë Stevens, William Schuman, Mary Martin, Harry Belafonte and other luminaries from the world of the performing arts. President Bush, moreover, has awarded the National Medal of the Arts to Katherine Dunham, John Birks ("Dizzy" Gillespie), Vladimir Horowitz, and dancer, choreographer and anthropologist Pearl Primus. On February 21, 1990, the first couple held a party at the White House for Mstislav Rostropovich, whom the president called a "national treasure." The renowned National Symphony conductor had just returned from a triumphant concert tour that included his native Soviet Union after a sixteen-year exile.

President and Mrs. Bush also continue the long White House tradition of the state dinner/musicale, holding ten to twelve of these events each year. (See Appendix B.) The finest artists from Broadway, jazz, concert and opera perform, but—as in the musicale tradition of Hayes, Theodore Roosevelt and other early administrations—ballet and staged productions are rare, and the East Room portable stage finds little use. Like the early days, the programs comprise short, encore-like pieces suitable for after-dinner entertainment. For her program on May 14, 1991, the celebrated Metropolitan Opera artist, Jessye Norman, sang works of Purcell, Poulenc, and "Habanera" from Bizet's *Carmen*. She closed with three expressive spirituals: "Ev'ry Time I Feel the Spirit," "Deep River," and "He's Got the Whole World in His Hand." The previous year, Roberta Peters—who has appeared at the White House eleven times since the Kennedy era—included a group of Italian arias on her program for Prime Minister Andreotti of Italy. Peter's presence reminded the president of another great singer and great American pastime. He told the story of Enrico Caruso who was once asked by a group of reporters what he thought of Babe Ruth. "Caruso replied politely that unfortunately he had never heard her sing," the president said.[21]

In many ways, the musical programs of the Bush administration carry us back full circle to the earliest days of White House entertaining, when a young American opera singer brightened the spirits of President Lincoln in the Red Room during the Civil War. Indeed tradition and history appear to be the hallmarks of the musical life of the White House as the twentieth century draws to a close—as the year 1992 marks both the quincentenary of the discovery of America and the bicentennial of the laying of the cornerstone of the White House. Nowhere is this more evident than in the extent and variety of the programs performed by the United States Marine Band at the White House today. Conducted by Colonel John Bourgeois, the band plays for White House concerts, dinners, receptions, and dances, and accompanies many of the guest artists, just as it did nearly two hundred years ago.

The nation's oldest musical organization, the U.S. Marine Band numbers 140 musicians, who play nearly six hundred programs a year, 150 of them at the White House. Band members are educated at the nation's finest music schools and must be able to sight read a wide variety of music. Women first

Marine Band Chamber Orchestra, Col. John Bourgeois, director, with President and Mrs. Bush after a Christmas program at the White House in 1990.

joined the band under President Nixon and today number thirty-six players. When she needs music for a particular event, moreover, the White House social secretary, Laurie Firestone, can select from at least sixteen musical units within the band: Concert Band, Marine Band Combo, Chamber Orchestra, Cordovox Trio, Piano Trio, Brass Choir, Brass Quintet, Guitarist, Dance Band, Woodwind Quintet, Harpist, Harp and Flute Duo, String Ensemble, Pianist, Dixieland Combo, and Baritone Vocalist Michael Ryan. There is no Marine choir, and when such a group is desired, the fine Army or Navy choirs assist. Strolling strings are provided by the Army and Air Force and have played in the state dining room during dinner from the time of Eisenhower.

Reminiscent of the early occupants of the White House, President and Mrs. Bush recognize music as a supreme American gesture, a vital symbol of American life as it underscores every national event, social cause, and ceremonial mood. Both the outdoor and indoor ceremonial practices of former administrations continue today. The Herald Trumpets and Fife and Drum Corps play, and the military bands from the four branches of service alternate for the various welcoming ceremonies for foreign dignitaries. Music is important in establishing good foreign relations, emphasizes Paul Miller, retired director of ceremonies for the Military District of Washington. "It really does have an effect on diplomacy," he says. "I can recall a foreign head of state coming to Washington to discuss some very, very serious problems. But the fellow was in such a good mood after the ceremony that the negotiations went very well. He said, 'I just want you to know that it had a great deal to do with the music you provided that morning at the arrival ceremony.' "[22]

And just what *is* the right music? Sometimes it is the favorite tune of the visiting dignitary, but more often it is music that captures the mood of the moment. Performing this music can be a complex enterprise, especially at a state dinner where the director of music must adapt his repertory to constantly shifting moods and casting, with the central characters the president and his honored visitor. "As the guests are arriving," Colonel Bourgeois explains,

the orchestra, stationed in the foyer, might play Gershwin, Leroy Anderson, Mozart, or the second movement of Schubert's C Major Symphony, which has a nice 'walking feeling.' When the guest of honor arrives, we

President and Mrs. Bush open the dancing after the state dinner for Queen Elizabeth II, May 14, 1991.

select something rather elegant and joyful—a bourée from one of the Bach suites, perhaps. As the president and his party come down the stairs, "Hail America" by George Drumm is played. This is traditional. The president and his party then pose for the press before entering the East Room, the band sounds four "Ruffles and Flourishes," the president, first lady and guest of honor are announced and "Hail to the Chief" follows. There is always considerable tension in getting this timing just right. For the receiving line, marches connected by drum cadences tend to move people into dinner.[23]

All these comments resemble those of John Philip Sousa when he led the Marine Band under President Hayes more than a hundred years ago— with a difference. As the presidential party enter the dining room, the orchestra now plays a work recognizable to the guest of honor. "For Queen Elizabeth recently," emphasizes Col. Bourgeois, "we used the British coronation march, 'Orb and Sceptre' by William Walton."[24]

While today's intriguing mélange of White House events tells a story of its own, its wonders lie ultimately in the music—in its kaleidoscopic powers on the human spirit. Isaac Stern once said, "The world weeps, cries, loves and laughs better through music than any other way." At the Reagans' first Christmas party for their senior staff, Jim Brady, severely injured during the assassination attempt on the president, was present. "Carols were played,"

Barbara Bush and Betty Ford enjoy the performance of the Harlem Boys Choir in the East Room after a Senate wives' luncheon.

recalls Mabel Brandon, "and we all gathered around the pianos in the grand foyer. . . . It was one of the most beautiful musical moments I have ever known. It was spontaneous, moving and really captured the essence of Christmas."[25] But it also caught the spirit of the White House, where music provides a vital bond among world leaders, princes, diplomats, visitors, staff—or just the family.

And if art offers a window to the soul, a blind young sculptor provided inspiration for President Bush's comments during the Very Special Arts International Festival at the White House in 1989. "All art is a vision that comes from within," he said. But it was a young musician, Phong Sak Meunchanai, who deeply moved the president with his glorious singing. "Maybe it's not such a long journey from the streets of Thailand to the South Lawn of the White House," the president said. "It tells us all that there's no limit to how far we can go or what we can achieve. And here at the White House we're very privileged—every President is—to have great artists come to this magnificent home, the people's home."[26]

For the music of the White House celebrates the American spirit. And while administrations change, tastes shift, and new currents explore fresh artistic terrain, in this music the image of America remains, reinforcing our heritage and glorifying our dreams. Music will always be a vital part of the American adventure of discovery, and the White House will remain a prime mover in the voyage. But even more important, America's noble home will guide us all on the journey, offering every man, woman and child a glimpse of that joyous "vision that comes from within."

EPILOGUE

This book has been a story of "the gradual emergence of the American national character through the growing acceptance of its diverse ethnic treasures and a lessening dependence upon European culture." But it has also been the tale of the American process of music-making—how music in a democracy was absorbed, shaped, transformed, and perceived from post-Revolutionary days to the present. Whether dramatic or abstract, vernacular or cultivated, music is a powerful voice that can charm as forcefully as it can repel. Ultimately, the manner in which music is perceived within the complexities of society determines its absorption, expression, and direction. The ancient Greeks recognized this in their doctrine of *ethos*, which claimed music had a vital effect on human character and conduct. Indeed, Plato in his *Republic* found in music certain mystical properties that could strengthen character, heal illness, spur men to action, and play a dominant role in the education and political system of Greek civilization.

In modern times, echoes from the doctrine of *ethos* appear in many guises—from the patriotic repertory of the U.S. Marine Band to the "subversive" American symphonic music of the 1950s, from the controversial messages of rock to the mind-expanding colors of music video. This book, then, is not only about history, the White House, or even music. It is about the human spirit. And it proves that the art of music can mold the political process, shape a historical event, and capture the human spirit in a manner like no other.

While the modern White House welcomes the arts of America more vigorously and visibly than ever before, it still maintains a certain moral obligation to the people to offer music that is appropriate or "right." But what is "right" or "wrong" often depends on the viewpoints and vicissitudes of the times. To a congressman of the 1870s, the "Athenian concept of music that ennobled the heart and purified the soul" shaped the music of the White House; to a critic a century later, "distinguished rock" was the cultural high point of the mansion. Might there be an echo from ancient Greece in the White House, then?—an image of a civilization that valued the *polis* or city-state as a source of moral, social, and political strength?—a symbol of a society's conviction that the sensuous powers of music could generate ethical values vital to the well being of the people? The answers are not hard to find. For as society moves into the future, this symbol gains power and vitality as the performing arts of all varieties become allied with American life more intimately than ever before. Thus the ancient image becomes a modern directive, transformed and rejuvenated by new dreams, fresh visions, and always a characteristic American spirit.

NINETEENTH-CENTURY PRESIDENTIAL FAMILY MUSIC COLLECTIONS

The following collections include music that family members most likely played and sang during their White House years. The largest collections of presidential music are those of George Washington and Thomas Jefferson, which are discussed further in Judith Britt, *Nothing More Agreeable* (Mt. Vernon, 1984), and Helen Cripe, *Thomas Jefferson and Music* (Charlottesville, 1974). The Rutherford B. Hayes Presidential Center holds hymnals used by the Hayeses during their White House tenure, notably *Songs for the Sanctuary* (New York, 1872), which has on its cover, stamped in gold: "Mrs. Hayes— Executive Mansion." In the President James A. Garfield Home, Mentor, Ohio, is a fine leather-bound piano/vocal copy of Gilbert and Sullivan's *Patience* dated 1881, the year of the London premiere, with "Garfield" printed on the cover (J. M. Stoddard, Philadelphia). Music belonging to White House children who played the piano—such as the Lincoln boys, Fannie Hayes, and Mollie and Hal Garfield—has yet to surface. Those collections that are available, however, provide a fine overview of nineteenth-century tastes and styles, as well as a springboard for further study of music's role within the diverse pastimes and pleasantries of the early American home.

George Washington (1789–1797)

Collection: Nelly Custis
Locations: Library of Congress
               Houghton Library, Harvard University
               Mount Vernon, Virginia
               Woodlawn Plantation, Virginia

Summary:

The collection of music belonging to Nelly Custis comprises more than ten books and represents publishers from Paris, London, Dublin, and America, especially Philadelphia. Many of the volumes bear Nelly's name on the flyleaves or nameplates: "Eleanor P. Custis," "E. P. Custis," "Eleanor Parke Lewis" (after her marriage), or the monogram "EPC." Of special interest are the works relating to Nelly's music education and her teacher, Alexander Reinagle, such as Reinagle's edition of *A Collection of Favorite Songs, divided into two books containing most of the airs in the Poor Soldier, Rosina etc. and the principal Songs sung at Vaux Hall* (ca. 1789). Published in Philadelphia, the collection includes "I've Kissed and I've Prattled," "The Spring with Smiling Face," "Out of My Sight or I'll Box your Ears," and "Good Morrow to your Night Cap." The arrangements are very simple, many with fingering written in, suggesting that they might have been used for Nelly's first lessons.

Also part of the collection are several four-hand works undoubtedly selected by Reinagle to instruct his young pupil. Among these are duets in A and F, op. 18 (1781) by Johann Christian Bach, and three sonatas for four hands by Ignace Pleyel (1796). As Nelly progressed, she was challenged by an array of composers popular at the time, though largely forgotten today: Johann Vanhal, Johann Sterkel, Leopold Kozeluch, and Theodore Smith. But Nelly's music also indicates that she played keyboard arrangements of the more enduring masterpieces, such as Joseph Haydn's Symphony no. 85 in B-flat, "La reine" (1785), and the overture to Gluck's *Iphigenia at Aulis* (1774).

Among other works in the volumes are patriotic pieces: "Hail Columbia," "La Marseillaise," Sicard's "The President of the United States March," "Adams and Liberty," and Reinagle's "Chorus Sung Before George Washington . . . at Trenton" (1789). There are also arrangements of opera arias by Pergolesi and Cimarosa; sonatas for violin and piano by Nicolai and Maurer; several sets of keyboard variations, and Kotzwara's ubiquitous "Battle of Prague" (1789). And neatly copied in Nelly's own hand are "Hope Told a Flattering Tale," "Hymn of Riego," and Thomas Moore's poem, "I Saw Thy Form in Youthful Prime"—works whose special secrets only Nelly can unlock.

Thomas Jefferson (1801–1809)

Collection: Thomas Jefferson, Martha Randolph, Mary Eppes.
Locations: Alderman Library, University of Virginia
               Monticello, Virginia

Summary:

The large Jefferson collection of several hundred musical pieces belonged to various family members, such as John Wales, Jefferson's father-in-law, Martha Wales Skelton, Jefferson's wife, and Jefferson's three granddaughters, Cornelia, Virginia and Septimia. Works among this vast archive that relate to the White House years, however, belonged either to Jefferson's talented daughters, Martha Randolph and Mary Eppes, both of whom lived in the mansion for a brief period, or to Jefferson himself. But like the musical instruments, the scores that may have been used in the White House during Jefferson's administration remain undocumented and problematic.

Most of the works in the Jefferson family collection were published in London, Paris, or Philadelphia during the middle to late eighteenth century, but often it is impossible to know just who in the family owned or played them. There are a number of works for keyboard, such as *Eight Lessons for the Harpsichord* by Giovanni Battista Pergolesi (London, ca. 1771), and several manuscript music notebooks in Martha's own hand. One is filled with songs ("Crazy Jane," Arne's "A Poor Little Gypsy"); another merely lists various arias, sonatas, rondos, and overtures by Scarlatti, Rameau, Pleyel and others. Martha also sketched in the words to a set of psalms for organ or harpsichord, which includes "St. David's Tune," a favorite of Jefferson. The period she and her sister spent in Paris when Jefferson was minister to France (1785–89) is reflected in selections from operas by Grétry, Piccinni and others, with notes and lyrics throughout in Martha's hand. As for Mary Jefferson's music, a large bound volume with "Miss Jefferson" stamped in gold on the cover contains sonatas and concertos with the inscription "Maria Jefferson."

There are many songs in the Jefferson family collection, most with accompaniments for harp, pianoforte, harpsichord or guitar. Perhaps the most interesting is the score of "Seven Songs" by Francis Hopkinson: both Jefferson and George Washington received copies from Hopkinson in 1788. But more than any genre in the archive, the large amount of instrumental ensemble music appears the most characteristic of Jefferson—works for flute, oboe, violin, cello, harpsichord or pianoforte. Composers represented include Handel, Pergolesi, Abel, Nicolai, Edelman, Johann Christian Bach, Pleyel, Mozart, Schobart, Clementi, Haydn, Kozeluch, and many others. These works, used in conjunction with Jefferson's own Catalogue (in the Massachusetts Historical Society, Boston), enlarge the image of America's third president and that "delightful recreation" that was the "favorite passion" of his soul.

James Madison (1809–1817)

Collection: Dolley Madison
Location: Library of Congress

Summary:

Dolley Madison's purchase of music for the White House is important not only to the mansion's history, but for its interesting contents. A voucher in the National Archives (#29.494, RG 217) indicates that on October 19, 1810, "12 numbers of Madame Le Pelletier's Musical Journal" were delivered to the "President's House." While the actual Madison music was probably destroyed in the 1814 fire, a Library of Congress edition provides details. In this copy the "numbers" are bound into a single volume; on the cover, expertly engraved by Godefroy and Tanner, is the designation: "Journal of Musick, Composed of Italian, French and English Songs, Romances and Duetts, and of Overtures, Rondos, etc. for the Forte Piano, Published by Madame Le Pelletier, Part II, 1810."

Printed by Willig in Philadelphia, the *Journal* was sold by subscription beginning in January 1810. Two "numbers" appeared each month for two years, and each number contained several pieces. Dolley Madison's copies were purchased for $12.00 through Joseph Milligan of Georgetown, who bound and sold books to Thomas Jefferson and gave a "treatise" on gardening to James Madison. As for the intriguing Mme. Le Pelletier, she remains a mystery, but her elegant *Journal* is an important early example of French culture within an American musical life that was predominantly English.

At a time when most American publishers were churning out simple songs on two staves, the *Journal's* airs are on three, with the vocal line on top supported by pianistic accompaniments. Most of the composers are French and include such names as Isouard, Berton, Catel, Méhul, and Boieldieu, with representative arias from their operas virtually unknown in America at this time. Illustrating the rare efforts of a serious woman composer in early America, many of the selections are composed, as well as arranged, by Mme. Pelletier herself. One of the most interesting is her set of variations, "Fantaisie sur un Air Russe, composée pour le Forte Piano et dédiée a Madame Daschkoff née Baronne de Preuzar." The work begins with a long introduction in C major that returns in shortened form at the closing. The simple main theme (Andante) in A minor is cast in a classical two-part, sixteen-measure mold allowing the eight variations to show off tremolo passages, rapid runs, octaves, trills, and other virtuosic embroidery in the style of Dussek or Pleyel.

John Quincy Adams (1825–1829)

Collection: Louisa Catherine Adams
Location: National Museum of American History, Smithsonian Institution

Summary:

A fine selection of the music that Louisa Catherine Adams owned and enjoyed is bound into two large albums, whose covers bear her name tooled in gold. The music is emblematic of the times, with pieces arranged for voice and piano from the operas of Andreozzi, Mayer, Paer, Martini and Guglielmi, composers whose operas Louisa and John Quincy had enjoyed in Europe during their betrothal. Included also in the collection is a copy of Handel's "Angels Ever Bright and Fair" and several arias from Mozart operas barely known in America, such as *The Magic Flute, The Abduction from the Seraglio,* and *The Clemency of Tito.*

But of special interest in this collection is the personal element reflected not only in the music itself, but in the various inscriptions. Who, for example, was the "Mlle Délieu" that had given the first lady several handwritten pieces of music? They bear the note (in French) that they were the "six pieces that she had requested" and she hoped Madame Adams would "sing and enjoy them many times." The songs are by Amadea de Beauplan and France's leading opera composer, Adrien Boieldieu. Délieu's note is signed: "20 Mai, 1824, EBD, Washington."

One interesting piece in the Adams collection bears Louisa's own doleful words to a song penned for her by the little-known Italian composer Carusi

(Gaetano, perhaps?). Called simply "Hymn," it begins: "Lord, listen to my great distress/Oh hear my feckle plaint./Could language all my griefs express/Those words that griefs could paint." The manuscript is dated April 21, 1828, shortly before Louisa's tormented son George Washington Adams committed suicide. Another segment of the collection includes a fine edition of the plaintive songs of Thomas Moore, whose singing had impressed the first lady deeply. Indeed her spirit seemed to share the "language of sorrow" expressed in Moore's songs, that "characteristic wildness and melting pathos of Irish music," as the early American composer James Hewitt once described them. The Adams edition is entitled: *A Selection of Irish Melodies with Symphonies and Accompaniments by Sir John Stevenson, Mus-Doc., and Characteristic words by Thomas Moore, Esq* (published by Blake, Philadelphia, ca. 1808).

Zachary Taylor (1849–1850)

Collection: Zachary Taylor Family
Location: Office of the Curator, The White House

Summary:

It is uncertain whether the three bound albums of music that comprise the Zachary Taylor collection were used in the White House or whether they were merely part of the family's aggregation of music over the years. The collection is from the estate of Betty Bliss Dandridge, Zachary Taylor's youngest daughter. Recent bride of Lt. Colonel William Bliss, Betty Taylor served as White House hostess for her mother, Margaret Smith Taylor, during the family's brief period in the mansion. The pieces date mainly from the White House period or earlier, most from the 1840s—such as Charles Grobe's programmatic memorial to the heroism of the Mexican War, "The Battle of Buena Vista" (Willig, 1847).

     Many of the pieces in this collection are linked to the city of Washington, notably "Washington's Favorite, the brave La Fayette [sic] written by a Gentleman of this city [Washington] to a Favourite Air arranged with a Chorus in three parts and an accompaniment for the piano." The composer's identity is not given, but the piece was published by John Cole of Baltimore in 1824. A rare copy of "French Air" by Nathaniel Carusi indicates that the piece was "Published and sold by Sam Carusi and Brothers, Washington." For a fine overview of dance styles and practices at this time, "Les Elegante Quadrilles" (Baltimore, John Cole) describes in detail the figures and steps at the head of each piece. "The New Vocal Instructor" (Baltimore, 1820) is also a revealing source for performance practice in early America. It contains exercises for improving and modulating the voice, various studies to enhance breathing and pronunciation, and lessons for the "acquirement of Graces, Ornaments and Cadenzas on the established precedent of the First Singers in Europe."

Millard Fillmore (1850–1853)

Collection: Abigail and Mary Abigail Fillmore
Location: Library of Congress

Summary:

The music that the Fillmores owned is bound into five large volumes (nos. 112–115 and 118) with "Mrs. M. Fillmore" or "M. A. Fillmore" (Mary Abigail) tooled in gold on the covers. The pieces date mainly from the 1830s and 1840s and are generally for piano alone or piano and voice. A large percentage of the selections are stamped: "Sold at J. D. Sheppard's Music and Fancy Store, Buffalo"—the city in which the Fillmores lived for many years. One of the volumes contains an index in a child's handwriting with the signature "Abbie Fillmore." Abbie was born in 1832 in Buffalo and undoubtedly studied and played a large quantity of the music, an indication of her talent and motivation. There are also many duets in the collection that Abbie and her mother may have enjoyed together, such as *Firth and Hall's Occasional Selections of Celebrated Duets for Two Performers on One Pianoforte* (New York, n.d.). Significantly, no music appears to have been added to the collection after the deaths of mother and daughter in the early 1850s.

    The five volumes of music in the Fillmore collection offer a fine representation of the tastes of an artistic and educated American family during the mid-nineteenth century. There are the ubiquitous Scotch and Irish airs, operatic transcriptions, patriotic songs, variations, battle pieces, and the popular Henry Russell tunes. But in addition are a number of piano method works, such as J. B. Cramer's sixty-three page "Instructions for the Piano Forte," and a variety of the day's "pop tunes." These include "Buy a Broom," "Comin' Thru' the Rye," "Sitting on a Rail, a Celebrated Comic Extravaganza," and, to captivate a young girl's imagination, "Fanny Grey," a jaunty little piece subtitled "a ballad of real life." Its verses begin: "I saw you making love to her/You see I know it all/I saw you making love to her/At Lady Glossop's ball!"

James Buchanan (1857–1861)

Collection: Harriet Lane
Location: James Buchanan Foundation for the Preservation of Wheatland, Lancaster, Pennsylvania

Summary:

James Buchanan's niece and ward, Harriet Lane, served as White House hostess during the administration of the bachelor president. Her album of music comprises twenty-four selections which reflect not only America's fascination with keyboard arrangements of Italian opera, but the young "first lady's" own abilities as a pianist. There are arrangements from Verdi, Donizetti, Balfe and others, but of special interest are the virtuosic piano pieces composed by famous European concert artists and teachers, such as Theodor Döhler, Henri Herz, Leopold de Meyer, and Franz Hünten. Both Herz and de Meyer were touring America as virtuoso pianists at this time, and their works in the collection were published primarily in Philadelphia, New York, or Cincinnati. Another showpiece for the piano among Miss Lane's music is an edition published in Baltimore by Frederick D. Benteen of Carl Maria von Weber's ever-popular "Invitation to the Dance" composed in 1819. Many of the pieces in the collection, however, date from the presidential period, such as "Beck & Lawton's New and Improved Method for the Piano Forte" (1857) and Eckhard Weber's "Souvenir de Rauschenberg" (1858), both published by Beck & Lawton of Philadelphia.

Benjamin Harrison (1889–1893)

Collection: Caroline Scott Harrison
Location: President Benjamin Harrison Memorial Home, Indianapolis, Indiana

Summary:

In addition to Gottschalk's "Last Hope" mentioned in Chapter Four, the Harrison Home possesses a collection of fifty-six pieces for piano, or voice and piano, bound into two volumes with "Carrie L. Scott" stamped on the covers. The pieces date primarily from the 1840s and 1850s, when Caroline Scott was studying and teaching music. Representative among them are "The Lament of the Irish Immigrant" (Dempster), "Susanna, from Songs of the Sable Harmonists" (Foster), "Empress Henrietta's Waltz" (Herz), "Chasse d'Amour" (Grobe), and various works of Hewitt, Strakosch, Willis, Henry Russell, and others. A few works date from the presidential period and were written for special occasions, such as "Pan-American Congress March" by Bernard Bloss. Secretary of State James Blaine headed the congress in 1889, the year the piece was composed. A similar work is "President's March Through Texas" by Charles Flick, which was composed in 1891, the year Harrison and his family made an official trip through many of the states to the west coast. Mrs. Harrison's name is written on this copy.

CHRONOLOGY OF SELECTED MUSICAL PROGRAMS HELD AT THE WHITE HOUSE FOR VISITING HEADS OF STATE

The practice of holding a short concert or musical program in the East Room after a state dinner honoring a visiting head of state is one of the most important traditions of the White House. Its origins can be traced to the "command performances" of Queen Victoria, who frequently invited famous artists to entertain for her honored guests. Before the age of air travel, visiting heads of state were relatively rare in America. King Kalakaua of Hawaii was the first to come in 1874 under President Grant, but during the Theodore Roosevelt–Hoover era, a period of thirty years, only eighteen heads of state visited the nation. While a foreign head of state was first entertained at the White House with a state dinner/musicale during the administration of Herbert Hoover, not until the Eisenhower administration did this practice become common. When a dinner and musicale took place under President Truman, American (rather than foreign) government leaders, such as the diplomatic corps and cabinet, were honored.

After-dinner musical programs in the East Room traditionally last about one-half hour and are presented by invited artists who usually perform without remuneration. The larger show scenes, such as the dance and musical theater numbers, are often accompanied by members of the US Marine Band. To keep the following chronology from becoming too unwieldy, only about one-half the programs have been included beginning with Eisenhower. The programs were chosen as a reflection of the political/cultural ambience of the various administrations, but they also offer a capsule image of the kaleidoscopic American musical scene during the second half of the twentieth century.

Herbert Hoover (1929–1933)

Apr. 29, 1931	Mildred Dilling, harpist Alexander Kisselburgh, baritone	King Prajadhipok of Siam

Franklin Roosevelt (1933–1945)

May 5, 1939	Enya Gonzales, soprano Stephen Hero, violinist	Pres. Somoza of Nicaragua
June 8, 1939	North Carolina Spiritual Singers Alan Lomax, folk singer Coon Creek Girls Soco Gap Square Dancers Kate Smith Marian Anderson Lawrence Tibbet	King George V and Queen Elizabeth of England

Dwight D. Eisenhower (1953–1961)

Jan. 27, 1954	Frank Guarrera, baritone	Pres. Bayar of Turkey
May 3, 1954	Thomas Redcay USMC, pianist	Gov. Gen. Massey of Canada
May 26, 1954	Patrice Munsel, soprano	Emperor Haile Selassie of Ethiopia
Jan. 26, 1955	Marian Anderson, contralto	Pres. Magloire of Haiti
Jan. 30, 1957	US Air Force Strolling Strings	King Saud of Saudi Arabia
May 8, 1957	Artur Rubinstein, pianist	Pres. Ngo Dinh Diem of Vietnam
Oct. 17, 1957	Fred Waring and the Pennsylvanians	Queen Elizabeth & Prince Philip of Great Britain
Nov. 25, 1957	US Air Force Band and Singing Sergeants	King Mohamed V of Morocco
June 17, 1958	The Sea Chanters and US Navy Band	Pres. Garcia of Philippines
Jan. 20, 1959	Voice of Firestone with Risë Stevens, Brian Sullivan and Oscar Shumsky	Pres. Frondizi of Argentina
Mar. 10, 1959	Paul Whiteman	Pres. Lemus of El Salvador
Mar. 17, 1959	Fred Waring and the Pennsylvanians	Pres. O'Kelly of Ireland
May 11, 1959	Leon Fleisher, pianist	King Baudouin of Belgium
Sept. 15, 1959	Fred Waring and the Pennsylvanians	Premier Khrushchev of The Soviet Union
Oct. 9, 1959	National Symphony Orchestra Howard Mitchell, conductor	Pres. Mateos of Mexico

Oct. 26, 1959	Gregor Piatigorsky, cellist	Pres. Touré of Guinea
Apr. 5, 1960	Leonard Bernstein and members of New York Philharmonic	Pres. Lleras of Columbia
Apr. 27, 1960	National Gallery Orchestra, Richard Bales, conductor	King Mahendra of Nepal
June 28, 1960	Guy Lombardo and his Royal Canadians	King Adulyadej of Thailand
Sept. 27, 1960	An Evening with Gershwin with Camilla Williams, Todd Duncan and Coleman Blumfield	Prime Minister Macmillan of Great Britain
Oct. 11, 1960	Malcolm Frager, pianist	King Frederick of Denmark

John F. Kennedy (1961–1963)

May 3, 1961	US Air Force Bagpipers	Pres. Bourguiba of Tunisia
July 11, 1961	National Symphony Orchestra	Pres. Ayub Khan of Pakistan
Sept. 19, 1961	Roberta Peters, soprano Jerome Hines, bass	Pres. Prado of Peru
Nov. 13, 1961	Pablo Casals, cellist with Mieczyslaw Horszowski, pianist and Alexander Schneider, violinist	Gov. Muñoz-Marín of Puerto Rico
Apr. 11, 1962	Jerome Robbins, Ballets: USA	Shah Reza Pahlevi of Iran
May 11, 1962	Eugene Istomin, pianist Isaac Stern, violinist Leonard Rose, cellist	André Malraux of France (Minister of Culture)
May 22, 1962	American Ballet Theater	Pres. Houphouet-Boigny of Ivory Coast
Mar. 27, 1963	New York City Center Light Opera Company	King Hassan II of Morocco
Apr. 30, 1963	Elizabethan Music and Poetry	Grand Duchess Charlotte of Luxembourg
June 3, 1963	Opera Society of Washington	Pres. Radhakrishnan of India
Oct. 1, 1963	Robert Joffrey Ballet	Emperor Haile Selassie of India
Sept. 5, 1963	US Marine Band and Drum and Bugle Corps US Air Force Bagpipers	King Zahir of Afghanistan

Lyndon Baines Johnson (1963–1969)

Jan. 14, 1964	Robert Merrill, tenor New Christy Minstrels	Pres. Segni of Italy
Apr. 14, 1964	Dave Brubeck Quartet	King Hussein of Jordan
May 27, 1964	Voices of Ireland	Pres. de Valera of Ireland
June 1, 1964	Mischa Elman, violinist Ward Swingle Singers	Prime Min. Eshkol of Israel
June 12, 1964	Maria Tallchief with National Symphony Orchestra	Chancellor Erhard of Germany
July 27, 1964	Scenes from *Oklahoma* with Shirley Jones and Air Force Band	Pres. Tsiranana of Malagasy Republic
Mar. 29, 1965	Indian Tribal Dancers	Pres. Yameogo of Upper Volta
Apr. 20, 1965	Leontyne Price, soprano	Pres. Marco of Italy
May 17, 1965	Walter Trampler, viola	Pres. Chung Hee Park of Korea
Dec. 14, 1965	Westminster Choir	Pres. Kahn of Pakistan
Dec. 20, 1965	American Light Opera Co.	Chan. Erhard of Germany
Feb. 14, 1966	Richard Tucker, tenor Nedda Casei, mezzo- soprano	Emperor Hailie Selassie of Ethiopia
Mar. 28, 1966	Isaac Stern, violinist Alexander Zakin, pianist	Prime Min. Indira Gandhi of India
Aug. 2, 1966	Rudolf Serkin, pianist	Pres. Shazar of Israel
Sept. 14, 1966	New York City Center Light Opera Company	Pres. Marcos of Philippines
Sept. 26, 1966	Washington Classical Symphony	Chan. Erhard of Germany
Feb. 9, 1967	Jose Limon, dancer	King Hassan II of Morocco
Apr. 3, 1967	Opera Company of Boston	Pres. Sunay of Turkey
June 1–2, 1967	Manhattan School of Music	Prime Min. Wilson of Great Britain
June 27, 1967	North Texas State University Lab Jazz Band	King Bhumibol Adulyadej of Thailand
Aug. 15, 1967	National Gallery Orchestra	Chan. Kiesinger of Germany
Nov. 14, 1967	Tony Bennett, singer	Prime Min. Sato of Japan
Apr. 10, 1968	Van Cliburn, pianist	Chancellor Klaus of Austria
Apr. 25, 1968	Joffrey Ballet	King Olav V of Norway

May 27, 1968	American Ballet Theater	Prime Min. Gorton of Australia
Oct. 2, 1968	Robert Goulet, singer	Pres. Tombalbaye of Chad
Oct. 9, 1968	Martha Graham Dance Company	Prime Min. Marshall of New Zealand

Richard Nixon (1969–1974)

May 6, 1969	Zara Nelsova, cellist Grant Johannesen, pianist	Prime Min. Gorton of Australia
July 8, 1969	Eugene List, pianist	Pres. Selassie of Ivory Coast
Aug. 7, 1969	Kyung-Wha Chung, violinist	Chan. Kiesinger of Germany
Sept. 25, 1969	Isaac Stern, violinist Leonard Bernstein, pianist	Prime Min. Golda Meir of Israel
Oct. 21, 1969	Modern Jazz Quartet	Shah Reza Pahlevi of Iran
Feb. 22, 1970	Peggy Lee	Pres. Pompidou of France
April 10, 1970	Pearl Bailey	Chan. Brandt of Germany
Aug. 4, 1970	André Watts, pianist	Pres. Mobutu of Republic of the Congo
Oct. 26, 1970	Anna Moffo, soprano	Pres. Ceausescu of Romania
Nov. 2, 1971	Richard Tucker, tenor	Prime Min. McMahon of Australia
Nov. 4, 1971	Patricia McBride, dancer Edward Villella, dancer	Prime Min. Indira Gandhi
Apr. 17, 1973	Frank Sinatra	Prime Min. Andreotti of Italy
May 3, 1973	Van Cliburn, pianist	Prime Min. Golda Meir of Israel
Oct. 9, 1973	Billy Taylor, pianist	Pres. Houphouet-Boigny of Ivory Coast

Gerald Ford (1974–1977)

Sept. 12, 1974	Eugene Fodor, pianist	Prime Min. Rabin of Israel
Sept. 25, 1974	New England Conservatory Ragtime Ensemble	Pres. Leone of Italy
Jan. 30, 1975	Beverly Sills, soprano	Prime Min. Wilson of Great Britain
Feb. 5, 1975	Billy Taylor	Prime Min. Bhutto of Pakistan

May 8, 1975	Edward Villella and Violet Verdy	Prime Min. Lee Kuan Yew of Singapore
May 15, 1975	Ann-Margret	Shah Reza Pahlevi of Iran
June 16, 1975	Tennessee Ernie Ford	Pres. Scheel of Germany
Sept. 25, 1975	Roberta Peters, soprano	Pres. Lopez of Columbia
Oct. 2, 1975	Van Cliburn, pianist	Emperor Hirohito of Japan
Jan. 27, 1976	Carol Burnett and Helen Reddy	Prime Min. Rabin of Israel
Mar. 30, 1976	Charlie Byrd	King Hussein of Jordan
May 17, 1976	Earl Hines	Pres. d'Estaing of France
July 7, 1976	Bob Hope and The Captain and Tennille	Queen Elizabeth of England
July 27, 1976	Sherrill Milnes, baritone	Prime Min. Fraser of Australia

James Earl Carter (1977–1981)

Feb. 14, 1977	Rudolph Serkin, pianist	Pres. Portillo of Mexico
June 28, 1977	Cynthia Gregory and Ted Kivitt, dancers	Pres. Perez of Venezuela
July 26, 1977	Shirley Verrett, soprano	Pres. Andreotti of Italy
Nov. 15, 1977	Sarah Vaughn, Dizzy Gillespie, and Earl Hines	Shah Reza Pahlevi of Iran
Mar. 7, 1978	The Romeros, classical guitarists	Pres. Tito of Yugoslavia
Apr. 12, 1978	George Shearing, pianist Clamma Dale, soprano	Pres. Ceausescu of Romania
Nov. 14, 1978	Alvin Ailey Dancers	King of Morocco
Feb. 6, 1979	American Dance Machine	Prime Min. Chomanan of Thailand
Dec. 17, 1979	Opera Company of Boston soloists	Prime Min. Thatcher of Great Britain
Jan. 24, 1980	Tom Hall, country singer	Prime Min. Cossiga of Italy
Feb. 4, 1980	Jerome Robbins and cast of 44	Queen Sirikit of Thailand
June 17, 1980	André Watts, pianist	King Hussein of Jordan

Ronald Reagan (1981–1989)

Feb. 26, 1981	Dance Theater of Harlem	Prime Min. Thatcher of Great Britain
Sept. 9, 1981	André-Michel Schub, pianist	Prime Min. Begin of Israel
Nov. 2, 1981	Benny Goodman	King Hussein of Jordan

Feb. 3, 1982	Itzhak Perlman, violinist	Pres. Mubarak of Egypt
Mar. 25, 1982	Perry Como, Frank Sinatra	Pres. Pertini of Italy
Apr. 19, 1982	George Shearing	Queen Claus of the Netherlands
July 29, 1982	New York Philharmonic, Zubin Mehta, cond.	Prime Min. Indira Gandhi of India
Nov. 15, 1982	Peter Nero, pianist	Chancellor Kohl of Germany
Dec. 7, 1982	Eugenia Zuckerman, flute Pinchas Zukerman, violin	Pres. Zia-ul-Haq of Pakistan
Apr. 12, 1983	Anna Moffo, soprano	Sultan of Oman
June 7, 1983	Chamber Music Society of Lincoln Center	Pres. Houphouet-Boigny of Ivory Coast
July 19, 1983	Byron Janis, pianist	Amir of Bahrain
Oct. 4, 1983	Sherrill Milnes, baritone	Pres. Carstens of Germany
Feb. 11, 1985	Montserrat Caballé, soprano	King Fahd of Saudi Arabia
Apr. 17, 1985	Marianna Tcherkassky and Fernando Bujones, dancers	Pres. Bendjedid of Algeria
June 12, 1985	Mstislav Rostropovich, cellist	Prime Min. Rajiv Gandhi of India
Jan. 14, 1986	Jessye Norman, soprano	Pres. Febres-Cordero of Ecuador
Mar. 18, 1986	Rosalyn Tureck, pianist	Prime Min. Mulroney of Canada
July 16, 1986	Eugene Fodor, violinist	Prime Min. Junejo of Pakistan
Apr. 30, 1987	Johnny Mathis, singer	Prime Min. Nakasone of Japan
Sept. 9, 1987	Marilyn Horne, soprano	Prime Min. Carlsson of Sweden
Oct. 14, 1987	Lionel Hampton, vibraphonist	Pres. Duarte of El Salvador
June 27, 1988	Christopher Parkening, guitarist	Pres. Evren of Turkey
Nov. 16, 1988	Michael Feinstein, pianist/ singer	Prime Min. Thatcher of Great Britain

George Bush (1989–)

Apr. 4, 1989	Maureen McGovern, singer	Pres. Mubarak of Egypt
Apr. 19, 1989	Mstislav Rostropovich, cellist	King Hussein of Jordan

June 6, 1989	Itzhak Perlman, violinist	Prime Min. Bhutto of Pakistan
June 27, 1989	Leontyne Price, soprano	Prime Min. Hawke of Australia
Oct. 11, 1989	Isaac Stern, violinist	Pres. Cossiga of Italy
Jan. 24, 1990	Alessandra Marc, singer	Pres. Salih of North Yemen
Feb. 12, 1990	Peter Nero, pianist	Pres. Sassou-Nguesso of People's Republic of the Congo
Mar. 6, 1990	Roberta Peters, soprano	Prime Min. Andreotti of Italy
May 15, 1990	Harry Connick, Jr., singer	Pres. Ben Ali of Tunisia
June 1, 1990	Frederica von Stade, soprano	Pres. Gorbachev of the Soviet Union
Oct. 18, 1990	Van Cliburn, pianist	Prime Min. Antall of Hungary
Feb. 20, 1991	Frederica von Stade, soprano	Queen Margrethe II of Denmark
Apr. 17, 1991	Johnny Mathis, singer	Pres. Chamorro of Nicaragua
May 14, 1991	Jessye Norman, soprano	Queen Elizabeth II of England
June 19, 1991	Gloria Estefan, singer	Pres. Collor de Mello of Brazil
July 2, 1991	Teri Bibb and Keith Buterbaugh from *Phantom of the Opera*	Pres. Roh Tae Woo of Korea
Sept. 10, 1991	Harlem Boys Choir	Pres. Diouf of Senegal
Sept. 26, 1991	Roberta Peters, soprano	King Hassan II of Morocco

APPENDIX C

DIRECTORS OF THE UNITED STATES MARINE BAND

William Farr .... January 21, 1799 to November 22, 1804
Charles S. Ashworth .... November 24, 1804 to October 16, 1816
Venerando Pulizzi .... October 17, 1816 to December 9, 1816
John Powley .... December 10, 1816 to February 18, 1818
Vererando Pulizzi .... February 19, 1818 to September 3, 1827
John B. Cuvillier .... September 3, 1827 to June 16, 1829
Joseph Cuvillier .... June 16, 1829 to February 25, 1835
Francis Schenig .... February 26, 1835 to December 9, 1836
Raphael R. Triay .... December 10, 1836 to May 22, 1843
Antonio Pons .... May 22, 1843 to May 1, 1844
Joseph Lucchesi .... May 1, 1844 to July 31, 1846
Raphael R. Triay .... July 8, 1848 to September 9, 1855
Francis Scala .... September 9, 1855 to December 13, 1871
Henry Fries .... December 14, 1871 to August 27, 1873
Louis Schneider .... September 2, 1873 to October 1, 1880
John Philip Sousa .... October 1, 1880 to July 30, 1892
Francesco Fanciulli .... November 1, 1892 to October 31, 1897
William H. Santelmann .... March 3, 1898 to May 1, 1927
Taylor Branson .... May 2, 1927 to April 1, 1940
William F. Santelmann .... April 3, 1940 to April 30, 1955
Albert F. Schoepper .... May 1, 1955 to April 28, 1972
Dale Harpham .... April 28, 1972 to October 31, 1974
Jack T. Kline .... November 1, 1974 to May 31, 1979
John R. Bourgeois .... May 31, 1979 to present

NOTES

List of abbreviations used in notes

DDEL	Dwight D. Eisenhower Library, Abilene, Kansas
Eisenhower Papers	Dwight D. Eisenhower Papers, DDEL
ER Papers	Eleanor Roosevelt Papers, FDRL
FDR Papers	Franklin D. Roosevelt Papers, FDRL
FDRL	Franklin D. Roosevelt Library, Hyde Park, New York
GRDN	General Records of the Department of the Navy, NARS
HHPL	Herbert Hoover Presidential Library, West Branch, Iowa
HSTL	Harry S Truman Library, Independence, Missouri
JFKL	John F. Kennedy Library, Boston, Massachusetts
Johnson Papers	Lyndon B. Johnson Papers, LBJL
Kennedy Papers	John F. Kennedy Papers, JFKL
Lady Bird Johnson Papers	LBJL
LBJL	Lyndon Baines Johnson Library, Austin, Texas
LC	Library of Congress, Washington, D.C.
MBL	Marine Band Library, U.S. Marine Barracks, Washington, D.C.
MCHC	Marine Corps Historical Center, Navy Yard, Washington, D.C.
MLKL	Martin Luther King Memorial Library, Washington, D.C.
MTA	Miscellaneous Treasury Accounts of the President's House, NARS
NARS	National Archives and Records Services, Washington, D.C.
NMAH, SI	National Museum of American History, Smithsonian Institution, Washington, D.C.
OPB&G	Office of Public Building and Grounds, NARS
OWHC	Office of the White House Curator, The White House, Washington, D.C.
OWHSF	Official White House Social Functions, NARS
RHPC	Rutherford B. Hayes Presidential Center, Fremont, Ohio
Truman Papers	Harry S. Truman Papers, HSTL
WHCF	White House Central Files, LBJL

Chapter 1. Musical Life in the President's House

1. Rufus Wilmot Griswold, *The Republican Court* (New York: Appleton, 1855), 313–14. George Washington Parke Custis, recalling his sister practicing "under the immediate eye of her grandmother," noted, "The poor girl would play and cry, and cry and play" (George Washington Parke Custis, *Recollections and Private Memoirs of Washington* [New York, 1860], 408*n*). For more on the musical life of the Washingtons, see Nicholas E. Tawa, "Music in the Washington Household," *Journal of American Culture* 1 (Spring 1978):21–43.

2. Martha Parke Custis had two children by a previous marriage: John Parke Custis (Jacky) and Martha Parke Custis (Patsy), who died in her teens before Washington became president. John was killed during the Revolution, leaving four children, two of whom President and Mrs. Washington raised (Nelly and Tub). George Washington never had children of his own.

3. Eleanor Parke Custis to Elizabeth Bordley, May 30 [1797], Mt. Vernon Archives, Mt. Vernon, Va.

4. Washington to Francis Hopkinson, Feb. 5, 1789, in John C. Fitzpatrick, ed., *The Writings of George Washington* . . . (Washington, D.C.: Government Printing Office, 1944), 30:196–97. For more on the Hopkinson songs, see Charles Hamm, *Yesterdays: Popular Song in America* (New York: W. W. Norton, 1979), 89–93.

5. "Invoice of Goods . . . ," July 20, 1767, in Fitzpatrick, ed., *Writings of Washington*, 2:463.

6. "Invoice of Sundrys . . . ," Oct. 12, 1761, ibid., 370.

7. Stephen Decatur, Jr., *Private Affairs of George Washington from the Records and Accounts of Tobias Lear, Esquire, His Secretary* (Boston: Houghton Mifflin, 1933), 33–34.

8. Decatur, *Private Affairs*, 35.

9. Arthur Loesser, *Men, Women and Pianos: A Social History* (New York: Simon and Schuster, 1954), 244.

10. Abigail Smith Adams, *Letters of Mrs. Adams, the Wife of John Adams*, introduction by Charles Francis Adams (Boston: Little, Brown 1840), 1:133. On Aug. 27, 1785, Abigail wrote to her sister from London that her favorite Scotch song was "There'e nae Luck about the House." Various arrangements of the song were published between 1812–24 in Baltimore, Philadelphia, and New York. See Richard J. Wolfe, *Secular Music in America 1801–1825*, 2 (New York: New York Public Library, 1964).

11. Adams, *Letters*, 432–35.

12. Page Smith, *John Adams* (New York: Doubleday, 1962), 1 (*1735–1784*): 685. John Quincy Adams was minister to Berlin at this time. Besides Charles and John Quincy, John and Abigail's children were Susanna, Abigail, and Thomas Boylston. For more on the history of the remarkable Adams family, see Jack Shepherd, *The Adams Chronicles: Four Generations of Greatness* (Boston: Little, Brown, 1975). Some authors, such as Gilson Willets and Marie Smith, claim that Abigail Adams brought to the President's Mansion her piano, harp, and guitar. They probably confused this first lady with Abigail Fillmore, whose daughter Mary Abigail played these instruments in the White House (see ch. 2, herein).

13. "Marine Band Chronology," compilation of clippings and reports from various government documents, July 11, 1798, to Mar. 8, 1954, 121 pp., typescript, MBL.

14. Handwritten list dated 1804 in files of Marine Band, MCHC; *National Intelligencer*, Sept. 25, 1805.

15. Shepherd, *Adams Chronicles*, xxiii.

16. Oscar Sonneck, "The Musical Side of Our First Presidents," in *Suum Cuique Essays in Music* (Freeport, NY: Books for Libraries Press, 1969), 37, reprinted from *New Music Review*, 1907.

17. L. H. Butterfield, ed., *Diary and Autobiography of John Adams* (Cambridge, Mass.: Harvard University Press, 1961) 4:104. See also H. Earl Johnson, "The Adams

Family and Good Listening," *Journal of the American Musicological Society* 11 (Summer-Fall 1958).

18. Adams, *Letters*, 82.

19. Ibid. Two days after the performance, *Porcupines Gazette* announced the publication, at Carr's Musical Repository, of "the very favourite New Federal Song." The first issue of the song bore the image of President John Adams neatly trimmed and pasted on the music above the words "Behold the Chief who now commands!" When Washington was appointed commander in chief of the American forces, on July 3, 1798, Carr substituted a portrait of Washington for Adams. See Oscar Sonneck, "The First Edition of Hail Columbia," *Miscellaneous Studies in the History of Music* (New York: AMS Press, 1970), 180–89; and Wendy C. Wick, *George Washington, an American Icon: The Eighteenth-Century Graphic Portraits* (Washington, D.C.: Barra Foundation, 1982), 125–27.

20. While Paine's verses are forgotten today, those of Francis Scott Key live on. Key's text, also set to the Anacreon tune, was written in 1814 after the bombardment of Fort McHenry by the British and published the same year as "The Star-Spangled Banner." It was not until 1931, however, that it was established as our national anthem (see ch. 5, herein). The earliest setting of the Anacreon tune is listed in Harry Dichter and Elliott Shapiro, *Handbook of Early American Sheet Music, 1768–1889* (New York: Dover, 1977), 35, as "'Freedom Triumphant,' B. Carr, NY & Phila. [1796]." For more on the origins of "The Star-Spangled Banner," see William Lichtenwanger, "The Music of the Star-Spangled Banner: From Ludgate Hill to Capitol Hill," *Quarterly Journal of the Library of Congress*, July 1977.

21. Charles William Janson, *The Stranger in America, 1793–1806* (New York: Press of the Pioneers, 1935), 213. Reprinted from the London edition of 1807.

22. John C. Haskins, "Music in the District of Columbia, 1800 to 1814" (M.A. thesis, Catholic University of America, 1952), 19.

23. Jefferson to Nathaniel Burwell, Mar. 14, 1818, in Andrew A. Lipscomb and Albert Ellery Bergh, eds., *The Writings of Thomas Jefferson* (Washington, D.C.: Government Printing Office, 1903–4), 15:135.

24. Jefferson's catalogue, the property of the Massachusetts Historical Society, Boston, is reprinted in Helen Cripe, *Thomas Jefferson and Music* (Charlottesville: University Press of Virginia, 1974), appendix I, 97–104.

25. Ibid., 114.

26. Thomas Jefferson to Martha Jefferson, Mar. 28, 1787, quoted in ibid., 30.

27. Esther Singleton, *The Story of the White House* (New York: McClure, 1907), I:25.

28. Mrs. Samuel Harrison Smith (Margaret Bayard), *The First Forty Years of Washington Society*, ed. Gaillard Hunt (New York: Scribner's, 1906), 399.

29. Ibid., 30.

30. *National Intelligencer*, July 5, 1801. Tingey's fine singing is mentioned in various other sources. Margaret Bayard Smith held a private gathering earlier in the year and recalled: "Captain T. [Tingey] sings a good song, his wife and two daughters accompany him . . . these songs very agreeably supplied the place of conversation" (Smith, *First Forty Years*, 18). As the British were entering Washington on Aug. 24, 1814, Tingey ordered the Navy Yard to be burned before evacuating it.

31. Jefferson to Fabbroni, June 8, 1778, in Julian P. Boyd et al., eds. *The Papers of Thomas Jefferson* (Princeton, N.J.: Princeton University Press, 1950–), 2:196.

32. Remarks of Hon. Fiorello H. LaGuardia, House of Representatives, *Congressional Record*, 71st Cong., 2d sess., Jan. 29, 1930. Mazzei and a group of Tuscan farmers had assisted Jefferson with agricultural experiments in Virginia in 1773. Mazzei also helped Jefferson meet the musicians Piccinni and Caravoglia when he arrived in Europe as minister to France.

33. "Narrative of Gaetano Carusi in Support of his Claim Before the Congress of the United States," typescript copy, n.d., 3.

34. Ibid.

35. Ibid., 11–12. See also "Report on the Committee on Naval Affairs," House of Representatives, *Congressional Report*, 24th Cong., 1st sess., Jan. 6, 1836: "Gaetano Carusi," House of Representatives, *Congressional Report*, 29th Cong., 1st sess., June 17, 1846.

36. John Clagett Proctor, "Dancing When the Capital Was Young," *Washington Sunday Star*, Dec. 3, 1933. The entrepreneurial Carusis rented the lower floor of the U.S. Post Office. When the post office moved out leaving the place in a shambles, the Carusis again sued the government. In the mid-1850s Samuel Carusi became a founder of the short-lived Washington Philharmonic Society. Gaetano's modern-day descendent, Eugene C. Carusi, became a prominent Washington lawyer, and his wife a patron of the John F. Kennedy Center for the Performing Arts.

37. "It is usual for him to have a dozen or 15 persons to dine every day." Catherine Mitchell to Margaret Miller, Apr. 8, 1806, Mitchell Papers, LC.

38. Nathan Schachner, *Thomas Jefferson: A Biography* (New York: Appleton-Century-Crofts, 1951), 2:68.

39. Cripe, *Jefferson and Music*, 89–90.

40. Claxton to Jefferson, June 13, 1800, Jefferson to Claxton, June 18, 1800, quoted in ibid., 42 (original letters in Massachusetts Historical Society). There is no musical instrument listed in Jefferson's inventory of government purchases for the White House compiled in 1809. The inventory is printed in Marie Kimball, "The Original Furnishings of the White House," Pt. I, *Magazine Antiques*, June 1929.

41. Cripe, *Jefferson and Music*, 129. The question of Jefferson's violins is discussed in appendix III and on 43–47.

42. The music stand now at Monticello is revolving and has five adjustable music rests. It accommodates four seated players and one standing. In a bound volume of manuscript music at Charlottesville is a copy of "Variations on the Sicilian Hymn, 'Life Let Us Cherish.'"

43. Jefferson to Martha Jefferson Randolph, Apr. 4, 1790, in Edwin Betts and James Bear, eds., *The Family Letters of Thomas Jefferson* (Columbia: University of Missouri Press, 1966), 51.

44. Dolley Madison remained a beloved social figure in the capital for many years after she left the White House. She died at eighty-one almost a pauper. She and James Monroe were childless. See Conover Hunt Jones, *Dolley and the "Great Little Madison"* (Washington, D.C.: American Institute of Architects Foundation, 1977), and Katherine Anthony, *Dolly Madison: Her Life and Times* (Garden City, N.Y.: Doubleday, 1949).

45. Catherine Mitchell to Margaret Miller, Jan. 2, 1811, Mitchell Papers, LC.

46. "Social Life in Washington during Mr. Madison's Presidency," *National Intelligencer*, Mar. 11, 1871. Mrs. William Seaton was the wife of the owner and manager of the *National Intelligencer*. Her memory of Mrs. Madison's first reception in the winter of 1812–13 is reprinted in this issue.

47. Latrobe to Dolley Madison, Mar. 17, 1809, in Edward C. Carter II, ed., *The Papers of Benjamin Henry Latrobe*, microfiche edition, 2 vols. (Clifton, N.J.: James T. White, 1976), fiche no. 198, row B, col. 10. Andrew Hazelhurst was the brother of Latrobe's wife, Mary. His father, Isaac Hazelhurst, ran a highly prosperous import/export business in Philadelphia. Correspondence from Latrobe to Dolley Madison, Mar. 22, 1809, indicates that Mary selected a guitar for Mrs. Madison in Philadelphia.

48. The piano was tuned shortly before the great fire, as the following voucher indicates.

Mrs. Madison for the President's House to F. A. Wagler

1814 Jan 8 to tuning grand piano	$2.00
regulating hammers	.37 1/2
1 broken string in the bass	.50
Aug 5, 1814 Rec. the above	$2.87 1/2

Account #29.494, Record Group 217, MTA, NARS.

49. United States for the President's House bot of Joseph Milligen [*sic*]
12 numbers of Madame Le Pelletier's Musical Journal $12
Delivered Oct. 19, 1810
Rec. payment Oct. 4, 1813
Account #29.494, Record Group 217.

50. Jones, *Dolley*, 43.

51. Account #37.131, May 8, 1818, Record Group 217. Writing to James Monroe from Le Havre on Sept. 15, 1817, Russell and Le Farge advises: "Being obliged to take piano of Erard, we could not get any other ready made but the one sent. He allowed us a very large discount on account of the many purchases we have made of him."

52. *National Intelligencer*, Mar. 26, 1819.

53. Allan Nevins, ed., *The Diary of John Quincy Adams, 1794–1855* (New York: Ungar, 1951), Nov. 7, 1830.

54. *Memoirs of John Quincy Adams* (New York, 1874), I:98–99, quoted in Johnson, "Adams Family," 172.

55. The diaries of John Quincy Adams are part of the Adams Family Papers, the property of the Massachusetts Historical Society. Hundreds of Louisa Catherine Adams's letters and other writings are part of this collection and are available on microfilm. Reels 264–69 contain her poems and a play, "Records of a Life, or My Story," 1825; "Adventures of a Nobody," begun 1840; and other autobiographical writings.

56. Joan Challinor, "Louisa Catherine Johnson Adams: The Price of Ambition" (Ph.D. diss., American University, 1982), 211.

57. Ibid., 589.

58. Margaret Bayard Smith, quoted in Anne Hollingsworth Wharton, "Social Life at the White House," *The Era*, July 1902, 85.

59. "March and Chorus in the Dramatic Romance of the Lady of the Lake, composed by Mr. Sanderson" (Philadelphia: G. E. Black, ca. 1812), LC. See also "Origins of Hail to the Chief," 1 page, typescript, Division of Political History, NMAH, SI.

60. "Oh! Say Not Woman's Heart Is Bought. A Favorite Ballad as sung with the greatest applause by Mrs. French, composed by John Whitaker" (Philadelphia: G. E. Blake) in Mrs. Adams's albums of music, property of Division of Political History, NMAH, SI. The larger album contains mainly published works (many by Americans, including Carr, Willig, and Blake); the smaller consists of handscribed pieces.

61. Margaret Brown Klapthor, *Official White House China 1789 to the Present* (Washington, D.C.: Smithsonian Institution Press, 1975), 49.

62. Spillane, *History of the American Pianoforte*, 84–86. The Babcock piano is a gift to the Smithsonian from the Juilliard School of Music. Association between the Mackay and Adams families goes back as far as Mungo Mackay's contacts with John Adams in 1798. See Dan Berwin Brockman, "Mackay-Hunt Family History," Cohasset, Mass., 1983, typescript, NMAH, SI. In the Smithsonian's Adams-Clement Collection is also a hymnal, *The Christian Psalter*, that contains several metrical versions of the psalms written by John Quincy Adams.

Chapter 2. Politics, Protest, and the Changing American Culture

1. *National Intelligencer*, Mar. 4, 1829. James Monroe was the first president to be honored with an inaugural concert (*National Intelligencer*, Mar. 4, 1817). See also Elise K. Kirk, "Celebrating the Presidency: The Inaugural Concert in the Nineteenth Century," in *Performing Arts Annual* (Washington, D.C.: Library of Congress, 1986).

2. Singleton, *Story of the White House* 1:198–99.

3. July 4, 1829, in "Marine Band Chronology," MBL.

4. Account #61.369, Record Group 217, MTA, NARS. See also "Furniture of the President's House," House of Representatives, *Congressional Report*, 27th Cong. 2d sess., Apr. 1, 1842. In this report is also listed: "1 music stool for circular room, first story."

5. Account #61.369, Record Group 217, MTA, NARS. Sorting out the pianos from government vouchers and records of this period is a complicated and often frustrating process. A "small pianof." was tuned for $1 on this same date, and on Dec. 12, 1829, "6 new mahogany feet, one pedal and other repairs and tuning" were provided by Jacob Hilbus for $18 (perhaps for Louisa Adams's Babcock if it had been a government purchase?). President Jackson also had a "grand piano" ("grand" in this case meaning "elegant") delivered on Sept. 9, 1833, and on Oct. 5, he sent it back to Professor Wagler. There is no indication as to whether this was rented, or bought and returned (voucher 17, #70.467, Record Group 217).

6. Lillian Moore, *Images of the Dance: Historical Treasures of the Dance Collection, 1581–1861* (New York: New York Public Library, 1965), 51.

7. Ivor Forbes Guest, *Fanny Elssler* (London: Adam & Black, 1970), 136–38.

8. "Speech of Mr. Ogle of Pennsylvania on The Regal Splendor of the President's Palace," delivered in the House of Representatives, Apr. 14, 1840, 12, 13, Rare Book Collection, LC. On May 31, 1839, the White House paid $1 "for varnishing one piano" ("Furniture," House Report 27/2, Apr. 1, 1842).

9. Benjamin Perley Poore, *Perley's Reminiscences of Sixty Years in the National Metropolis* (Philadelphia: Hubbard Bros., 1886), 1:229.

10. Arrangements of "Hail to the Chief" and "Wha'll be King but Charlie" appear with "The Blue Bells of Montrose" in a small book of piano pieces in the Scala Collection, LC. Francis Scala joined the Marine Band in 1842, but some of the pieces from the earlier years of the band may have made their way into his collection. See David M. Ingals, "Francis Scala: Leader of the Marine Band from 1855 to 1871" (Ph.D. diss., Catholic University of America, 1957).

11. "When Tyler Ruled: Recollections of White House Life in the Forties—Told by His Daughter," *Washington Evening Star*, June 10, 1893. Letitia Tyler Semple served briefly as first lady before the president remarried.

12. Mary Ormsbee Whitton, *First First Ladies* (New York: Hastings House, 1948), 193; Laura C. Holloway, *The Ladies of the White House* (Philadelphia: Brailey & Co., 1881), 395; "Recollections of Scala," *Morning Times*, Jan. 19, 1896, Scala Collection, LC.

13. Voucher 1, account #87.086, Record Group 217, MTA, NARS. The term "concert piano" probably implied a large square at this time. The term "double grand action" undoubtedly means double escapement. The voucher also described the piano's "Metallic plate," a metal hitchpin plate, and its "Tablet front" in which the keyboard was flanked by rectangular recessed vertical panels (tablets) that were placed slightly forward of the fronts of the keys.

14. John Tasker Howard, *Our American Music* (New York: Crowell, 1946), 231–232.

15. Carol Ryrie Brink, *Harps in the Wind: The Story of the Singing Hutchinsons* (New York: Macmillan, 1947), 82.

16. Mrs. Polk's Astor and Harewood square pianoforte (9 Cornhill Rd., London) and her music book are the property of the James K. Polk Home, Columbia, Tenn.

17. Milo Milton Quaife, ed., *The Diary of James K. Polk during His Presidency, 1845 to 1849* (Chicago: McClurg, 1910), 1:366–67.

18. Scala, "Recollections."

19. Holman Hamilton, *Zachary Taylor: Soldier in the White House* (Hamden, Conn: Archon Books, 1966), 223.

20. Quoted in Samuel Eliot Morison, *The Oxford History of the American People* (New York: Oxford University Press, 1965), 516.

21. Ibid., 574.

22. Sept. 9, 1850, in Allan Nevins and Milton Halsey Thomas, eds., *The Diary of George Templeton Strong* (New York: Octagon Books, 1974), 2:18.

23. Jenny Lind, concert program, Dec. 18, 1850, given at National Hall, Washington, D.C.; a copy of the program is in the Library of Congress.

24. Charles G. Rosenberg, *Jenny Lind in America* (New York: Stringer and Townsend, 1851), 88.

25. Margaret Brown Klapthor, *The First Ladies* (Washington, D.C.: White House Historical Association, 1975), 35.

26. Christine Saddler, *Children of the White House* (New York: Putnam, 1969), 135.

27. Voucher 8, account #107.778, Record Group 217, MTA, NARS.

28. Voucher 27, account #109.073, ibid.

29. Singleton, *Story of the White House*, 2:53–54.

30. "The Blind Boy Pianist," *Dwight's Journal of Music*, Sept. 17, 22, 1860; *The Albany Argus*, Jan. 1866, in "Thomas Greene Bethune (1849–1908)," *Black Perspective in Music* 3 (1975).

31. Eileen Southern, *Music of Black Americans* (New York: W. W. Norton, 1971), 252; Richard Badolph, *The New Vanguard* (New York: Vintage Books, 1959), 121.

32. Geneva Southall, "Blind Tom: A Misrepresented and Neglected Composer-Pianist," *Black Perspective in Music* 3 (1975). Southall discusses Blind Tom's compositions and musical style (partly deriving from Chopin and Field) and includes musical examples.

33. Ibid. Today Tom would probably be analyzed as an idiot savant, a mentally defective person with rare gifts in a special field.

34. Blake to Chickering, June 22, 1857, Chickering to Blake, June 27, 1857, Blake to Chickering, July 3, 1857, Letters Sent/Received, Record Group 42, OPB&G, NARS. A Chickering grand piano stands today at Buchanan's Wheatland home in Lancaster, Pa.: however, it is believed to have been purchased by Buchanan in 1865 after he left office.

35. Alistair Cooke, *Alistair Cooke's America* (New York: Knopf, 1977), 200.

36. From Lincoln's campaign speech, June 16, 1858, quoted in Morison, *Oxford History of the American People*, 595.

37. James P. Shenton, preface to William Barney, *Flawed Victory: A New Perspective on the Civil War* (New York: Praeger, 1975), vii. Shenton observed that Americans had inflicted upon one another more casualties than had ever been sustained in a previous, or subsequent, foreign war.

38. Kenneth A. Bernard, *Lincoln and the Music of the Civil War* (Caldwell, Idaho: Caxton Printers, 1966), 312–13.

39. John Lair, *Songs Lincoln Loved* (New York: Duell, Sloan and Pearce, 1954), ix. See also Philip D. Jordan, "Some Lincoln and Civil War Songs," *Abraham Lincoln Quarterly*, Sept. 1942.

40. Kenneth A. Bernard, *Abraham Lincoln: The Song in His Heart* (Worchester, Mass.: Achille J. St. Onge, 1970), 49–51. In the Scala Collection are copies for band of "Annie Laurie, as sung in the opera *La dame blanche*. Arr. by P. K. Moran"; "Kathleen Mavourneen" by Frederick Crouch; and "Mary of Argyle," composer unknown. The last two are arranged by Scala as quicksteps. Other songs especially enjoyed by Lincoln were "The Doxology," Newman's "Lead, Kindly Light," Foster's "Gentle Annie," Dempster's "The Lament of the Irish Immigrant," Hewitt's "Rock Me to Sleep, Mother," Willing's "Twenty Years Ago," Bishop's "Home, Sweet Home," and Hopkins's "Silver Bell Waltz." See Lair, *Songs Lincoln Loved*, and Bernard, *Abraham Lincoln*.

41. Lincoln was known to have heard *Faust* three times while he was president. He appeared at the opera twice during the one-week opera season in Washington in April 1863, and in the hectic month of March 1865 he heard three operas the last two days before his departure for City Point (Bernard, *Abraham Lincoln*, 36–39).

42. *New York Herald*, Apr. 23, 1863.

43. Washington *Daily Morning Chronicle*, Mar. 24, 25, 1864; *National Intelligencer*, Mar. 24, 1864.

44. Irving Lowens, "Louis Moreau Gottschalk," *New Grove*, 6th ed., 7:570–74.

45. W. S. Wood, commissioner of Public Buildings and Grounds, to Henry W. Gray, Esq., June 21, 1861, Letters Sent, Record Group 42, OPB&G, NARS. Another letter (in the Chicago Historical Society) from Stanley McClure to Paul Angle, director, Oct. 1, 1948, indicates that the piano (#1900) was delivered to the White House sometime after June 21, 1861, by the firm of William H. Carryl and Bros., 719 Chestnut Street, Philadelphia. This piano stands in the Chicago Historical Society today.

46. *Philadelphia Press*, Sept. 27, 1865; *National Intelligencer*, Oct. 6, 1862.

47. Bernard, *Lincoln and the Music of the Civil War*, 36.

48. Ibid., 16–17.

49. *National Republican*, Oct. 17, 1862; Bernard, *Lincoln and the Music of the Civil War*, 114–15; *History of Commodore Nutt, Now Exhibiting at Barnum's Museum, New York* (pamphlet, 1862), Hoblitzelle Theater Arts Library, Austin, Tex.; C. Percy Powell, ed., *Lincoln Day by Day* (Washington: Lincoln Sesquicentennial Commission, 1960), 3:145. The Lincolns also entertained General and Mrs. Tom Thumb at the White House reception in Feb. 1863.

50. "Living Stage Folk Who Knew and Cheered Lincolns," *Montgomery Advertiser*, Feb. 12, 1911. See also M. Milinowski, *Teresa Carreño* (New Haven, Conn.: Yale University Press, 1940), 61–62. Carreño, described at the height of her illustrious career as "the Valkyrie of the piano," also became a fine singer, conductor, and composer. The article in the *Montgomery Advertiser* includes an interview with (supposedly) Adelina Patti, who tells of her performance in the White House for Lincoln. The date of Patti's appearance is not corroborated by her biography, however, which indicates she was in London and Paris during the fall of 1862. There is also nothing mentioned in the papers to substantiate that she was even singing in Washington at this time. There may have been some confusion with Carlotta Patti, also a fine singer, whose career paralleled her sister's. Carlotta was presenting a program in the capital during the period in question.

51. John Wallace Hutchinson, *The Story of the Hutchinsons* (Boston: Lee & Shepherd, 1896), 2:380. The Hutchinsons were in Washington singing for the Union soldiers. During one of their programs they caused a near riot by singing "Hymn of Liberty" with its powerful antislavery lyrics by John Greenleaf Whittier. General George B. McClellan promptly forbad their further appearances before the soldiers, but Lincoln declared he saw nothing wrong with the song and gave permission for the Hutchinsons to continue their programs (Lair, *Songs Lincoln Loved*, 60).

52. Bernard, *Lincoln and the Music of the Civil War*, 298–99. "The first favorite of all is 'Dixie's Land,' and its music has sounded almost day and night until it has taken on a weird, spell-like influence, and it seems a part and a voice of this horrible glamour that sweeps in upon the souls and hearts of men." William O. Stoddard, *Inside the White House in War Times* (New York: Webster, 1890), 17–18.

53. Lair, *Songs Lincoln Loved*, 15, "Your Mission" was composed by S. M. Grannis with words by Mrs. Ellen H. Gates.

54. Ona Griffin Jeffries, *In and Out of the White House* (New York: Wilfred Funk, 1960), 178.

55. F. B. Carpenter, *The Inner Life of Abraham Lincoln: Six Months at the White House* (New York: Hurd and Houghton, 1867), 143.

56. *Washington Evening Star*, Apr. 20, 25, 1865; *Illinois State Journal*, May 3, 5, 1865.

Chapter 3: The White House Musicale—Whimsical And Sublime

1. Hamm, *Yesterdays* 254. The Hutchinsons comprised a seven-member team at this time: "Mr. and Mrs. John W. Hutchinson, Henry Hutchinson, Mrs. Lillie Phillips,

Ludlow Patton, Mrs. Abby Hutchinson Patton and C. M. Parks" (*National Republican*, Apr. 19, 1878). Hayes was the last of seven presidents that the famous family entertained during its long career.

2. Klapthor, *First Ladies*, 42.

3. Saddler, *Children of the White House*, 168.

4. Inventory of the President's House," Feb. 28, 1867, Letters Sent/Received, Record Group 42, OPB&G, NARS.

5. Steinway #16,214, property of the Tennessee State Museum, Nashville; a bill of sale for #16,651 (patented in 1859) is at the Andrew Johnson National Historic Site. Each piano has a rosewood veneer case, a seven-octave compass, two pedals, and a one-piece cast iron frame.

6. Thomas Hillgrove, "A Complete Guide to the Art of Dancing," 1863. Portions of the guide are reprinted in the program booklet for the 100th anniversary of the opening of the Renwick Gallery, Washington, D.C., Feb. 20, 1981, Division of Musical Instruments, NMAH, SI.

7. *Washington Evening Star*, Dec. 19, 1864.

8. See Odell, *Annals of the New York Stage*, vol. 8, for the Pauls' various engagements in New York City.

9. *National Intelligencer*, Jan. 21, 1867.

10. Hutchinson, *Story of the Hutchinsons*, 2:34.

11. Singleton, *Story of the White House*, 2:130.

12. "Entertainment at the White House," *Report of the Board of Indian Commissioners*, Washington, June 9, 1870, a two-page clipping in the file "Washington, D.C.—Social," MLKL.

13. Quoted in Bess Furman, *White House Profile: A Social History of the White House and Its Occupants* (New York: Bobbs Merrill, 1951), 328–29. Mary Arthur McElroy, youngest sister of Chester Arthur, served as White House hostess for the bachelor president.

14. For more on the origins of "The Marines' Hymn," see "History of 'The Marines' Hymn,'" typescript, n.d., 3pp., MBL.

15. Major Augustus A. Nicholson to Vice-Admiral David P. Porter, Jan. 13, 1870, entry 14, vol. of 1870, Record Group 80, GRDN, NARS. Microfilm copies of documents cited from Record Group 80 are in MCHC. The leader of the Marine Band earned $79 per month, the salary of the leader of the West Point Band.

16. Col. Comdt. McCawley to Secretary of the Navy Thompson, June 25, 1877, entry 14, vol. of Jan.–June 1877, Record Group 80, GRDN, NARS.

17. Section 12 of Whitthorne's bill printed in the *Army and Navy Journal* June 1876, in "Marine Band Chronology," MBL.

18. Lillian Hegermann-Lindencrone, *The Sunny Side of Diplomatic Life* (New York: Harper & Bros., 1914), 112.

19. Rutherford B. Hayes to Fanny Hayes, Jan. 24, 1886, RHPC. The earliest of our first ladies to have been a college graduate, Lucy Hayes attended Wesleyan Female College in Cincinnati.

20. Hayes Scrapbook, 3:2, RHPC.

21. *Cincinnati Gazette*, Feb. 22, 1879.

22. *National Republican*, Nov. 14, 1878.

23. Harold Rosenthal, ed., *The Mapleson Memoirs: The Career of an Operatic Impresario 1858–1888* (New York: Appleton-Century, 1966), 218.

24. Widdows to Mrs. Hayes, Feb. 12, 1879, RHPC.

25. Dated July 18, 1879, and quoted in *Hayes Historical Journal* 2, nos. 3–4 (1979).

26. *Washington Post*, Mar. 8, 1893.

27. *National Republican*, Feb. 10, 1880; "Grand Musical Entertainment: The McGibney Family," [1881–82], Emil Seifert, musical director, formerly concert master of Berlin. The leaflet is the property of the Hoblitzelle Theater Arts Library.

28. Telegram from George A. Gustin to Honorable Carl Schurz, Mar. 1880, RHPC.

29. "Miss Grundy's Letters," Mar. 28, 1878, clipping in Hayes Scrapbooks, Vol. 112, RHPC. Miss Grundy (Austine Snead) was a New York correspondent.

30. Casey to Wm. Knabe & Co., June 25, 1878, Knabe to Casey, June ?, 1878, Letters Sent/Received, Record Group 42, OPB&G, NARS.

31. Casey to Knabe, Mar. 15, 1879, ibid.

32. Knabe to Rockwell, Dec. 11, 1882, ibid. "List of furniture from data furnished by T. J. Pendle, Usher, April 15, 1898." Letters Received, Nov. 21, 1929, ibid. Listed as "Green Room Knabe bought during Arthur." The discarded White House furnishings were usually sold at auction, and the funds received were used to purchase new furniture. Arthur's famous auction of 1882 included twenty-four wagon loads of goods.

33. William Bradbury, who had directed his choir in works by Handel and Rossini for President Buchanan, founded his New York piano company in 1854. Freeborn G. Smith served as Bradbury's superintendent before he purchased the company, continuing the name of Bradbury. In 1917 the Bradbury Piano Company was absorbed by the William Knabe firm.

34. Smith to Casey, Mar. 22, 1877, Letters Sent, Record Group 42, OPB&G, NARS. See also "Miss Grundy's Letters," Mar. 28, 1878, RHPC. The Bradbury eagle inlay does not show in the sketch made of Carl Schurz playing for the Hayes in the oval library, but artists in those days took many liberties. (Notice Frances Cleveland's wedding gown, which appears different in three newspapers.) The eagle Bradbury stands in the Hayes Presidential Center as a donation from the Girls' Club of Ohio.

35. *New York Times*, Aug. 23, 1976. Sousa also compiled, at the direction of Secretary of the Navy Tracy, a book of "representative melodies" of the world's cultures, which included "airs" of Abyssinia, Boa Vista, Celebes, Dalecarlia, East Indies, Fiji Isles, Lapland, Moldavia, Nukahivah, Pfalz, and Samoa. See Sousa, *National and Patriotic Airs of All Lands, with copious notes* (Philadelphia: Coleman, 1890). The book is the property of the Benjamin Harrison Home, Indianapolis. Several of Sousa's marches were arranged for dancing; "The Washington Post" was commonly known as the "Two-step" in Europe.

36. John Philip Sousa, *Marching Along: Recollections of Men, Women, and Music* (Boston: Hale, Cushman and Flint, 1928), 70–71.

37. *Catalogue of Music, Band, U.S. Marine Corps* (Washington: Government Printing Office, 1885), 18. The number of selections in the other categories, presumably for band, were: overtures, 151; waltzes, 76; songs, duets, trios, and quartets, 68; polkas and galops, 50; gavottes, 9; patrols and dances, 28; miscellaneous (solos, quadrilles, etc.), 21. The *Catalogue* is the property of the Marine Band Library.

38. Emma Foote to Florence Carlisle, Apr. 21, 1877, RHPC. A Navy Department memo of Feb. 25, 1878, indicates that the president was to have "a state dinner at which the Band will be present as an orchestra." It was signed "P. W. Thompson, Sect. of the Navy" (Record Group 80, NARS).

39. Saddler, *Children of the White House*, 191–92.

40. William H. Crook, *Memories of the White House*, comp. and ed. Henry Rood (Boston: Little, Brown, 1911), 163.

41. Albani's fine recording of this piece is a collector's item. The soprano died in 1930 at the age of eighty-three. See Emma Albani, *Forty Years of Song, with a discography by W. R. Moran*, ed. Andrew Farkas (New York: Arno Press, 1977).

42. *Washington Post* Mar. 30, 1883. For more on Nilsson at the White House, see Edna Coleman, *White House Gossip from Andrew Johnson to Calvin Coolidge* (Garden City, N.Y.: Doubleday, 1927), 159, and undated newspaper clipping in White House Social File, MLKL. Another famous singer, Minnie Hauk, saw Arthur at the White House on Oct. 11, 1883, and expressed her hopes that a National Opera Company could be

formed similar to those in Europe. "Your idea has my full approbation," said the president, "but you see we are still too young a nation for such an enterprise." Minnie Hauk, *Memories of a Singer* (London: N.p., 1925), 193.

43. *Washington Post*, Feb. 17, 1882.

44. Ibid., Feb. 18, 1882.

45. Sousa, *Marching Along*, 85.

46. *Washington Weekly Star*, Apr. 14, 1882.

47. Ibid.

48. Ibid., June 4, 1886.

Chapter 4. Familiar Tunes with a New Message

1. William H. Crook, *Memories of the White House* (Boston: Little, Brown, 1911), 177.

2. Carpenter, *Carp's Washington*, 256; *Washington Post*, Mar. 8, 1885.

3. *Washington Weekly Star*, June 11, 1886. See also Wilbur Cross and Ann Novotny, *White House Weddings* (New York: David McKay, 1967), 120–27.

4. *New York Times*, Sept. 18, 1890.

5. Theodore E. Steinway, *People and Pianos: A Century of Service to Music* (New York: Steinway and Sons, 1961), 39; John Steinway in an interview with Elise Kirk, Steinway Place, New York City, Mar. 14, 1979. The letter from Grover Cleveland to William Steinway expressing appreciation for the wedding gift is at Steinway Hall, New York City. According to Steinway records, the piano came back to the plant as a trade-in as recently as 1951 and was sold to Brodwin Piano Company, now no longer in business. Chester and Ellen Arthur also owned a Steinway piano. Accounts show that it had been tuned on Mar. 15 and Oct. 25, 1880, before Arthur became president and shortly after Ellen died. Receipt, Schlegel, Steinway and Sons, Dec. 31, 1880, reel 1, Arthur Papers, LC.

6. *Washington Star*, Oct. 5, 1897.

7. *Chicago Daily News*, Sept. 27, 1892, Sousa Papers, MCHC.

8. *Cleveland Daily Telegraph*, Nov. 10, 1886.

9. The piano is the property of Benjamin Harrison Memorial Home. See also *Frank Leslie's Illustrated Newspaper*, May 3, 1890, for Russell's letter to the Fisher Company praising the piano.

10. Loesser, *Men, Women and Pianos*, 500.

11. Undated clipping from *The Inland*, Benjamin Harrison Home.

12. Programs in "White House Receptions"—scrapbook, 1889–91, Benjamin Harrison Papers, LC. The musicale did not follow a dinner party, but was the featured evening event with "light refreshments" served afterwards.

13. *Washington Evening Star*, Apr. 19, 1890.

14. *Washington Post*, Oct. 22, 1891, *New York Times*, Sept. 29, 1891.

15. The scrapbook is in the possession of the Mooreland-Spingarn Research Center, Howard University, Washington, D.C. See also Willia E. Daughtry, "Sissieretta Jones: A Study of the Negro's Contributions to Nineteenth Century American Concert and Theatrical Life" (Ph.D. diss., Syracuse University, 1957).

16. *Washington Evening Star*, Feb. 5, 1890. The funeral of Caroline Harrison, who died at age sixty, was also held in the East Room (on October 25, 1892). The service was shorter, but the choir of St. John's again sang "Lead, Kindly Light"—"Cardinal Newman's beautiful hymn, which Mrs. Harrison so much admired" (*Washington Post*, Oct. 28, 1892). St. John's Church on Lafayette Square was named "the Church of the Presidents," although neither Benjamin Harrison nor Grover Cleveland worshiped there regularly.

17. *Washington Evening Star*, June 27, 1891.

18. "Memorandum on Winter Receptions at the White House," Nov. 1897. T. A. Bingham Papers, LC.

19. "When the Band Plays: In the White House Grounds on Saturday Afternoons," *Washington Evening Star*, June 27, 1891, clipping in White House Social Files, Washingtoniana Collection, MLKL.

20. *Richmond Times*, Mar. ?, 1893; scrapbook of programs of U.S. Marine Band, July 30, 1898 to Aug. 27, 1910: programs (typescript) comprise mainly concerts at the White House, U.S. Capitol, and Marine Barracks. Scrapbook, scores, and manuscripts of many of the "descriptives" are the property of the Marine Band Library. A large Fanciulli collection is at the New York Public Library at Lincoln Center.

21. It is interesting that nowhere within the Commonwealth are drum ruffles and the two-note bugle call used in this manner today, though the tradition is still carried on in our country. Four ruffles and flourishes are rendered to many foreign and American dignitaries and officials. However, these honors are followed by "Hail to the Chief" only for the president of the United States. See "Ruffles and Flourishes," typescript, n.d., MBL; Camus, *Military Music*, 114–15; and "Personnel General Salutes, Honors and Visits of Courtesy," Publication Department of the Army, Washington , D.C., Aug. 15, 1980.

22. Reports for dinners at the Executive Mansion: dinner to Admiral Dewey, Oct. 3, 1899. Bingham Papers, LC.

23. Autograph manuscript possession of Marine Band Library. The library also holds manuscripts, printed scores, and parts for Sousa, Santelmann, and other Marine Band leaders. Additional Sousa materials are at the Library of Congress and the University of Illinois at Urbana–Champaign.

24. Southern, *The Music of Black Americans*, 306. The details of Douglass's performances in the White House are not known.

25. *Washington Post*, Feb. 9, 1898. Ernest Lent was born in Germany in 1856. He toured Europe as a concert cellist before settling in Washington as a teacher in 1884, where he lived until his death in 1922. Arriving in America from Prague, Czechoslovakia, in 1892 as a young man, Joseph Cadek took residence in Chattanooga, Tenn. He died in 1927 after having founded the Chattanooga Conservatory of Music and playing a long and important role in the city's cultural development. See Donald Clyde Runyan, "The Influence of Joseph O. Cadek and His Family on the Musical Life of Chattanooga, Tennessee (1893–1973)" (Ph.D. diss., Vanderbilt University, 1980).

26. Program in Bingham Papers, LC.

27. Droop to Mrs. McKinley, Nov. 5, 1897, William McKinley Papers, LC. Droop delivered a piano stool specifically made by Henry Holtzman and Sons of Columbus, Ohio, to go with the piano. An A. B. Chase electric player piano was presented to President and Mrs. Warren Harding in 1921 and used in the West Sitting Room.

28. The Kimball Company originated in Chicago and concentrated on the production of medium-priced, quick-selling instruments. A Kimball salesman writing in 1880 said that the name of Kimball was as familiar in the western states as that of Grant. McKinley's Kimball developed a crack in the plate and was repaired on Jan. 3, 1901. Conway to McKinley, Feb. 27, 1897, Nov. 1, 1899, Jan. 3, 1901. McKinley Papers, LC. The piano is property of Elizabeth D. Martin of Bolivar, Ohio, a grandniece of Ida McKinley.

29. Davis to McKinley, Sept. 17, 1895, Letters Received, Record Group 42, OPB&G, NARS. A leaflet showing this instrument is enclosed with Davis's correspondence.

30. Droop to Cortelyou, Apr. 24, 1901, McKinley Papers, LC.

31. Program, Feb. 14, 1901, McKinley Papers, LC.

Chapter 5. Lyrical Images of a Growing Nation

1. "White House Social Aides," undated clipping in OWHSF, in Record Group 42, OPB&G, NARS. These records follow the Bingham Papers as a comprehensive set of sources for White House entertaining from 1902 through 1915. In the twenty-one large, leather-bound scrapbooks are programs, guest lists, invitations, newspaper clippings, correspondence, photographs, and memoranda by the officers in charge. See also Lillian Lohmeyer Soules, "Music at the White House during the Administration of Theodore Roosevelt" (M.M.Ed. thesis, Catholic University of America, 1968).

2. Mabel P. Daggett, "Mrs. Roosevelt, the Woman in the Background," *The Delineator*, Mar. 1909, as quoted in Sylvia Jukes Morris, *Edith Kermit Roosevelt: Portrait of a First Lady* (New York: Coward, McCann and Geoghegan, 1980), 541. The president is reputed to have liked Caruso's singing and once commented, "There have been many presidents, but only one Caruso." It is uncertain whether the great tenor ever visited the White House, but he cherished the autographed photo given to him by Roosevelt after the president heard him sing *Tosca* at the National Theater.

3. See the copy of John A. Lomax, *Cowboy Songs and Other Frontier Ballads* (New York: Sturgis and Walton, 1916), vii–viii, in the Library of Congress, Music Division.

4. "Steinway in the White House," *National Magazine* 50 (May 1921):93.

5. The Washington Steinway dealer Edward H. Droop also occasionally assisted with the musical arrangements during this period, which raises the possibility that he may have earlier, too. Accounts are conflicting as to just when Junge began his association with the White House. His obituary (*New York Times*, July 19, 1939) mentions his being in charge of the White House musicales "soon after their beginning under President Theodore Roosevelt." Correspondence in the TR Papers clearly shows only J. Burr Tiffany's involvement in the White House programs, but Junge might have served as an advisor or assistant.

6. Cecilia Beaux, *Background with Figures* (New York: Houghton Mifflin, 1930), 230–31, as quoted in Morris, *Edith Kermit Roosevelt*, 236.

7. I. J. Paderewski and Mary Lawton, *The Paderewski Memoirs* (London: Collins, 1939), 365. Paderewski's printed White House Program in Scrapbook, 1902, OWHSF, Record Group 42, OPB&G, NARS.

8. Loeb to Tiffany, Jan. 23, 1904, TR Papers, LC.

9. Margaret Campbell, *Dolmetsch, the Man and His Work* (Seattle: University of Washington Press, 1975), 175. See also Mabel Dolmetsch, *Personal Recollections of Arnold Dolmetsch* (London: Routledge and Paul, 1958), 170.

10. Pablo Casals, *Joys and Sorrows: Reflections*, as told to Albert E. Kahn (New York: Simon and Schuster, 1970), 109.

11. "White House Social Aides," Scrapbook, 1902, OWHSF, Record Group 42, OPB&G, NARS.

12. David Bispham, *A Quaker Singer's Recollections* (New York: Macmillan, 1920), 317. Printed program in Scrapbook, 1904, OWHSF, Record Group 42, OPB&G, NARS. Set to a text of Rudyard Kipling's, "Danny Deever" (1897) was composed by Walter Damrosch, conductor of the New York Philharmonic.

13. Ole May, "How Alice Roosevelt Converted the Marine Band Leader to Ragtime," Nov. 27, 1915, newspaper source unknown, MCHC. The Marine Band archives hold handwritten parts for the "Maple Leaf Rag" that date from 1904. From their 5 × 7 size, they were probably intended for marching band lyres.

14. Only four performances were given, however, and the composer attributed this failure to the hostile anti-American Berlin group. E. E. Hipsher, *American Opera and Its Composers* (Philadelphia: Presser, 1927), 334–43.

15. Dorin K. Antrim, "The Part Music Has Played in the Lives of Our Presidents," *Musical Observer* 33 (Oct. 1924).

16. *Washington Star*, Oct. 17, 1908; *Washington Post*, Oct. 17, 1908.

17. Memorandum: "Performance of the Ben Greet Woodland Players in the White House Grounds, October 16–17, 1908," Scrapbook, 1908, OWHSF, Record Group 42, OPB&G, NARS. Decorative printed program on p. 186.

18. "Musicales at the White House," *Christian Herald*, Apr. 6, 1910. For more on the Baldwin piano, see letters from Lucien Wulsin, chairman of the Baldwin Company, to Mrs. Taft from Feb. 2 to Mar. 29, 1909, located at the Cincinnati Historical Society.

19. Olga Samaroff Stokowski, *An American Musician's Story* (New York: W. W. Norton, 1939), 74.

20. Hofmann became an American citizen in 1926. He performed twice for President Roosevelt in the White House: with Frieda Hempel on Dec. 14, 1933, and at the presentation of the new Steinway piano on Dec. 10, 1938. He died in Los Angeles in 1957 after an illustrious, legendary career.

21. Hofmann's program is in OWHSF, Record Group 42, OPB&G, NARS.

22. Memorandum, Mar. 25, 1911, ibid.

23. Gwen Bagni and Paul Dubor, *Backstairs at the White House* (New York: Bantam, 1979), 105–6, based upon Lillian Rogers Parks's *My Thirty Years Backstairs at the White House.* Mrs. Parks and her mother, Maggie, served as maids from the Taft through Eisenhower administrations.

24. Ibid., 90.

25. Bispham, *Quaker Singer*, 318; Paderewski and Lawton, *Paderewski Memoirs*, 365. Paderewski played for Wilson in the White House on Feb. 22, 1916, and on May 16, 1919. A patriot and statesman, Paderewski pleaded the cause for Poland.

26. Doron K. Antrim, "Our Musical Presidents," *Etude*, May 1940. Wilson's violin, as well as his mother's guitar, are in the Woodrow Wilson Birthplace, Staunton, Va. The guitar is a six-stringed instrument, beautifully inlaid and possessing a soft, mellow tone. It was made in France about 1850.

27. Memorandum and printed program, OWHSF, Record Group 42, OPB&G, NARS.

28. Grainger also played for Franklin Roosevelt at the White House on Jan. 6, 1938.

29. Melville Clark, "I Played the Harp for Wilson," *Christian Science Monitor*, May 19, 1945.

30. Edith Wilson, *My Memoir* (Indianapolis: Bobbs-Merrill, 1939), 121.

31. Ibid., 145. The president's Victrola from the White House is believed to be the one in the Wilson Home in Washington, D.C. (Victor Talking Machine Company, Camden, N.J.).

32. Minstrel and ragtime songs were spirited, often syncopated, reflections of black folk culture. Their earthiness and vitality had great impact on the popular music industry in America at the turn of the century. Reputedly, Roosevelt adopted such a piece—"A Hot Time in the Old Town Tonight" (1896) by Theodore Metz—as the official song of his Rough Riders during the Spanish-American War. Dialect songs generally dealt with minorities, such as the Irish, Germans, or Italians, and were especially popular in beer halls and saloons.

33. Earl Godwin, "They Make our Presidents Laugh," *Philadelphia Public Ledger*, June 14, 1925. The George O'Connor archive consists of three large scrapbooks, photographs, clippings, and song texts and is the property of the Lauinger Memorial Library, Georgetown University, Washington, D.C.

34. Jim Walsh, "Favorite Pioneer Recording Artists: George H. O'Connor," *Hobbies*, Mar. 1955.

35. "Al Jolson Leads Actor Band in Pledge of Support at Breakfast Party," *Washington Star*, Oct. 17, 1924. See also Ishbel Ross, *Grace Coolidge and Her Era* (New York: Dodd, Mead and Co., 1962), 164–65.

36. "George Cohan Gives President Copy of His Bicentennial Song," *Washington Star*, July 29, 1931.

37. *New York Times*, June 2, 1921.

38. Baldwin piano #37024, style K., Baldwin Company to McClure, Jan. 24, 1950, OWHC.

39. "Boy Pianist Plays at White House," *New York Herald*, May 18, 1923. Harding Scrapbook, OWHC. Cherkassy later studied with Josef Hofmann at the Curtis Institute in Philadelphia and has given concerts all over the world.

40. "Gifted Musicians Eagerly Await Bid to White House," source unknown, Mar. 15, 1937. White House scrapbook, Washingtoniana Collection, MLKL.

41. The pianoforte was borrowed on Apr. 4, 1932, and returned to the Smithsonian at the beginning of Franklin D. Roosevelt's administration, probably in 1937 with the other White House furniture on loan from the Smithsonian (receipt, Apr. 4, 1932; memorandum of packing, Apr. 1, 1932; memorandum, Chief Usher Hoover to Goldsmith, Apr. 1, 1932, Accession file #118796, NMAH, SI). James Monroe's Astor is in the James Monroe Museum and Memorial Library, Fredericksburg, Va.

42. Marguerite D'Alvarez, the great Peruvian contralto, was the sister of J. Alvarez de Buenavista of the Peruvian Embassy. *Herald*, Mar. 25, 1924. All Harding and Coolidge printed musicale programs, OWHC.

43. Sergei Bertensson and Jay Lerner, *Rachmaninoff: A Lifetime in Music* (New York: New York University Press, 1956), 194–95.

44. Harold Schonberg, *The Great Pianists* (New York: Simon and Schuster, 1963), 371.

45. Ross, *Grace Coolidge*, 162.

46. Two pages of explanatory notes were printed in the small, seven-page program. In listing the selections, Fellowes's name was misspelled, and the word "circa" was appended to Tomkins, as if it were part of his name. However, the program was finely executed and each stringed instrument with its date and maker was included.

47. Glen Plaskin, *Horowitz, a Biography* (New York: William Morrow, 1983), 142; *New York Times*, Jan. 7, 1931; *Chicago Tribune*, Feb. 25, 1931.

48. Campbell to Kirk, Mar. 9, 1981.

49. Jerome Kern, *The Jerome Kern Song Book* (New York: Simon and Schuster 1955), 3.

50. E. Clark to R. Weeks, Dec., 1923, Coolidge Papers, LC.

51. The letters are property of the Herbert Hoover Presidential Library.

Chapter 6. Music in a Wartime White House

1. Arthur P. Molella, curator, "Introduction," in *FDR: The Intimate Presidency* (Washington, D.C.: National Museum of American History, Smithsonian Institution 1982), a catalogue of exhibition commemorating the 100th anniversary of FDR's birth.

2. Oct. 18, 1899, in Elliott Roosevelt, ed. *FDR: His Personal Letters, Early Years* (New York: Duell, Sloan and Pearce, 1947), 347.

3. FDR to Sarnoff, Jan. 31, 1940, PPF 764, FDR Papers.

4. FDR to Davenport, May 4, 1942, President's Personal Files [PPF] 100, FDR Papers. Printed program, "A Thanksgiving Day Service at the White House," Wilkinson Collection, Division of Political History, NMAH, SI. All other programs mentioned in this chapter are the property of the FDRL and NMAH, SI.

5. Interview with Marian Anderson by Mary McAlpine for the Canadian Broadcasting Co., Sept. 26, 1973, FDR Papers; Mrs. Roosevelt's "My Day" column often contained comments about her White House musicales.

6. Article written for Frank B. Cookson of the *Educational Music Magazine*, July 22, 1938, Eleanor Roosevelt [ER] Papers 3031–51, FDRL. Especially interesting are Mrs. Roosevelt's handwritten revisions on this typescript, characteristic of her personal interest in the content and expression of her texts.

7. John Steinway in an interview with Elise Kirk, Steinway & Sons, New York City, Mar. 14, 1979.

8. For the 1938–39 season a list of seventy names of performers with Junge's comments ("Nice for Lent," "Too many pianists already," "Solo saxophonist—a novel idea") was submitted to Mrs. Roosevelt for her perusal.

9. Junge to Mrs. Roosevelt, Dec. 13, 1937, ER Papers, 80.3, #986.

10. Junge to Mrs. Roosevelt, Apr. 12, 1939, Junge to Helm, Apr. 3, 1934, White House Office of Chief of Social Entertainments, Box 204, Junge, ER Papers.

11. All letters Helm to Junge, ER Papers, 80.3, #986. Edith Helm had been social secretary under Woodrow Wilson and would also serve under the Trumans.

12. May 24, 1939, ER Papers, 60.9.

13. *New York Times*, Jan. 21, 1935. The Gullah Negros reputedly originated the popular new dance of the 1930s, the "Big Apple," which they danced barefoot.

14. Todd Duncan in an interview with Elise Kirk, Washington, D.C., Feb. 24, 1982.

15. Anderson/McAlpine interview.

16. Graham to Mrs. Roosevelt, Feb. 22, 1937, Helm to Hawkins, Feb. 25, 1937, ER Papers, 80.9, #993.

17. Crim to Greiner, Nov. 8 1939, Steinway and Sons, New York City.

18. "Folk Music in the Roosevelt White House: An Evening of Song, Recollections and Dance," a booklet accompanying the concert held at the National Museum of American History, Smithsonian Institution, Jan. 31, 1982. The twenty-eight-page booklet contains excellent oral histories of Alan Lomax, Wade Mainer, Lily May Ledford, and Charles Seegar.

19. Helm to Dornbush, Mar. 5, 1939, Of. Ch. Soc. Entertainments 91–197; Helm to Junge, Nov. 2, 1935, Of. Soc. Entertainments, Box 204, ER Papers; Helm to Dornbush, Apr. 13, 1939, Of. Ch. Soc. Entertainments 91–197. See also Dornbush to Mrs. Roosevelt, Apr. 18, 1939. Transportation and per diem was $5 apiece. Cost for the Negro chorus was given as $2040.30; the Coon Creek Girls, $390; the Cowboy Singers were replaced by Alan Lomax. The expenses were to be paid by the State Department.

20. Junge to Helm, May 23, June 1, and June 3, 1939, ER Papers, 80.3, #986. See also June 6, 1939, Of. Ch. Soc. Entertainments, 91–197. Junge also brought two American Indian singers to Hyde Park for the picnic for the king and queen on June 11, 1939: Princess Te Ata and Ish-Ti-Opi.

21. The complete program has been reprinted in "Folk Music in the Roosevelt White House," 23–28.

22. The Lincoln Memorial program was arranged after Anderson was refused a singing engagement at DAR's Constitution Hall because she was black. Mrs. Roosevelt resigned from membership in the Daughters of the American Revolution as a result of this infamous incident.

23. "Folk Music in the Roosevelt White House," 12, 22, 13. Lily May adds: "After we got off stage and went back to our dressing room, we noticed that Sis had a $20 bill that had slipped down her leg and was flattened out right in front under the silk hose. She had put it in her garter for safe keeping, before performing, and it had worked loose. Now we realized that it had been there while we were out on stage and it had been seen by all!"

24. All letters are the property of the FDRL. The collection also includes correspondence between the president and Lauritz Melchior, Basil O'Connor, Jose Iturbi, Ignacy Jan Paderewski, Ernestine Schumann-Heink, Lawrence Tibbett, Hans Kindler, Douglas Fairbanks, Rosa Ponselle, Edwin Hughes, and Schuyler Chapin.

25. William Santelmann in an interview with Elise Kirk, Arlington, Va, Jan. 21, 1982.

26. Barnett Lester, "What the Roosevelts Like in Swing Music," *The Senator* (June 17, 1939): 23–24, Washingtoniana Division, MLKL. After someone once sent him a copy of Alex Templeton's new recording, "Bach Goes to Town," the president commented that he hoped he'd never be converted "from Bach to Boogie-Woogie." Struther PPF 100.

27. "1600 Peppermint Lounge," *Washington Evening Star*, Nov. 13, 1961. Seideman also recalls playing for the Hoovers while they danced the Charleston.

28. "Grave Is in Garden," *New York Times*, Apr. 16, 1945.

29. HST to Mrs. John Truman and Mary Jane, June 13, 1945, Truman Papers. The portion of this chapter dealing with Harry Truman is reprinted with modification in Brian Lingham, ed., *Harry Truman: The Man . . . His Music* (Kansas City: Lowell, 1985).

30. HST to Mrs. John Truman and Mary Jane, April 16, 1945, Truman Papers.

31. HST to Mary Jane, Apr. 12, 1948, ibid.

32. HST to Margaret Truman, Feb. 14, 1948, ibid.

33. HST to Bessie Wallace, Jan. 10, 1910, ibid.

34. Rex Scouten, in an interview with Elise Kirk, The White House, Aug. 5, 1982. Scouten, who became White House chief usher in 1969, was Truman's Secret Service agent during the interim at Blair House.

35. "Music and Art," p. 8 of a nine-page typed questionnaire, n.d., President's Personal Files (PPF), Truman Papers. Truman jotted down, in his usual terse, breezy style, his own views on subjects ranging from his health and dress to music and painting; also Margaret Truman, in a telephone conversation with Elise Kirk, Apr. 6, 1982.

36. "Music and Art," 8.

37. Truman's remarks to Guy Lombardo are quoted in Robert H. Farrell, *Off the Record: The Private Papers of Harry S. Truman* (New York: Harper and Row, 1980), 356. Frederic Logan's "The Missouri Waltz" (1914) became the official state song on June 30, 1949.

38. Ibid., 23.

39. Margaret Truman, *Harry S. Truman* (New York: William Morrow, 1973), 336.

40. Howard Mitchell, in an interview with Elise Kirk, Apr. 18, 1982.

41. HST to MT, Oct. 23, 1946, ibid. Greiner's list included sixteen pianists, eight violinists, and twenty-four vocalists. Those who were available were marked "A." The president's original choices for pianists were: 1. Eugene List, 2. Sylvia Zaremba, 3. Rudolph Ganz, 4. Percy Grainger, 5. William Kapell. Violinists marked were: 1. Jascha Heifetz, 2. Yehudi Menuhin, 3. Albert Spalding, 4. Patricia Travers. Margaret had not yet checked her choices for the singers.

42. HST to BT and Mary, Jan. 30, 1947, Truman Papers.

43. Eugene List, in an interview with Elise Kirk, Dallas, Mar. 21, 1981. After List's performance, Truman played Paderewski's "Minuet," often confused in accounts of this event with Beethoven's "Minuet in G." In a typed copy of a letter to his mother and sister, Truman has crossed off the reference to Beethoven and written in "Paderewski." See also "Log of the President's Trip to the Berlin Conference (July 6 to Aug. 7, 1945)" compiled by Lt. William M. Rigdon, USN, typescripts, HSTL. A copy of the Chopin score, played by List and later autographed by him, was presented to the president on Jan. 4, 1946.

44. Truman, *Harry S. Truman*, 280; HST to BT, July 22, 1945, Truman Papers.

45. Truman, *Harry S. Truman*, 342.

46. Hume's review appeared in the *Washington Post* on Dec. 6, 1950. With Truman's reply it was reprinted in the *New York Times*, Dec. 9, 1950, and in other

papers across the country. Truman's original letter eventually made its way to the collection of a New Haven businessman and was auctioned for $15,000 in 1967.

47. HST to Philip Graham, Feb. 4, 1952, ibid. The documents concerning this incident are clipped together with the top page marked "Music—Personal. See me. *Important—Personal*," in Truman's hand.

48. The distinguishing feature of the Baldwin was its large sterling silver spread eagle and thirteen stars on the fallboard, designed by Sidney Waugh with the approval of the president. On the back of the fallboard was the presidential seal. After the piano was moved to the White House Library in March 1953, the press of Cincinnati, the home of the Baldwin firm, expressed indignation over the instrument's new location in the "basement." In 1965 the piano was loaned to the State Department and an identical copy placed in the Harry S. Truman Library (also a gift of the Baldwin Company).

49. Entry for June 4, 1956, in Ferrell, *Off the Record*, 331.

Chapter 7. America's Musical Showcase

1. Julia Pels, "Art for Whose Sake?" *American Legion Magazine*, Oct. 1955, Box 209, 236J, Eisenhower Papers.

2. Mary Jane McCaffree (Mrs. Henry Monroe, Jr.), in an interview with Elise Kirk, Washington, D.C., Mar. 10, 1982. Mrs. McCaffree was not only social secretary but also press and personal secretary for Mrs. Eisenhower.

3. Howard Mitchell, in an interview with Elise Kirk, Washington, D.C., Apr. 18, 1982.

4. "White House Guests See Broadway Acts," *New York Times*, May 9, 1958; Harry MacArthur, "White House Musicale Was Well-Kept Secret," *Washington Sunday Star*, May 11, 1958.

5. Mary Jane McCaffree interview. Wiley Buchanan, *Red Carpet at the White House* (New York: Dutton, 1964), 232. The program was larger than the usual 3½ × 5 inches, had a drawing of the White House on the cover, and was decorated with a red, white, and blue ribbon. All Eisenhower White House programs in Mamie Dowd Eisenhower Papers, Social Records, DDEL.

6. Steinway/Kirk interview. Thirty-year-old Fleisher became the first American to win a major foreign competition when he was awarded the Queen of Belgium Prize in 1952. Another Steinway artist and 1960 Belgium prize winner, Malcolm Frager, performed for the king of Denmark at a state dinner on Oct. 11, 1960.

7. Greiner to Henry Steinway, May 3, 1957, Steinway & Sons.

8. Ibid.

9. Piatigorsky had been first cellist with the Imperial Opera, Moscow, at the age of fifteen. It is said that after his arrival in the United States in 1929, he brought about a cello renaissance. He was considered the greatest cellist after Casals.

10. MJM to JE, Mar. 10, 1960; DDE to Bernstein, Apr. 6, 1960, OF 101-B-6, Eisenhower Papers.

11. William K. Wyant, Jr., "Federal Aid for the Arts," *Music and the Arts*, Dec. 9, 1956, reprinted from the St. Louis *Post-Dispatch*, Eisenhower Papers. An attempt was made to bring the entire *Porgy and Bess* company to the White House to be received by the president, but this did not materialize. See Robert Breen to Maxwell M. Rabb, May 31, 1956, and ff., OF 111, ibid.

12. Mahalia Jackson, *Movin' On Up* (New York: Hawthorn Books, 1966), 139.

13. From words of John F. Kennedy written on the facade of the John F. Kennedy Center for the Performing Arts, Washington, D.C.

14. John F. Kennedy; Government and the Arts, "*John F. Kennedy Center for the Performing Arts Inaugural Program*, Sept. 8, 1971.

15. This concept was formulated by Salinger, Schlesinger, and Mrs. Kennedy shortly after the inauguration. Arthur and Barbara Gelb, "Culture Makes a Hit at the White House," *New York Times*, Jan. 28, 1962. Stephen Birmingham in his *Jacqueline Bouvier Kennedy Onassis* (New York: Grosset & Dunlap, 1978), 106, notes that Jacqueline Kennedy was a decided political asset to the president, and he let her do pretty much what she wanted.

16. Jacqueline Kennedy Onassis to Elise Kirk, Feb. 3, 1984.

17. The program on Apr. 30, 1963, was presented for Grand Duchess Charlotte of Luxembourg by Basil Rathbone and the Consort Players. The early music group was organized in 1953 by Sydney Beck, head of the Rare Book and Manuscript Section of the Music Division of the New York Public Library. Another tribute to musical scholarship took place when the president sent a letter to the Eighth Congress of the International Musicological Society congratulating the IMS on its achievements.

18. *New York Times*, Aug. 10, 1962.

19. Oral history interview with August Heckscher, by Wolf von Eckhardt, Dec. 10, 1965, New York, Kennedy Papers, JFKL.

20. Bernard West in an interview with Elise Kirk, Washington, D.C., July 22, 1981; Klapthor, *First Ladies*, 79. See also "Jackie Brings Culture to the White House," *New York–Journal American*, Nov. 23, 1960. "A Tour of the White House with Mrs. John F. Kennedy" was broadcast on the CBS Television Network, Feb. 14, 1962.

21. Oral history interview with Leonard Bernstein, composer and music director of the New York Philharmonic, by Nelson Aldrich, July 21, 1965, New York, 2–4, Kennedy Papers, JFKL.

22. Col. John Bourgeois, in an interview with Elise Kirk, Washington, D.C., Feb. 12, 1982. For more on Casals event, see Marta Istomin interview with Elise Kirk, Washington, D.C., July 20, 1982; Casals, *Joys and Sorrows*, 289–94; and jacket notes "Concert at the White House," Columbia AKL 5726.

23. Lowens, "Move to East Room Solves 'Magic Flute,'" *Washington Evening Star*, June 4, 1963.

24. Letitia Baldrige, *Of Diamonds and Diplomats* (New York: Ballantine Books, 1968), 196–97.

25. Ibid., 194.

26. West/Kirk interview.

27. Ann H. Lincoln, *The Kennedy White House Parties* (New York: Viking, 1967), 176.

28. The complete listing of the musical selections and organizations performing on the day of the funeral appears in the *Washington Star*, Dec. 1, 1963, compiled by Irving Lowens. Capt. Gilbert H. Mitchell, assistant conductor of the Army Band, served as music coordinator for the Military District of Washington during the ceremonies.

29. *New York Times*, July 12, 1964.

30. *New York Times*, Nov. 27, 1963.

31. Copyright © 1965 by W. H. Auden. Reprinted from Edward Mendelson, ed. *W. H. Auden: Collected Poems*, by permission of Random House, Inc.

32. Jack Valenti, *A Very Human President* (New York: W. W. Norton, 1975).

33. Mrs. Lyndon Johnson to Elise Kirk, Aug. 20, 1980.

34. See also Roger Stevens, "Report on the Formation of the Arts Foundation," typescript, 20, File—National Endowment for the Arts (NEA), Administrative History, White House Central Files (WHCF), Johnson Papers, LBJL, Austin, Tex. See also Elise Kirk, "Presidents and the Performing Arts—a Tribute to LBJ," *Dallas Civic Opera Magazine* 3 (1980): 72; Roger Stevens, "The First Annual Report of the National Council on the Arts, 1964–1965," typescript, File—NEA, Ad. Hist., WHCF, Johnson Papers. Sixty-three million dollars was appropriated to finance the first three years of the foundation program.

35. Transcript, oral history interview with Abe Fortas by Joe Frantz, on Aug. 14, 1969, 19, Johnson Papers, LBJL.

36. Lady Bird Johnson, *A White House Diary* (New York: Holt, Rinehart & Winston, 1970), 25–26. The barbecue was held on Dec. 29, 1963.

37. Luci Johnson Turpin to Elise Kirk during "Modern First Ladies" conference, Gerald R. Ford Museum, Grand Rapids, Mich., Apr. 18–20, 1984.

38. Memo, Office of the White House Press Secretary, July 2, 1964, Social Files, Liz Carpenter's Files, Lady Bird Johnson Papers. Among the other recipients were Helen Keller, Carl Sandburg, T. S. Eliot, Walter Disney, Paul Dudley White, Reinhold Niebuhr, and Helen Taussig.

39. Johnson to Kirk, Aug. 20, 1980.

40. Elizabeth Carpenter, *Ruffles and Flourishes* (New York: Doubleday, 1970), 200–201. Merrill's program with Veronica Tyler was on Feb. 8, 1968. The president joked about the fuss made on the morning radio during his toast to the prime minister that evening: "Well, there they go again, always wanting me to dance to their tune." Press release, Feb. 8, 1968, Office of the White House Press Secretary, Social Files—Bess Abell, Box 23, Lady Bird Johnson Papers.

41. Typed script, Salute to Congress File, Social Files—Bess Abell, Box 6. NBC-TV planned to cover portions of the event for inclusion in a special preconvention show on Aug. 19.

42. Memorandum, n.d., Social Files—Bess Abell, Box 29, #4014, ibid; press release, Office of the Press Secretary to Mrs. Johnson, Dec. 7, 1968, James Webb Folder, Social Files—Carpenter, Box 58, ibid.

43. Johnson, *White House Diary*, 738; Johnson to Kirk.

44. *Washington Post*, Sept. 30, 1965. See also "Fact Sheet on New Stage for East Room," Sept. 27, 1965, Social Files—Carpenter Press Releases, Lady Bird Johnson Papers; West/Kirk interview.

45. Excerpt from Carpenter, *Ruffles and Flourishes*, reprinted in *Washington Evening Star*, Feb. 3, 1970.

46. *New York Times*, Jan. 19–23, 27, 1968; *Washington Evening Star*, Jan. 19, 1968; Carpenter, *Ruffles and Flourishes*, 206–7.

47. Letter to Mrs. Johnson, Jan. 23, 1968, Social Files, Alpha–Eartha Kitt, Box 1305, Lady Bird Johnson Papers.

48. Barbaralee D. Diamonstein to Eric F. Goldman, "Some Recollections of the White House Festival of the Arts" (typescript), May 11, 1966, GEN AR 7/26/65, Box 2, WHCF, Johnson Papers.

49. Ellington had played for President Eisenhower at a White House Correspondents dinner in Washington about ten years earlier. For more on Ellington at the White House, see Edward Kennedy Ellington, *Music Is My Mistress* (New York: Doubleday, 1973), 424–33.

50. Abell to Carpenter, hand-draft of memo, n.d., ibid. Carpenter, *Ruffles and Flourishes*, 208; Abell to Goldman, May 28, 1965, GEN AR 7/26/65, Box 2, WHCF, Johnson Papers.

51. Goldman to LBJ, Feb. 25, 1965, GEN AR 7/26/65, Box 2, WHCF, Johnson Papers.

52. *New York Herald Tribune*, June 15, 1965.

53. Paul Miller, in an interview with Elise Kirk, Ft. McNair, Washington, D.C., July 21, 1982.

54. Isabelle Shelton, "The President's Trumpeters," *Washington Sunday Star*, Mar. 22, 1970. See also George Farmer, *Rise and Development of Military Music* (London: W. Reeves, 1912), 18–19.

55. *The Memoirs of Richard Nixon* (New York: Grosset and Dunlap, 1978), 9.

56. Frank Getlein, "Nixon and the Arts," *New York Times Magazine*, Feb. 14, 1971.

57. Thomas Meehan, "Washington Society Isn't Exactly Swinging," *New York Times Magazine*, Mar. 8, 1970.

58. Mel Gussow, "Mrs. Stuart: White House Impresario," *New York Times*, Feb. 24, 1970. Connie Stuart also served as Mrs. Nixon's press secretary until she was succeeded by Helen Smith in early 1973.

59. Alan Frank, *Sinatra* (New York: Hamlyn, 1978), 140–41. Anthony Ripley, "Sinatra at White House Gets Standing Ovation," *New York Times*, Apr. 18, 1973.

60. Nixon had twenty-six non-denominational Sunday worship services at the White House during his period in office. The Vienna Choir Boys, Danish Boys' Choir, several Hebrew choruses, and many other choirs performed. Programs are the property of the Office of the White House Curator.

61. *Memoirs of Nixon*, 540.

62. Ted Thackery, Jr., "Star-Spangled Fete for Moon Pioneers," *Los Angeles Times*, Aug. 14, 1969.

63. Rex Scouten and Nelson Pierce, in an interview with Elise Kirk, The White House, Aug. 5, 1982. The Fords had Scouten construct a tent with a floor and carpet for the queen of England's visit, in order to avoid the muddy ground and guests' ruined shoes when Ford was vice-president.

64. Isabella Shelton, "Music Salutes Israel's Leader," *Washington Evening Star*, Sept. 26, 1969.

65. *Washington Evening Star*, Feb. 6, Jan. 29, 1972.

66. Betty Beale, "Topless at the White House?" *Washington Sunday Star*, Feb. 6, 1972; Isabelle Shelton, "Moffo's Moorings Slip," *Washington Evening Star*, Oct. 27, 1970; Carpenter, *Ruffles and Flourishes*, 201; Christopher Lydon, "Beverly Sills Sings at the White House," *New York Times*, Feb. 3, 1971; Beverly Sills to Elise Kirk, Nov. 20, 1981.

67. Bruce Howard, "Wiffenpoofs Turn Deaf Ear to Nixon," *Washington Star-News*, Dec. 14, 1973.

68. Eugene List, in an interview with Elise Kirk, Dallas, Mar. 21, 1981.

69. Isabelle Shelton, "Host on the Ivories," *Washington Evening Star*, Mar. 8, 1974; "Notes on People," *New York Times*, Mar. 22, 1973.

70. Andrew Glass, "The Fords as Impresarios: Who Plays the White House— And Why?" *New York Times*, Sept. 14, 1975.

71. Ibid.

72. Betty Ford, *The Times of My Life* (New York: Harper and Row, 1978), 230.

73. Billy Taylor, in an interview with Elise Kirk, Washington, D.C., June 24, 1982.

74. "Remarks upon Presenting the Presidential Medal of Freedom to Artur Rubinstein," Apr. 1, 1976, in *Public Papers of the Presidents of the United States: Gerald R. Ford*, 1 (Washington: Government Printing Office, 1979), 881–82. Artur Rubinstein's response to the president's remarks appear on an audio recording cassette, the property of the Ford Library.

75. Anna Kisselgolff, "Martha Graham Hailed by Nation; Given Freedom Medal by Ford," *New York Times*, Oct. 15, 1976. "It is interesting that Martha Graham had pursued her career almost exclusively without government subsidy until only recently," the *Times* reported. The day that Ford presented the Medal of Freedom to Graham he announced at a news conference that he was asking Congress for $50 million more for a new "challenge" grant program for the NEA.

76. Video cassette of the program, property of the Gerald R. Ford Library, Ann Arbor, Mich. Bob Hope, a native of England, was master of ceremonies. There was no biographical information about Captain and Tennille on the printed program, but Hope had four long paragraphs, "the only performer who has triumphed in all five show business media: vaudeville, stage, radio, motion pictures and television."

77. Betty Beale, "'Lowbrow' Entertainment at the White House," *Washington Sunday Star*, July 29, 1973; Charlie McCollum, "What's the Matter with Rock at the White House Anyway?" *Washington Sunday Star*, July 18, 1976.

78. Ibid.

Chapter 8. Music, Mass Media, and the Modern White House

1. Col. John Bourgeois in an interview with Elise Kirk, Marine Barracks, Washington, D.C., Feb. 12, 1982. Bourgeois was especially impressed with the genuine attention and recognition President Carter gave the Marine Band.

2. Ibid.

165–1703. Rosalynn Carter in a telephone interview with Elise Kirk, Dallas/Atlanta, Feb. 22, 1984. See also Rosalynn Carter, *First Lady from Plains* (Boston: Houghton Mifflin, 1984).

4. Guest list for Horowitz concert, courtesy of Irving and Margery Lowens. See also Glenn Plaskin, *Horowitz* (New York: William Morrow, 1983), 435.

5. Scouten/Kirk interview; Carter/Kirk interview.

6. Harold Schonberg, "Horowitz Plays for Carter," *New York Times*, Feb. 27, 1978. "For this event, they roll out the carpet," *Washington Star*, Feb. 27, 1978; Irving Lowens review in ibid.

7. Gretchen Poston in an interview with Elise Kirk, Washington, D.C., July 7, 1981.

8. MSgt. James Kessler in an interview with Elise Kirk, Brucker Hall, Ft. Myer, Va. Aug. 6, 1982.

9. John Wilson, "Carter Opens Home to Jazz as an Art," *New York Times*, June 19, 1978. See also Jacqueline Trescott and Joseph McLellan, "A Who's Who of Jazz on the South Lawn," *Washington Post*, June 19, 1978, and Taylor/Kirk interview.

10. Gospel Music Association. Remarks at a White House Performance, Sept. 9, 1979, in *Public Papers of the Presidents of the United States: Jimmy Carter* (Washington: Government Printing Office, 1979–80), 2:1614–15.

11. Poston/Kirk inteview.

12. Ibid.

13. Mabel Brandon in an interview with Elise Kirk, the White House, Jan. 8, 1982.

14. Remarks made by Mrs. Reagan introducing the program, "In Performance at the White House," Nov. 22, 1981. Unless otherwise indicated, all quotations and information from the "In Performance at the White House" series have been drawn from the author's attendance at the concerts and rehearsals as well as viewing the telecasts.

15. The following details were part of the notes printed on the White House program for this concert: "Presumed lost for more than two centuries, the Symphony was written in 1765, when Mozart was nine years old. It was known only as a fifteen-measure fragment scribbled in his father's hand on the back of another composition's title page until it was discovered among some private papers in West Germany last fall. The original manuscript was subsequently sold to the Bavarian State Library, and arrangements for the Mostly Mozart Festival performances have been made through the German music publishing house of Barenreiter Verlag, owners of the worldwide copyright."

16. *Washington Post*, June 13, 14, 1983.

17. Scouten/Kirk interview. Scouten, who became White House curator, was succeeded by the new chief usher, Gary Walters, in January 1986.

18. Remarks in letter from Anna Perez, Press Secretary to Mrs. Bush, to Elise Kirk, Oct. 29, 1991.

19. Donnie Radcliffe, *Simply Barbara Bush* (New York: Warner Books, 1989), 223.

20. Alan Kriegsman, "Exuberant Houstonians," *Washington Post*, June 22, 1991. Donnie Radcliffe and Roxanne Roberts, "Pastimes and Politics," *Washington Post*, March 7, 1990.

21. Paul Miller in an interview with Elise Kirk, Ft. McNair, Washington, D.C., July 21, 1982.

22. Bourgeois/Kirk interview.

23. Bourgeois/Kirk interview, Sept. 28, 1991.

24. Brandon/Kirk interview.

25. "Remarks at a Reception for Participants in the Very Special Arts International Festival," June 15, 1989, *Public Papers of the Presidents of the United States: George Bush*, (Washington: Government Printing Office, 1989), I:745–46.

BIBLIOGRAPHICAL ESSAY

Accompanying each chapter of this text, notes present details of the sources most directly related to the project. This survey is offered primarily to guide the reader through the general categories of materials consulted, at the same time noting their relevance and accessibility. The most important single tool for researching White House history is Ann Duncan Brown's *The White House: A Bibliographical List* (Washington, D.C.: Library of Congress 1953; suppl., 1960), which contains almost every article, book, and monograph on the White House furnishings, the presidents, first families, and life at the mansion. This valuable index needs to be updated, however, and also to include works relating to music. The important materials that should be added are Helen Cripe's *Thomas Jefferson and Music* (Charlottesville: University Press of Virginia, 1974); Kenneth Bernard's *Lincoln and the Music of the Civil War* (Caldwell, Idaho: Caxton, 1966); and H. Earle Johnson's "The Adams Family and Good Listening" (*JAMS*, summer-fall, 1958). For George Washington, Nicholas Tawa's "Music in the Washington Household" (*Journal of American Culture* [Spring 1978]) and Judith Britt's *Nothing More Agreeable* (Mt. Vernon: Mt. Vernon Ladies Association, 1984) are relevant.

The handful of other books and articles on early White House social life, including a few articles on presidents and music, must be read with caution, since the authors rarely have considered primary sources and tend to pass down the same anecdotal errors (the production of *La traviata* for James Buchanan, for instance). The best early book on the White House is Esther Singleton's pioneer study, *The Story of the White House*, 2 volumes (New York: McClure, 1907). While this was a fine source for its day and utilizes primary materials, it lacks documentation and leaves the reader wondering where all those marvelous quotations originated. The series of guide books published by the White House Historical Association are excellent for the general reader. The association has also issued a new journal, *White House History*, and in 1986 published a comprehensive history of the mansion, William Seale's *The President's House*. Another valuable book on the White House is Margaret Klapthor's scholarly and fascinating *Official White House China 1789 to the Present* (Washington, D.C.: Smithsonian Institution Press, 1975). For government records relating to the mansion's furnishings, this study is a remarkable source. These records led me to the identification of numerous pianos that were placed in the White House during the nineteenth century and thus reinforced my conviction that the mansion was indeed a musically active home from its earliest days.

To locate information about the pianos (often derived from tuning receipts), and anything else musical that I could find, I spent several months plowing through inventories at the National Archives. These records included the vouchers and expense accounts of Record Group 217, Miscellaneous Treasury Accounts for the President's House (1800–1867), and Record Group 42, correspondence relating to purchases filed with the Office of Public Buildings and Grounds (1867–1901). In order to locate the account, one must be familiar with the names of those who served as commissioners of public buildings during the early history of Washington, and here Klapthor's book and her personal suggestions were invaluable. Somehow through all of this I kept hearing the late Irving Lowen's words that I would encounter a great deal of "negative" research in writing on White House musical history. No truer words were spoken. And so I opened with great care the hundreds of musty, crumbling inventories with their chipped wax seals, untying their faded red ribbons hopefully. If I found few piano vouchers, I was sure I had located the *original* government "red tape." Among all these White House expenses were every gold spittoon, picture hook, and chimney sweeping and water closet repair bill possible. Imagine my delight when there appeared evidence of the earliest collection of music purchased for the mansion— Madame Le Pelletier's exquisite *Journal of Musick*, published in Philadelphia in 1810!

Other important materials consulted were the biographies, diaries, memoirs, and state papers, both published and in manuscript, of the presidents and first ladies. The most useful of *The Public Papers of the Presidents of the United States*, comprising speeches, statements, and reports arranged chronologically for each president, were the later series for Lyndon Johnson, Richard Nixon, Gerald Ford, Jimmy Carter, Ronald Reagan, and George Bush, in which the various presidents' remarks about music were often included. But the real gems were found in the unpublished papers. In myriads of fascinating nooks, crannies, and byways lay the memos, correspondence, clippings, programs, and guest lists relating to musical events at the White House. The papers of the presidents before Herbert Hoover are housed at the Library of Congress (the Adams family at the Massachusetts Historical Society) and available on microfilm. Indices to the papers are helpful, but frequently a musical matter will be hidden in letters to now obscure personages.

The true legwork for my research began with extended visits to each of the presidential libraries where the archives of the modern chief executives are housed. Beginning with Herbert Hoover, these libraries with their accompanying museums are located in towns and cities associated with the presidents and are spread across the country. But these libraries (Hoover, Roosevelt, Truman, Eisenhower, Kennedy, Johnson, and Ford) enabled me to sense the immediacy of the presidential office and become familiar with the flow of changing administrations, unequaled by any other means. The papers for Nixon and Carter were contained in the National Archives, and only the audio-visual materials were open to the public at the time of my research. By the close of 1991, however, the Carter, Nixon, and Reagan libraries were opened. Systems of filing and retrieving information vary from library to library and grow more complex with the later administrations. At the Johnson library, for example, the White House Central Files, which contain most of the presidential papers, are subdivided according to Name, Subject (Executive and General), and Confidential files with a detailed system of cross-reference. One must learn the names of important members of the White

House staffs under each administration, moreover, since needed materials are often filed under their names.

There were moments when I had the feeling I was spying on the intricate memoing network of the White House. Where else could one find, on an official memo that had passed through several channels, the president's own handwriting vetoing a musical group that asked to play at the White House? The Papers of Harry S. Truman, moreover, are especially revealing. Reflecting his keen interest in music, President Truman's letters, diaries, and memoranda in his own hand occasionally contain some titillating notes: on one file, "Music—Personal. See me. *Important—Personal*." Another fascinating body of materials in the presidential libraries comprises the autograph letters from prominent concert artists, composers, and entertainers filed alphabetically—and inconspicuously—along with John Doe and everyone else in America who wrote to the president.

For White House programs and details surrounding a musical event, the superb staffs of each of the libraries managed to review and pull materials for me from files not yet opened, mainly those of the first ladies. Only Eleanor Roosevelt's papers were available at the time of my research, although those of Mrs. Lyndon Johnson and Mrs. Herbert Hoover are now open for general research. Perusing the day-by-day schedules of each of the presidents, moreover, reveals that the musical life of the mansion seemed to go on regardless of the onerous duties of the chief of state.

A study of the audio-visual materials in the presidential libraries illustrates the increased importance and visibility of the concerts from the period of John F. Kennedy onward. Photographs of performers appearing at the White House do not exist before this administration. Beginning with Lyndon Johnson, recordings and films were made of selected programs by the White House Communications Agency; however, the sound was often discontinued after the president's speech, leaving singers with their mouths open and famous pianists with their arms wildly thrashing. Tape recordings of many of the concerts during the 1960s are in the Music Division of the Library of Congress, and the Pablo Casals concert under the Kennedys is available commercially (Co. AKL5926). Historic early engravings, lithographs, photographs, and drawings were found in the collections of the Library of Congress, New York Public Library, Associated Press, United Press International, White House Curator's Office, Bettmann Archive, the Marine Band Library, Smithsonian Institution, Hoblitzelle Theater Arts Library, and other sources listed in the Picture Credits.

Like the photographs and recordings, newspaper coverage of White House entertainment reflects changing attitudes on the part of both the public and the first families as to their significance. Rutherford Hayes, conscious of his dignified image after the corruptions of the Ulysses Grant administration, probably encouraged the press to cover his many musicales, because the *National Republican* of this period scarcely missed an event. Reporters began regularly reviewing the state dinners as social affairs under William McKinley, but music was rarely mentioned. Calvin Coolidge flatly refused to allow a choir concert to be broadcast from the White House via radio, and FDR, first of the "media monarchs," allowed not one of the 300 musicales to be covered by the papers, although Eleanor Roosevelt mentioned many of them in her "My Day" column. The first music critics came under Dwight Eisenhower's last years during America's great cultural boom, continued prominently through Kennedy's administration, but reviewed only occasionally under Johnson's tenure. The Nixon, Ford, and Carter programs received front-page coverage with photographs, but the Reagan and Bush state dinner concerts have had less press attention. The president and first lady, however, have chosen an artistic and effective alternative to show their support of the performing arts through their series of PBS telecasts.

The printed programs for White House musical entertainment are obviously rich sources for the study of the repertory itself. The earliest in this genre is the program of dances for Andrew Johnson's Juvenile Soirée on December 28, 1868, property of the White House Curator's Office. Programs for the musicales began with those printed on satin during the Benjamin Harrison period and are located among the Harrison Presidential Papers housed at the Library of Congress. For programs during the administrations of McKinley through Coolidge the presidential papers are also useful, as are the manuscript collections of White House social aides, T.A. Bingham and Irwin Hood Hoover, also in the Library of Congress. From the turn of the century to the present, White House entertainment records and programs were pasted into large leather-bound scrapbooks. The first of these series is entitled "Official White House Social Functions" (1902–15) and comprises twenty-one volumes contained in the National Archives relating to the active social life of Theodore Roosevelt, William Howard Taft, and Woodrow Wilson's earlier years. The remaining series are in the White House Curator's Office and the various presidential libraries. A collection of programs from various administrations beginning with Franklin Roosevelt is in the Ralph E. Becker Collection, Division of Political History at the Smithsonian. For the Reagan administration I received printed programs from the White House Social Office and from three events that I attended: the Itzak Perlman/Ken Noda "Young Performers" telecast on November 7, 1982; the Congressional Children's concert on July 13, 1982; and the arrival ceremony for Prime Minister Indira Gandhi of India on the South Lawn, July 28, 1982. From Mrs. Bush's Press Office and the Marine Band Library I received copies of important programs and other relevant information.

To locate musical instruments, scores, and memorabilia associated with presidential families, I wrote to over 200 historic sites commemorating the presidency—birthplaces, residences, monuments, and other structures—most operated by the National Park Service. The result was gratifying, and the collections described in Appendix A I personally perused and studied. The music at the presidential libraries from Hoover on, especially the large collection of scores at the Truman and FDR libraries, ranges from pieces sent in by the public to early family sheet music. All were not necessarily used at the White House. Sorting out the function and significance of this music was problematic, often frustrating.

One of the most important collections for this study was the archive of the U.S. Marine Band housed in the Marine Band Library and at the Marine Corps Historical Center. These archives contain scores, early band programs, government records on microfilm, leader's logs from 1917 to the present, a compendium of useful clippings entitled "Marine Band Chronology, 1798–1954," and other items valuable for rounding out the ceremonial and musical history of the White House. Additional sources for this project are too numerous to cite in detail. They comprise American political and musical histories; early histories of military bands in both Europe and America; studies of social and theatrical life in Washington, D.C.; theses; congressional records; recollections and diaries of former first ladies, Washington socialites, diplomats, and reporters; and various oral histories located in the presidential libraries. Published biographies of famous performers often mention a program they presented at the White House, and I had a busy time in Washington, linking and verifying leads, clues, and hunches in the manuscripts housed in the magnificent Jefferson, Adams, and Madison buildings of the Library of Congress. The joy of having at my disposal the wonders of those resources cannot be overemphasized, and the recollections, moods, and ambience of our nation's capital will remain key elements in the message of this book.

ACKNOWLEDGMENTS

This book could not have been realized without the help and support of many curators, archivists, librarians, friends, and others who generously shared with me their recollections about White House musical life. Regretfully, I cannot mention them all without embarking on another book in itself, but their dedication and assistance have been deeply appreciated. The main organization that sponsored my project was the Smithsonian Institution. A postdoctoral fellowship enabled me to spend a year and four summers in the Division of Political History, National Museum of American History, consulting with the excellent staff and utilizing the vast resources of this prestigious museum. I am also grateful to the Lyndon Baines Johnson Foundation for its assistance and to Southern Methodist University for granting me a leave from teaching for two semesters to work on my project in Washington.

A word of thanks is hardly adequate to express to Margaret Klapthor—my advisor, mentor, and friend at the Smithsonian—all that her help has meant to my spirit as well as scholarship. As curator emeritus of the Division of Political History, Mrs. Klapthor has been responsible for the First Ladies Hall for many years, and her knowledge and writings on the White House are well known. In spite of rigorous professional demands on her time, she was never too busy to talk with me, answer questions, and care about my work when I needed such assurance desperately. Other Smithsonian curators to whom I am indebted are Herbert Collins (Political History), Helen Hollis and Bob Sheldon (Musical Instruments), Carl Scheele (Community Life), Harold Langley (Naval History), and Rodris Roth (Domestic Life). Eleanor Boynge, former secretary of the Division of Political History, kindly answered phone calls and took messages that kept me in touch with the outside world while I was buried in secluded archives.

In addition to the Smithsonian, the White House staff itself was a patient, supportive, and authoritative pillar for my work. The associate curator, Betty Monkman, not only allowed me to consult and photocopy programs, records of social events, photographs, and documents in the Office of the White House Curator, but also answered my questions about the mansion with her characteristic expertise. The first social secretary under the Reagans, Mable ("Muffie") Brandon, and her assistant, Linda Faulkner, who became social secretary in 1985, provided programs and arranged for me to attend certain White House rehearsals and concerts and—most exciting of all—to meet the president and first lady. Diane Powers, Carol Greenawalt, and Janet McConnell in the White House Photo Office were most gracious, and my interviews with the chief usher, Rex Scouten, who later became curator of the White House, were invaluable.

Interviewing important personalities added a touch of humanity to my manuscript that cannot be measured. I recall with sincerest gratitude my long conversation with Rosalynn Carter and interviews with Todd Duncan, Eugene List, James McCracken, Mstislav Rostropovich, Isaac Stern, Billy Taylor, and many other artists. The following persons also associated with White House entertainment kindly allowed me to interview them:

Letitia Baldrige, social secretary under John F. Kennedy
Colonel John Bourgeois, leader, U.S. Marine Band
Mabel Brandon, social secretary under Ronald Reagan
Mildred Hall Campbell, secretary for Mrs. Herbert Hoover
Marta Istomin, artistic director, John F. Kennedy Center
Mary Jane McCaffree (Mrs. Henry Monroe, Jr.), secretary for Mrs. Dwight Eisenhower
Paul Miller, director of ceremonies, Military District of Washington
Gilbert Mitchell, coordinator of music, funeral of John F. Kennedy
Howard Mitchell, former conductor, National Symphony Orchestra
Gretchen Poston, social secretary under Jimmy Carter
William Santelmann, former leader, U.S. Marine Band
John Steinway, former chairman, Steinway & Sons, New York
Bernard M. West, former chief usher, the White House.

Impressive to me was the personal attention I received from archivists associated with specific resources. Special thanks is offered to Frank Byrne, chief librarian of the Marine Band Library, for his fine cooperation and to the following helpful individuals associated with the presidential libraries.

Cora F. Pederson and Dale Mayer, Herbert Hoover Library, West Branch, Iowa
John Ferris and Mark Renovitch, Franklin D. Roosevelt Library; Susan Brown, Roosevelt Home, Hyde Park, New York
Elizabeth Safly, Warren Ohrvall, and Erwin Mueller, Harry S. Truman Library, Independence, Missouri
James Leyerzapf and Kathy Novak, Dwight D. Eisenhower Library, Abilene, Kansas
William Johnson, Megan Desnoyers, and Allan Goodrich, John F. Kennedy Library, Boston, Massachusetts
Nancy Smith, Tina Lawson, Linda Hanson, and E. Philip Scott, Lyndon B. Johnson Library, Austin, Texas
Holley Wilson, Richard McNiel, Fynette Eaton, and Robert Bohanan, Nixon and Carter Projects, National Archives and Records Services, Washington, D.C.
Leesa Tobin, Dennis Daellenbach, and Richard Holzhausen, Gerald R. Ford Library, Ann Arbor, Michigan.

Other individuals were also of great assistance:

Esme E. Bahn, Mooreland-Spingarn Research Center, Howard University, Washington, D.C.
Paul M. Bailey, Hoblitzelle Theater Arts Library, University of Texas, Austin

Joseph Barnes, chief musician, Public Affairs, U.S. Navy Band, Washington, D.C.

James A. Bear, Jr., curator, Monticello, Virginia

Judson E. Bennett, Richard Long, Charles Wood, and Carol Nowicke, Marine Corps Historical Center, Washington, D.C.

Robert L. Brubaker, curator of Special Collections, Chicago Historical Society

Thomas Burney, Rare Books; Oliver Orr, Lincoln specialist; and John McConough, director, Manuscript Division, Library of Congress

Sally Smith Cahalan, James Buchanan, Foundation for the Preservation of Wheatland, Lancaster, Pennsylvania

Theora David, White House Photographers Association, Washington, D.C.

Roxanna Dean, supervisor, Washingtoniana Collection, Martin Luther King Memorial Library, Washington, D.C.

Perry Gerard Fisher, executive director, Columbia Historical Society, Washington, D.C.

Joyce Goulait, Photographic Services, Smithsonian Institution

Wilhelmina S. Harris, Adams National Historic Site, Quincy, Massachusetts

James J. Hestin, former director, New–York Historical Society

Jane Holahan, Fine Arts Division, Dallas Public Library

Richard Jackson, head, Americana Division, Music Reading Room, Performing Arts Research Center, New York Public Library

James Kessler, arranger, U.S. Army Band, Ft. Myer, Virginia

James Ketchum, curator of the Senate, U.S. Capitol

Hugh A. Lawing, park historian, Andrew Johnson National Historic Site, Greeneville, Tennessee

Donald Leavitt, chief, Jon Newsom and staff, Music Division, Library of Congress

Watt P. Marchman, former director, and Leslie H. Fishel, director, Rutherford B. Hayes Presidential Center, Fremont, Ohio

Frances D. McClure, Walter Havighurst Special Collections, Miami University, Oxford, Ohio

Bernard Meyer, executive vice-president, White House Historical Association, Washington, D.C.

George H. O'Connor, George O'Connor Collection, Lauinger Memorial Library, Georgetown University, Washington, D.C.

Genevieve Oswald, Dance Collection, Performing Arts Research Center, New York Public Library

Anna Perez, Press Secretary to Mrs. Bush

Dorothy Provine, Record Group 42, National Archives and Records Service

Francis Rainey, Home of James K. Polk, Columbia, Tennessee

Mike Ressler, Marine Band Library

Pat Ronsheim, President Benjamin Harrison Memorial Home, Indianapolis, Indiana

Herman Sass, senior librarian, Buffalo and Erie County Historical Association, Buffalo, New York

Anne B. Shepherd, curator of manuscripts, Cincinnati Historical Society

Jay Suchan, Mrs. Bush's Press Office

Florian Thayne, architect of the Capitol, U.S. Capitol

Gary Walters, chief usher, The White House.

Wendy Weber, Mrs. Reagan's Press Office, The White House
David Zeidberg, director, Special Collections, George Washington University Library, Washington, D.C.

To the following individuals, who kindly answered my queries and provided important specific pieces of information, many, many thanks: Elizabeth C. Abell (Bess), Mary Aladj, Ralph Becker, Judith Britt, John S. Burroughs, John Challinor, Eliott Chapo, Francis Grover Cleveland, John Coolidge, Clement Conger, Margaret Truman Daniel, Mrs. Gerald Ford, Malcolm Frager, Martha Graham, Dale Harpham, Queen Noor al Hussein of the Hashimite Kingdom of Jordan, Mrs. Lyndon Johnson, Gene Kelly, Estelle Ball Kuhl, William Lichtenwanger, Ruth Lipman, Irving and Margery Lowens, Charles Francis Lombard, Betty Martin, Mrs. Jacqueline Onassis, Vivian Perlis, Roberta Peters, Ronald Prescott Reagan, James Roosevelt, Francis B. Sayer, Harold Schonberg, Eleanor Seagraves, Beverly Sills, Bobby Short, Henry Z. Steinway, John R. Truman, Nancy Tuckerman, Luci Johnson Turpin, D. Gardiner Tyler, Fred Waring, Helen White, and the fine staffs of numerous presidential historic sites.

I am grateful to the following publications for material that I drew from my own articles: *Opera News* ("Nightingales at the White House," Nov. 1, 1980); *American Way* ("Playing the White House," Apr. 1983); *The Magazine Antiques* ("Pianos in the White House," May 1984); *Kennedy Center Stagebill* ("American Celebration," Jan. 21, 1985); and the Library of Congress's *Performing Arts Annual*, premier issue ("The Inaugural Concert in the Nineteenth Century," 1986). Among my other articles on the subject are "Music at the White House—Lyrical Images of America" in *Prologue*, Quarterly of the National Archives (22/3), fall 1990; and "Voices of Glory: Opera for American Presidents," Pts. I and II, in *Washington Opera Magazine* (55 and 56), 1991. Finally, I offer thanks to my family and many friends, whose interest and enthusiasm provided a loving, human continuum during the many years of my research for *Music at the White House*.

PICTURE CREDITS

Services; page 156, Carter Projects, National Archives and Records Services; page 158, Donald J. Crump, *National Geographic* staff, White House Historical Association; page 159, Marine Band Library; page 161, Bill Fitz-Patrick, The White House; page 162, Michael Evans, The White House; page 163, Steven Purcell, The White House; page 165, Michael Sargent, The White House; page 166, Susan Biddle, The White House; page 168, Carol Powers, The White House; page 169, David Valdez, The White House; page 170, Carol T. Powers, The White House.

The color illustrations in signature one are courtesy of: first page, top, Mount Vernon Ladies Association; first page, bottom, National Museum of American History, Smithsonian Institution; second page, top, I. N. Phelps Stokes Collection, New York Public Library at Lincoln Center, Astor, Lenox and Tilden Foundations; second page, bottom, Adams-Clement Collection, National Museum of American Art; third page, Dance Collections, New York Public Library at Lincoln Center, Astor, Lenox and Tilden Foundations; fourth page, Music Division, New York Public Library at Lincoln Center, Astor, Lenox and Tilden Foundations; fifth page, Hoblitzelle Theater Arts Collection; sixth page, Rutherford B. Hayes Presidential Center; seventh page, top, Hoblitzelle Theater Arts Collection; seventh page, bottom, White House Historical Association; eighth page, Marine Band Library.

The color illustrations in signature two are courtesy of: first page, top and bottom, John F. Kennedy Library; second page, top, Lyndon Baines Johnson Library; second page, bottom, Joseph J. Scherschel, White House Historical Association; third page, top and bottom, Nixon Projects, National Archives and Records Services; fourth page, top and bottom, Gerald R. Ford Library; fifth page, Gerald R. Ford Library; sixth page, top and bottom, Carter Projects, National Archives and Records Services; seventh page, Jack Kightlinger, The White House; eighth page, top and bottom, Jack Kightlinger, The White House.

INDEX